GEGE AKUTAMI

Hamburger!!!

GEGE AKUTAMI published a few short
works before starting *Jujutsu Kaisen*, which began
serialization in *Weekly Shonen Jump* in 2018.

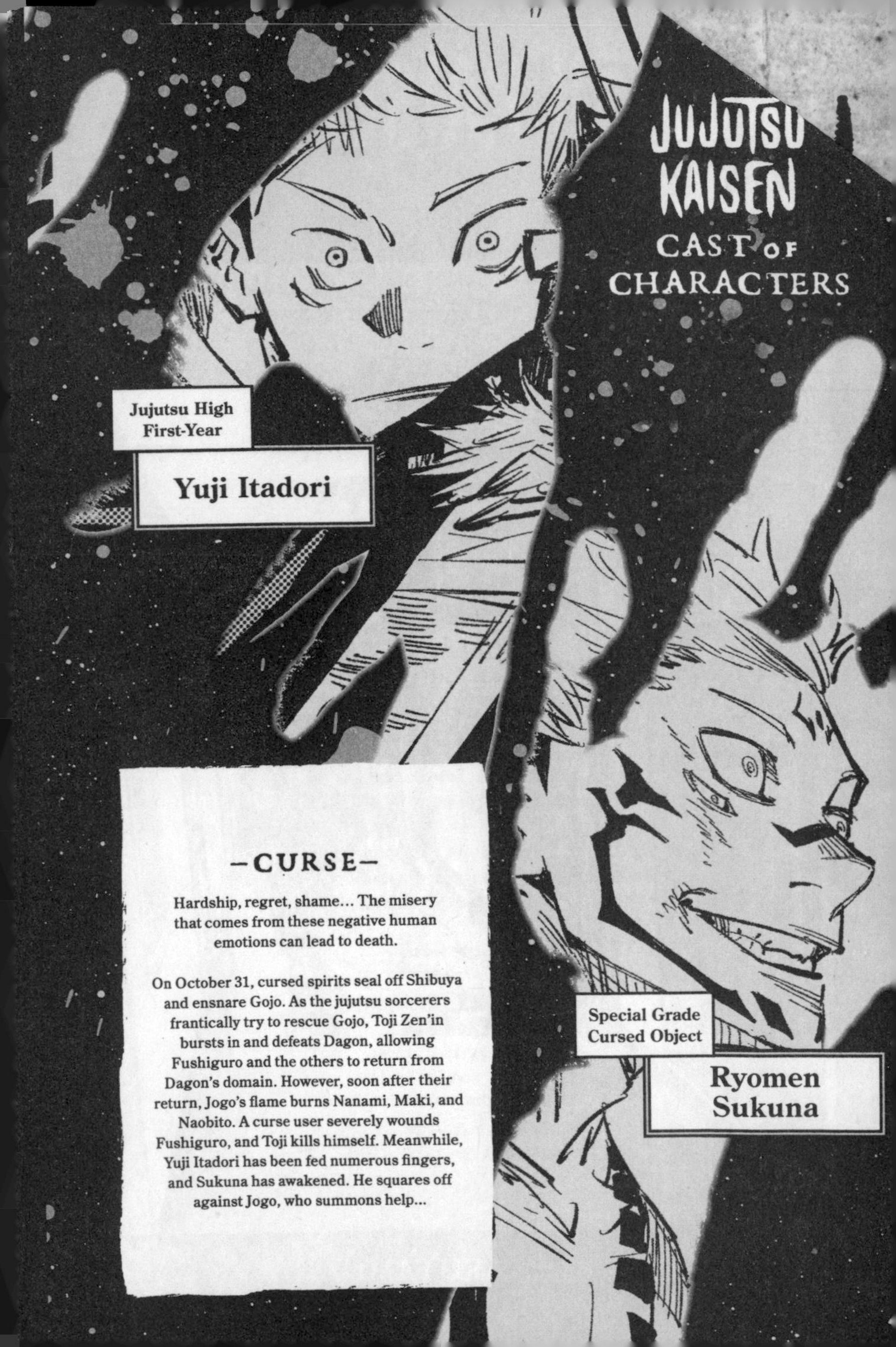
JUJUTSU KAISEN
CAST OF CHARACTERS
Jujutsu High First-Year
Yuji Itadori
Special Grade Cursed Object
Ryomen Sukuna

—CURSE—

Hardship, regret, shame… The misery that comes from these negative human emotions can lead to death.

On October 31, cursed spirits seal off Shibuya and ensnare Gojo. As the jujutsu sorcerers frantically try to rescue Gojo, Toji Zen'in bursts in and defeats Dagon, allowing Fushiguro and the others to return from Dagon's domain. However, soon after their return, Jogo's flame burns Nanami, Maki, and Naobito. A curse user severely wounds Fushiguro, and Toji kills himself. Meanwhile, Yuji Itadori has been fed numerous fingers, and Sukuna has awakened. He squares off against Jogo, who summons help…

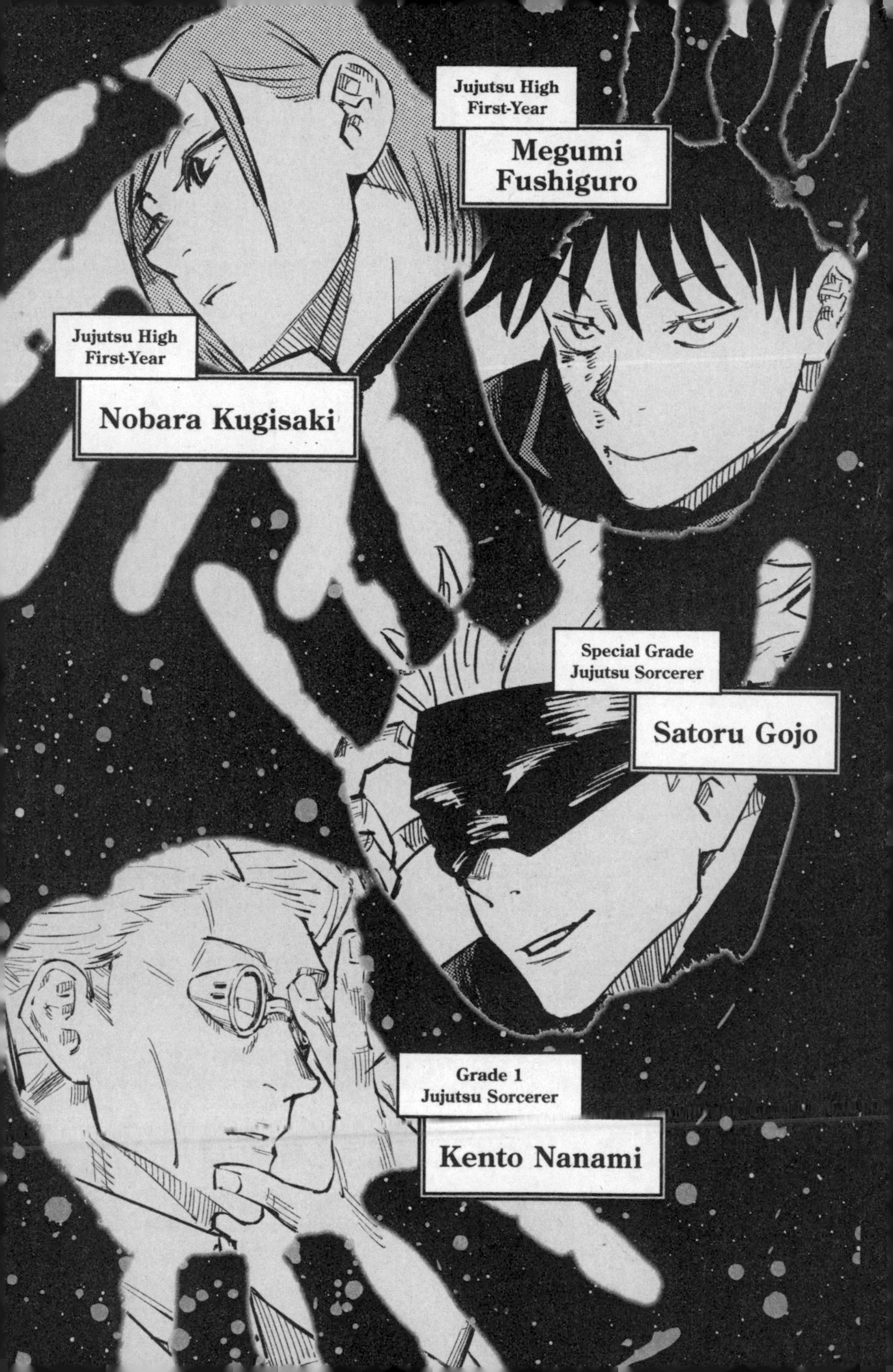
Jujutsu High
First-Year
Megumi
Fushiguro
Jujutsu High
First-Year
Nobara Kugisaki
Special Grade
Jujutsu Sorcerer
Satoru Gojo
Grade 1
Jujutsu Sorcerer
Kento Nanami

JUJUTSU KAISEN

14

THE SHIBUYA INCIDENT
—RIGHT AND WRONG—

Chapter 116: The Shibuya Incident, Part 34

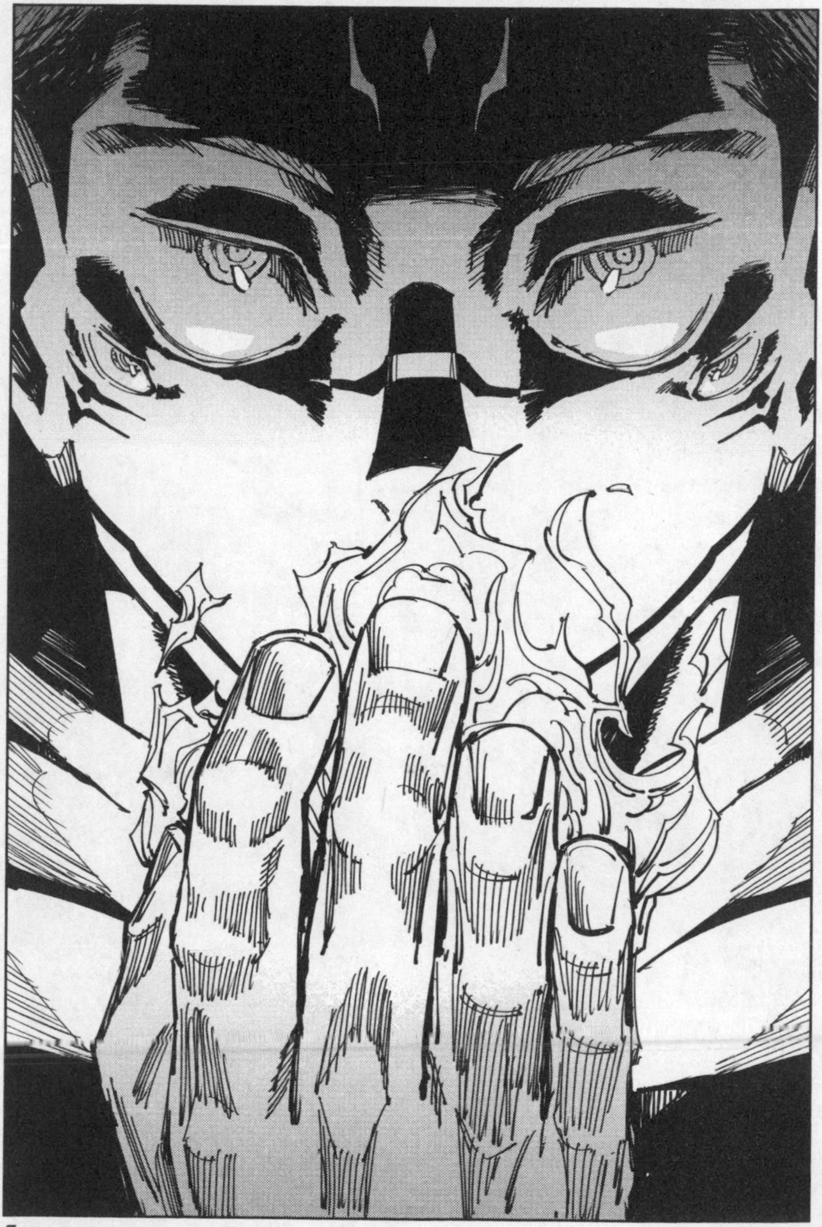

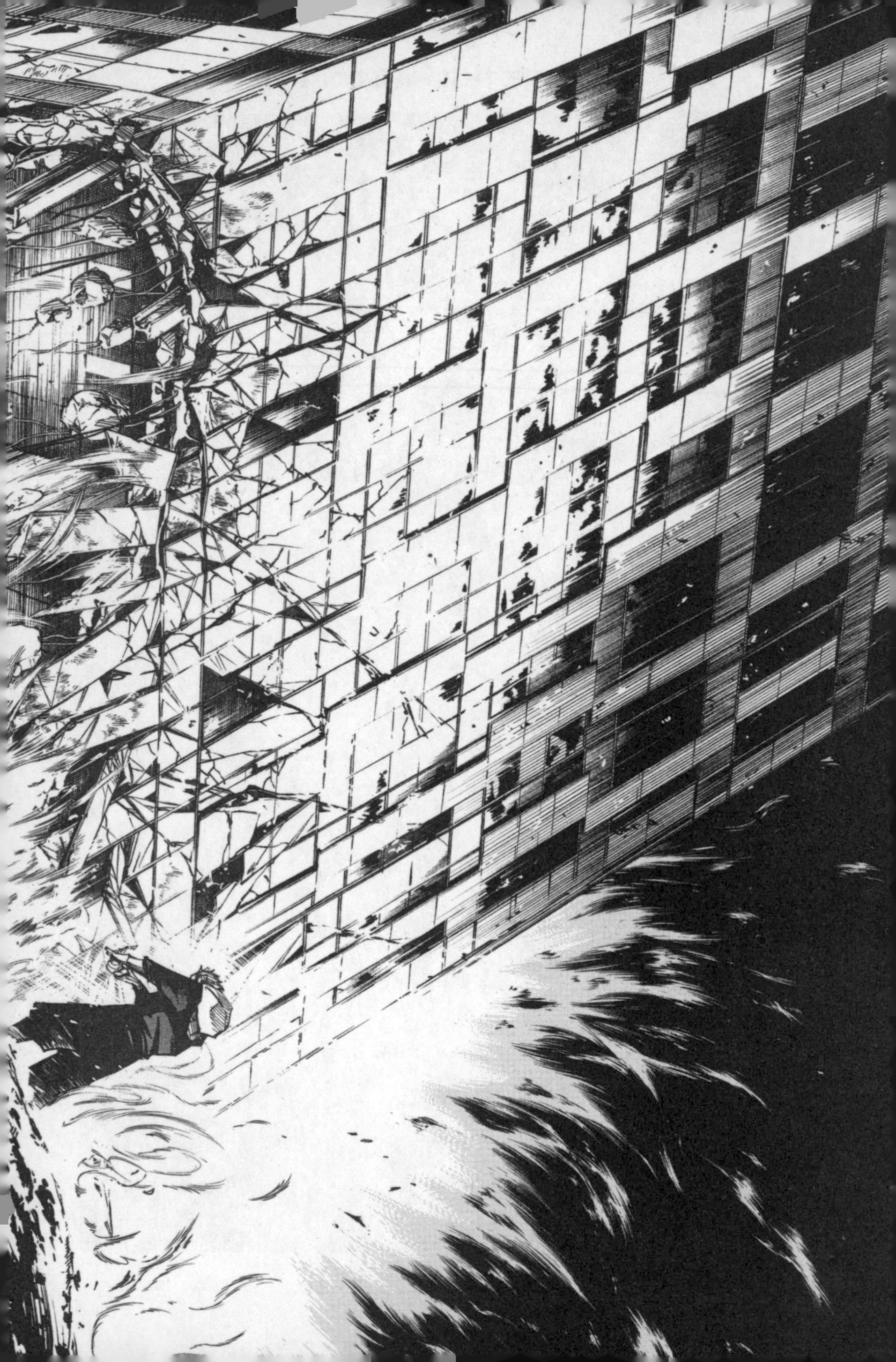

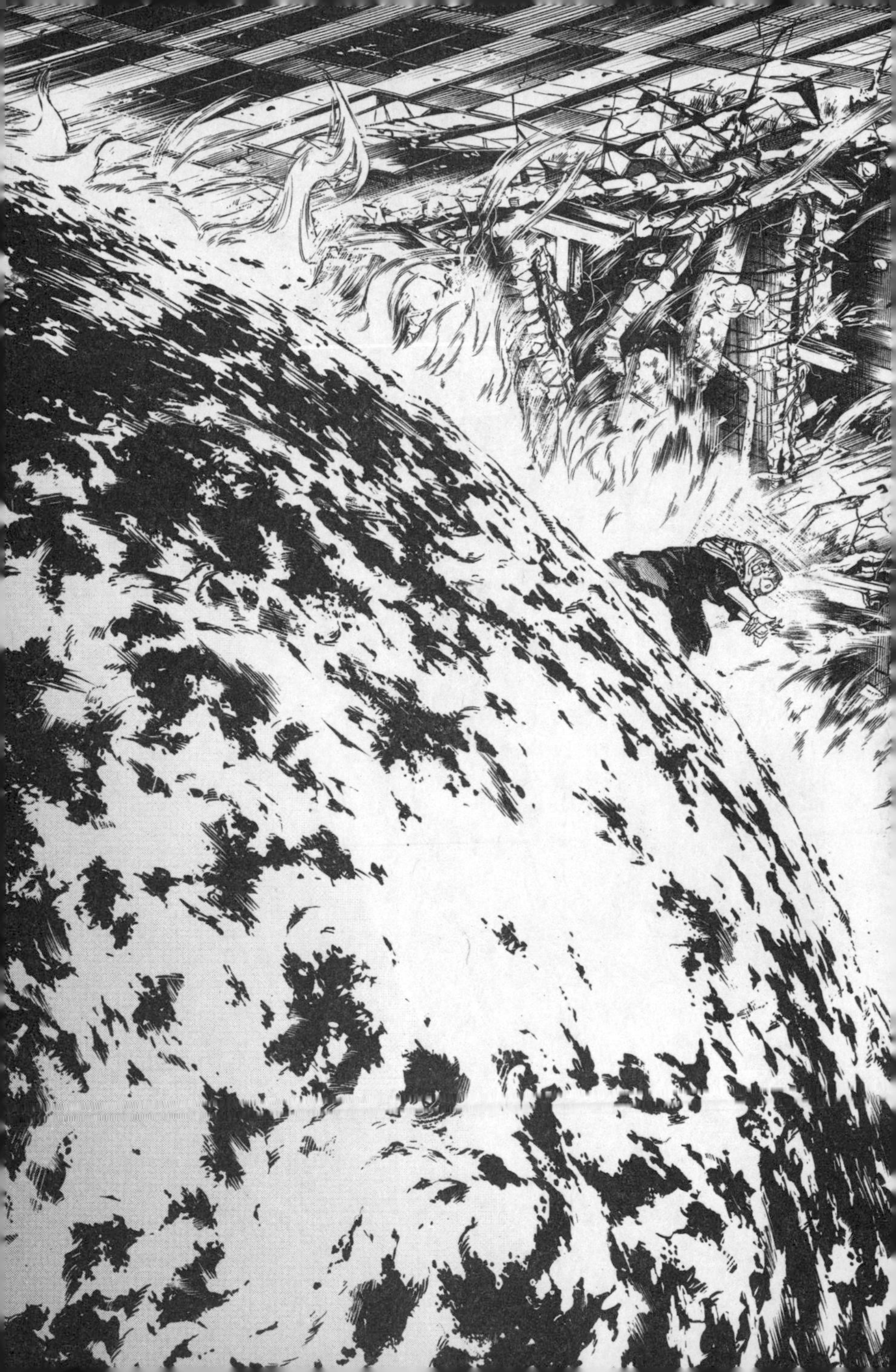

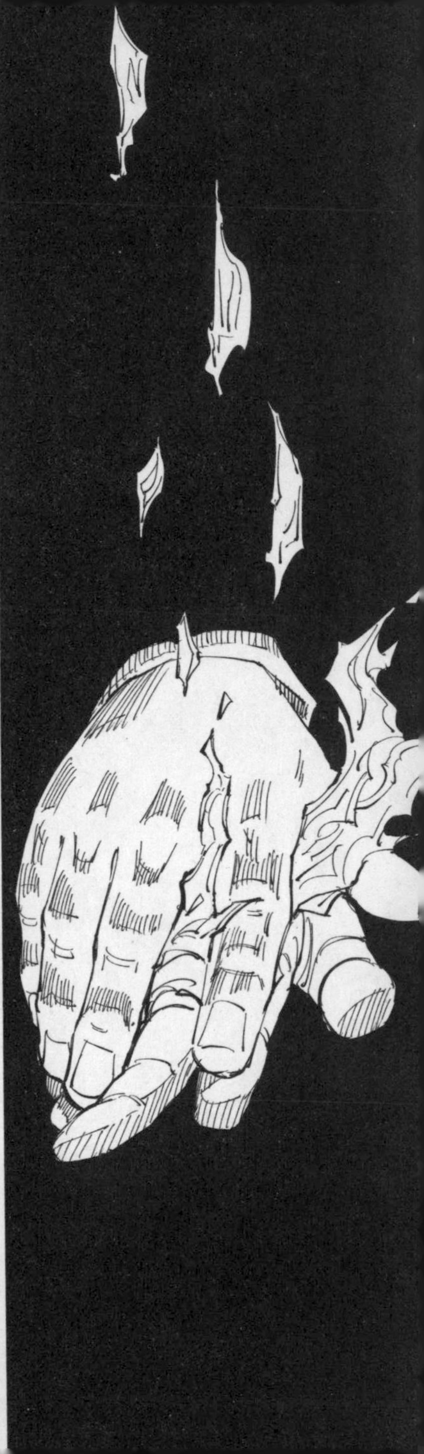
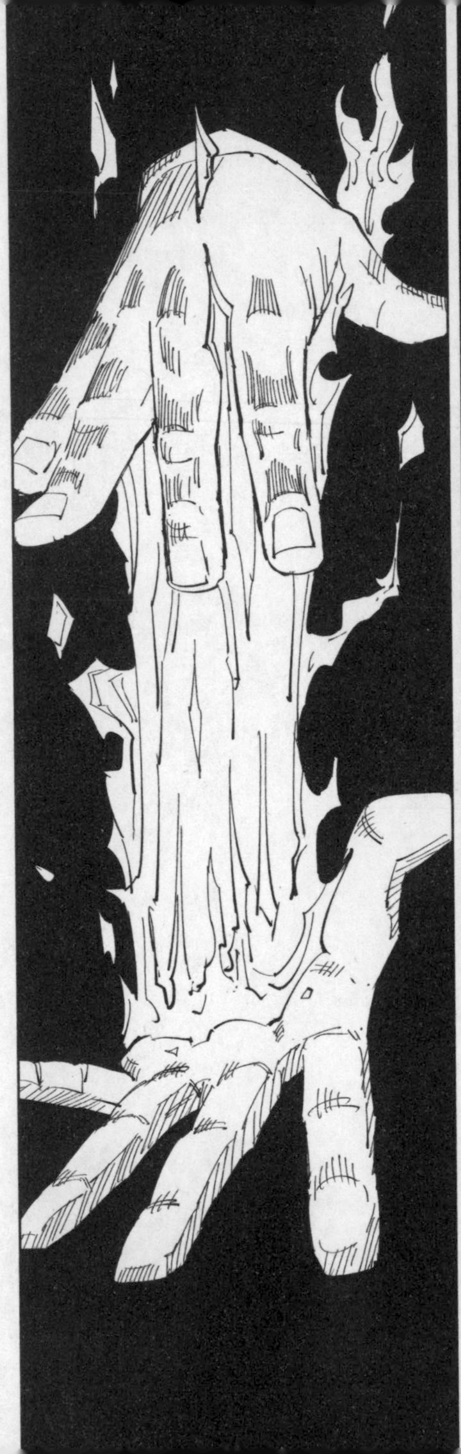

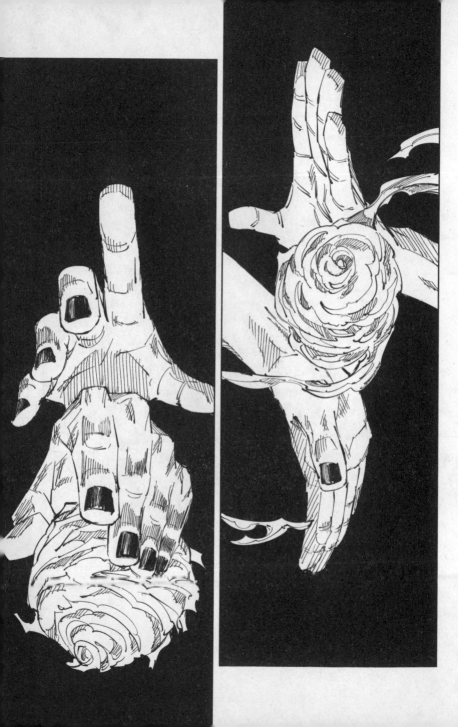

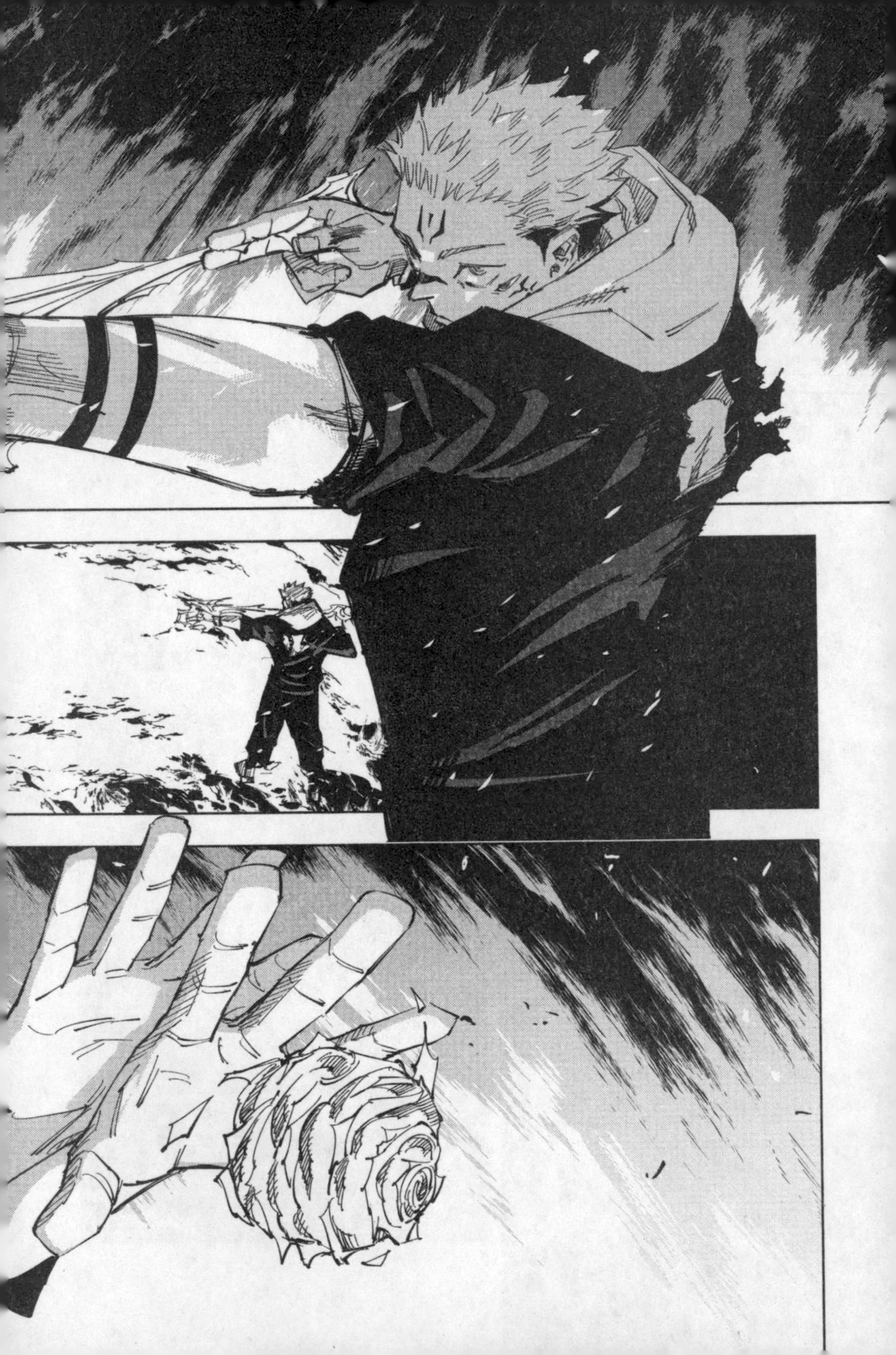

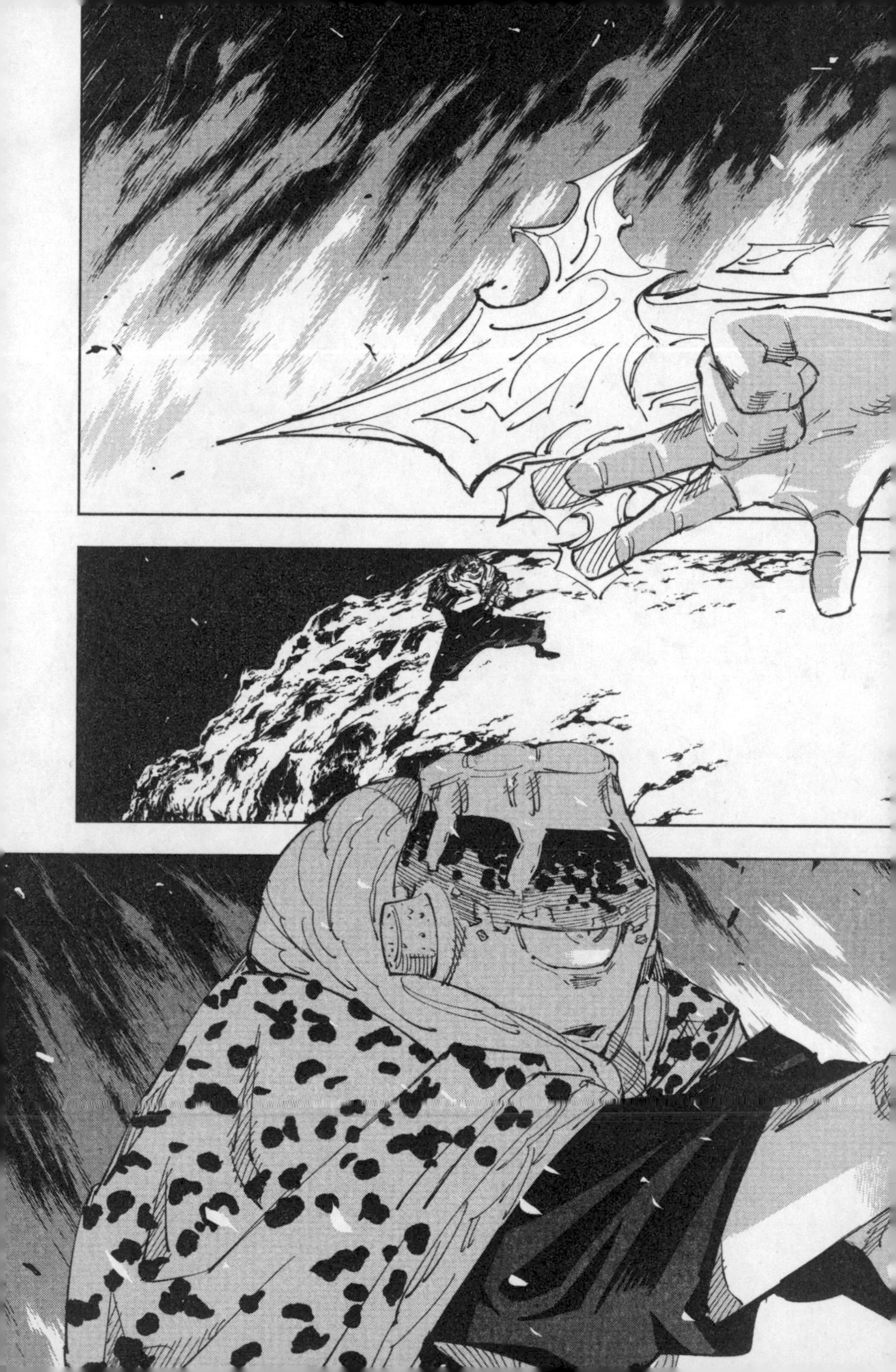

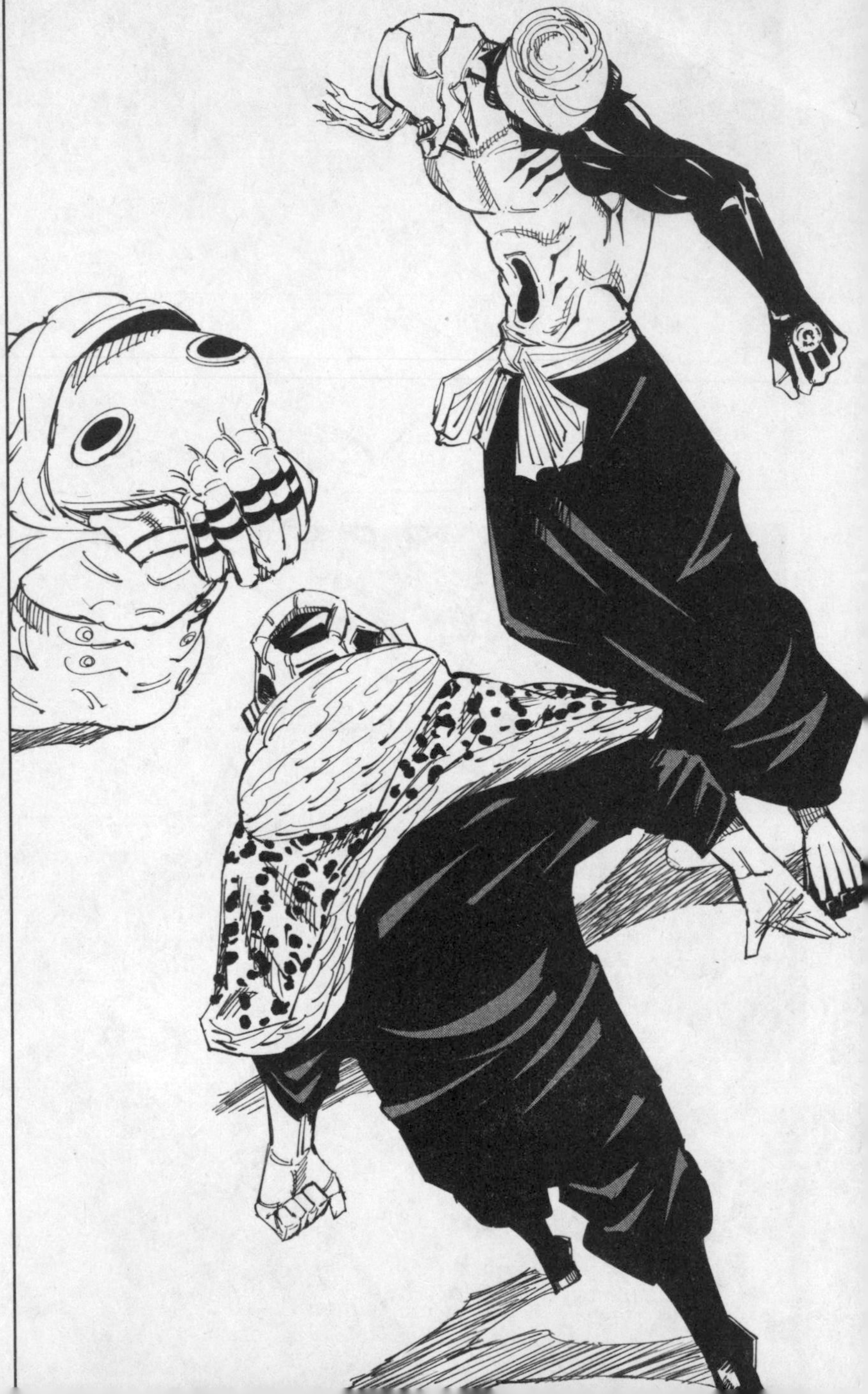

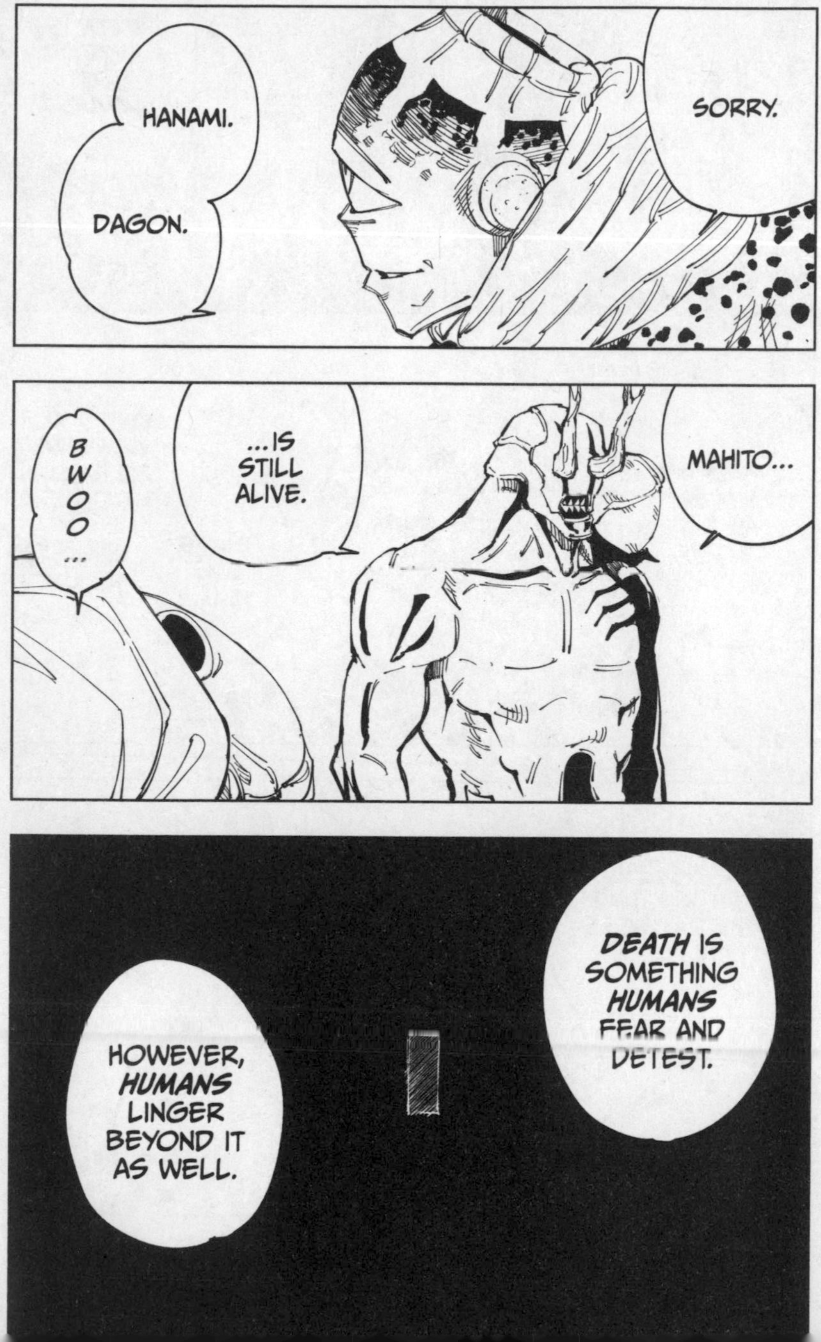
SORRY.
HANAMI. DAGON.
MAHITO...
...IS STILL ALIVE.
BWOO...
DEATH IS SOMETHING *HUMANS* FEAR AND DETEST.
HOWEVER, *HUMANS* LINGER BEYOND IT AS WELL.

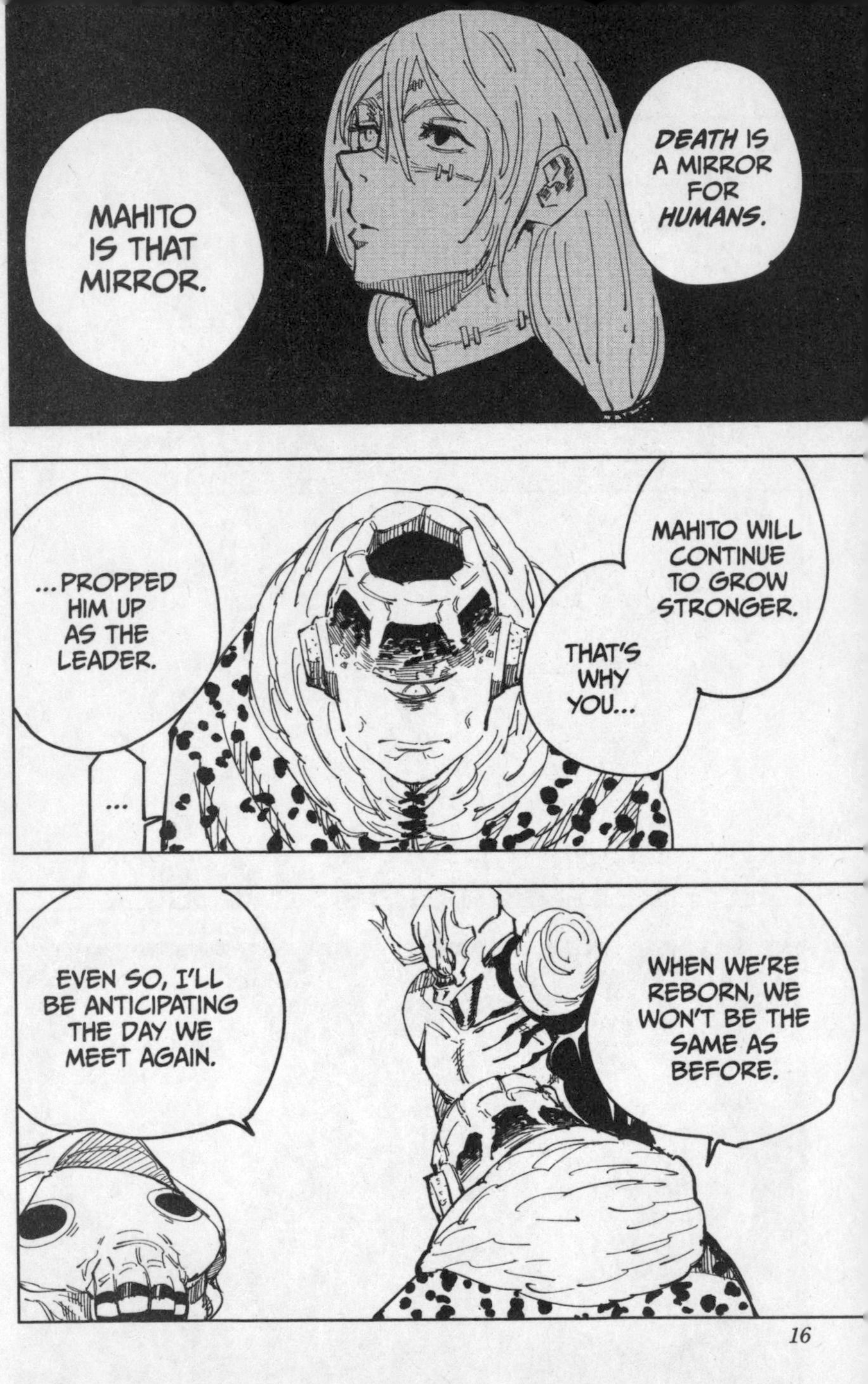
DEATH IS A MIRROR FOR HUMANS.
MAHITO IS THAT MIRROR.
MAHITO WILL CONTINUE TO GROW STRONGER.
THAT'S WHY YOU...
...PROPPED HIM UP AS THE LEADER.
...
WHEN WE'RE REBORN, WE WON'T BE THE SAME AS BEFORE.
EVEN SO, I'LL BE ANTICIPATING THE DAY WE MEET AGAIN.

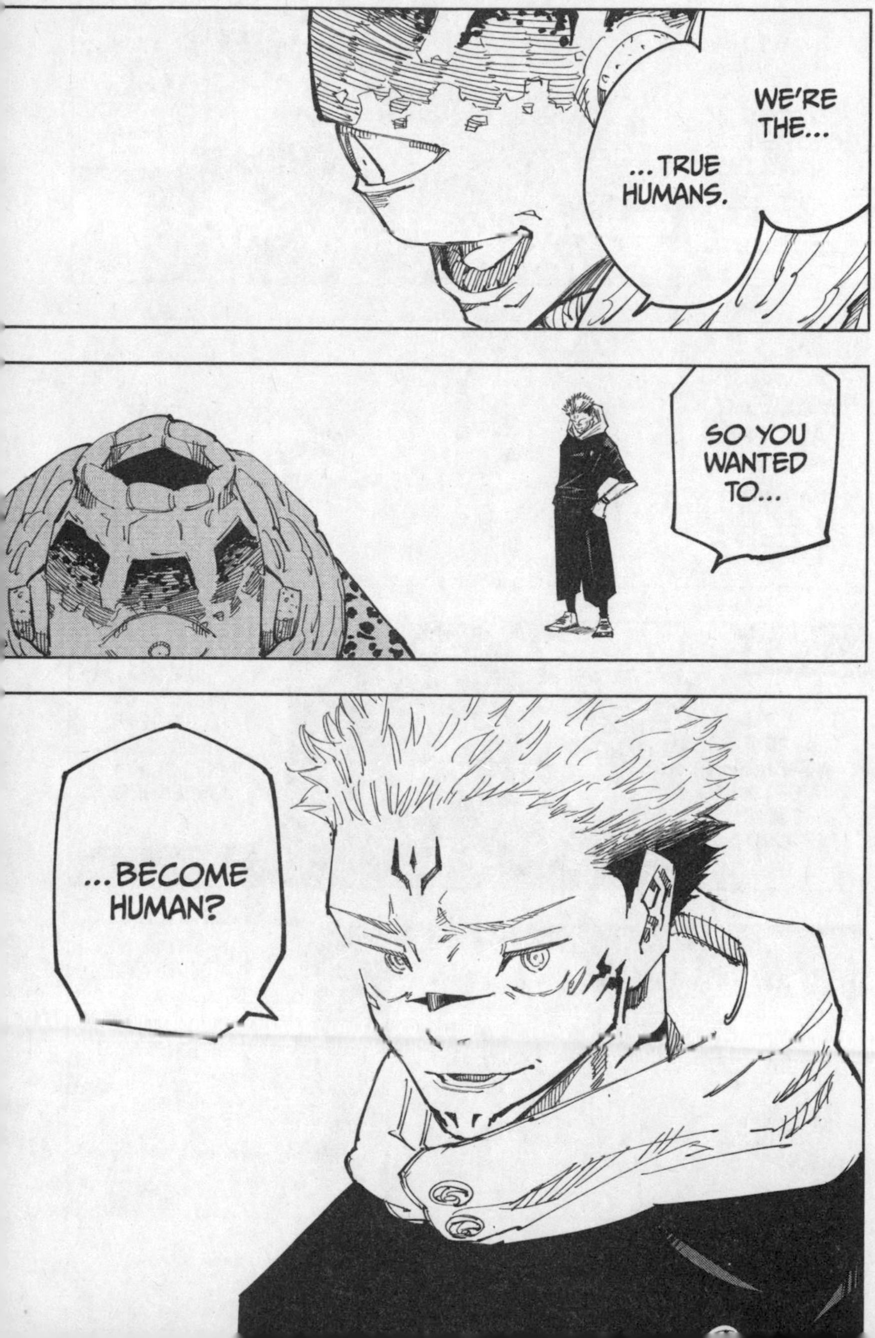
WE'RE THE...
...TRUE HUMANS.
SO YOU WANTED TO...
...BECOME HUMAN?

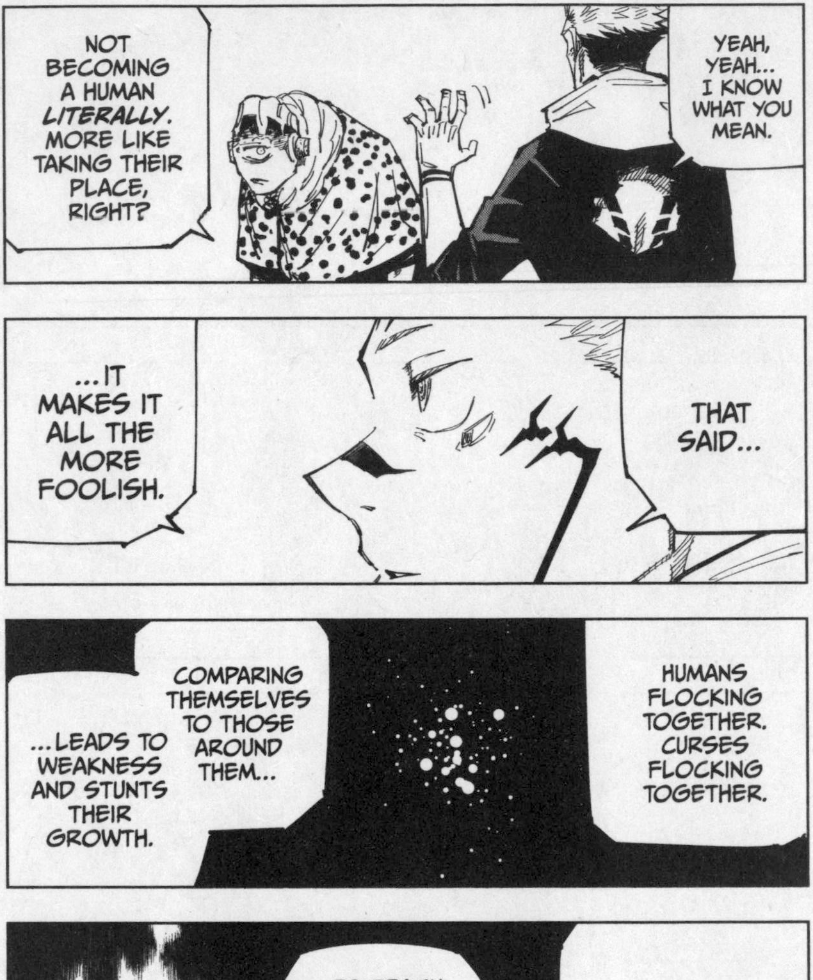
YEAH, YEAH... I KNOW WHAT YOU MEAN.
NOT BECOMING A HUMAN *LITERALLY*. MORE LIKE TAKING THEIR PLACE, RIGHT?
THAT SAID...
...IT MAKES IT ALL THE MORE FOOLISH.
HUMANS FLOCKING TOGETHER. CURSES FLOCKING TOGETHER.
COMPARING THEMSELVES TO THOSE AROUND THEM...
...LEADS TO WEAKNESS AND STUNTS THEIR GROWTH.
YOU SHOULD HAVE BURNT EVERYTHING YOU DESIRED TO A CINDER.
TO REACH THE HEIGHTS OF SATORU GOJO AND NOT WORRY ABOUT YOUR FUTURE OR IDENTITY.
BUT YOU LACKED THE *HUNGER* TO TAKE HOLD OF YOUR DESIRES.

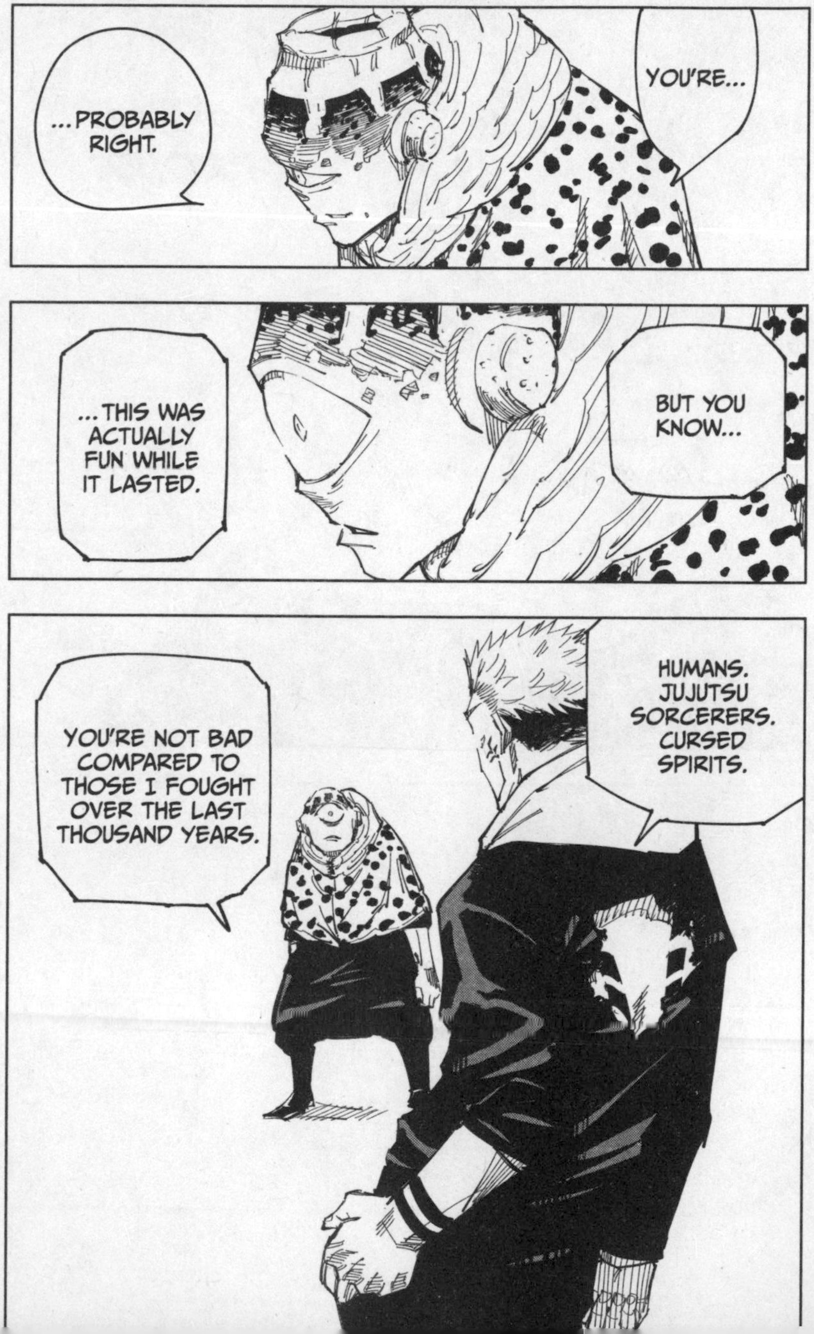
YOU'RE...
...PROBABLY RIGHT.
BUT YOU KNOW...
...THIS WAS ACTUALLY FUN WHILE IT LASTED.
HUMANS. JUJUTSU SORCERERS. CURSED SPIRITS.
YOU'RE NOT BAD COMPARED TO THOSE I FOUGHT OVER THE LAST THOUSAND YEARS.

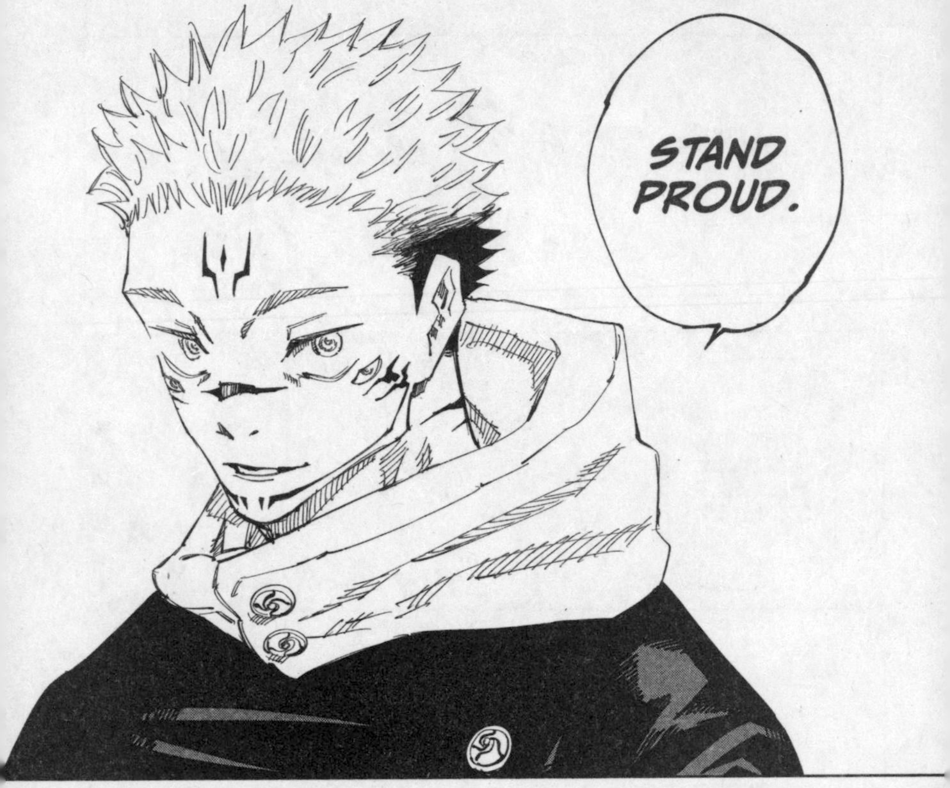
STAND PROUD.
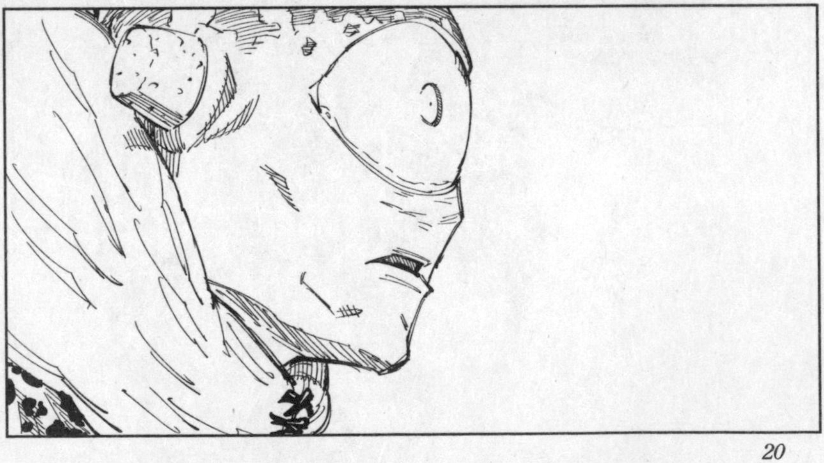

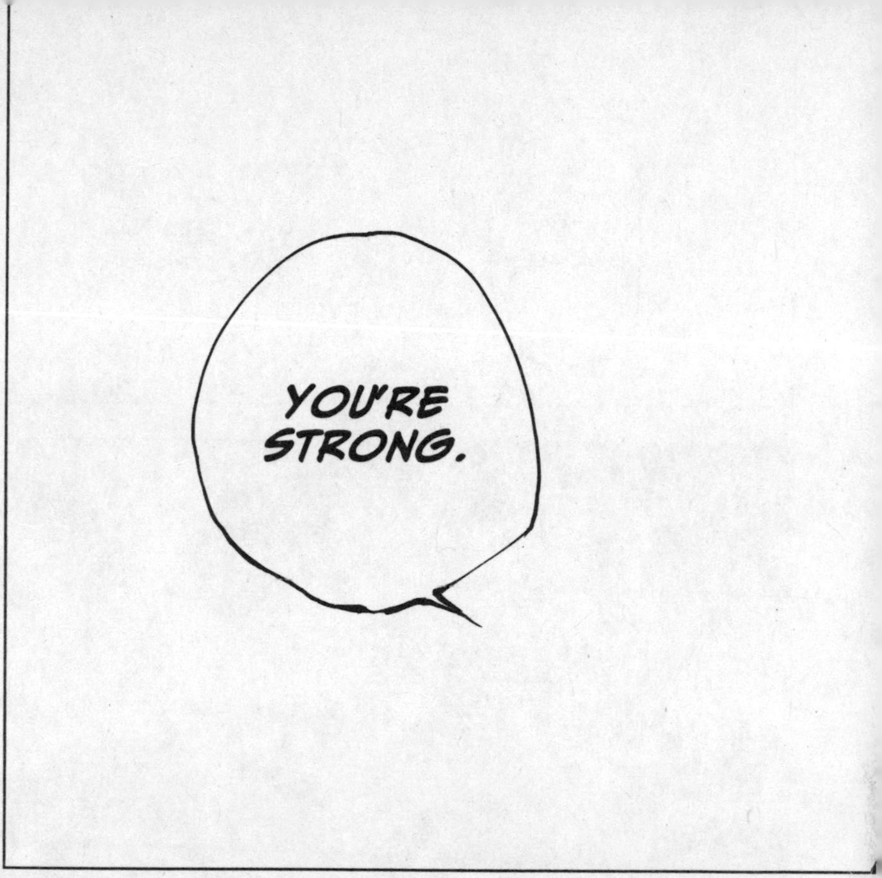
YOU'RE STRONG.
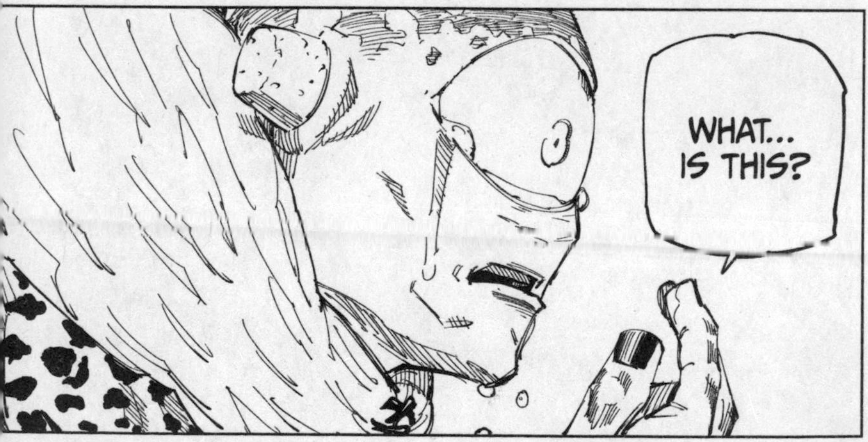
WHAT... IS THIS?

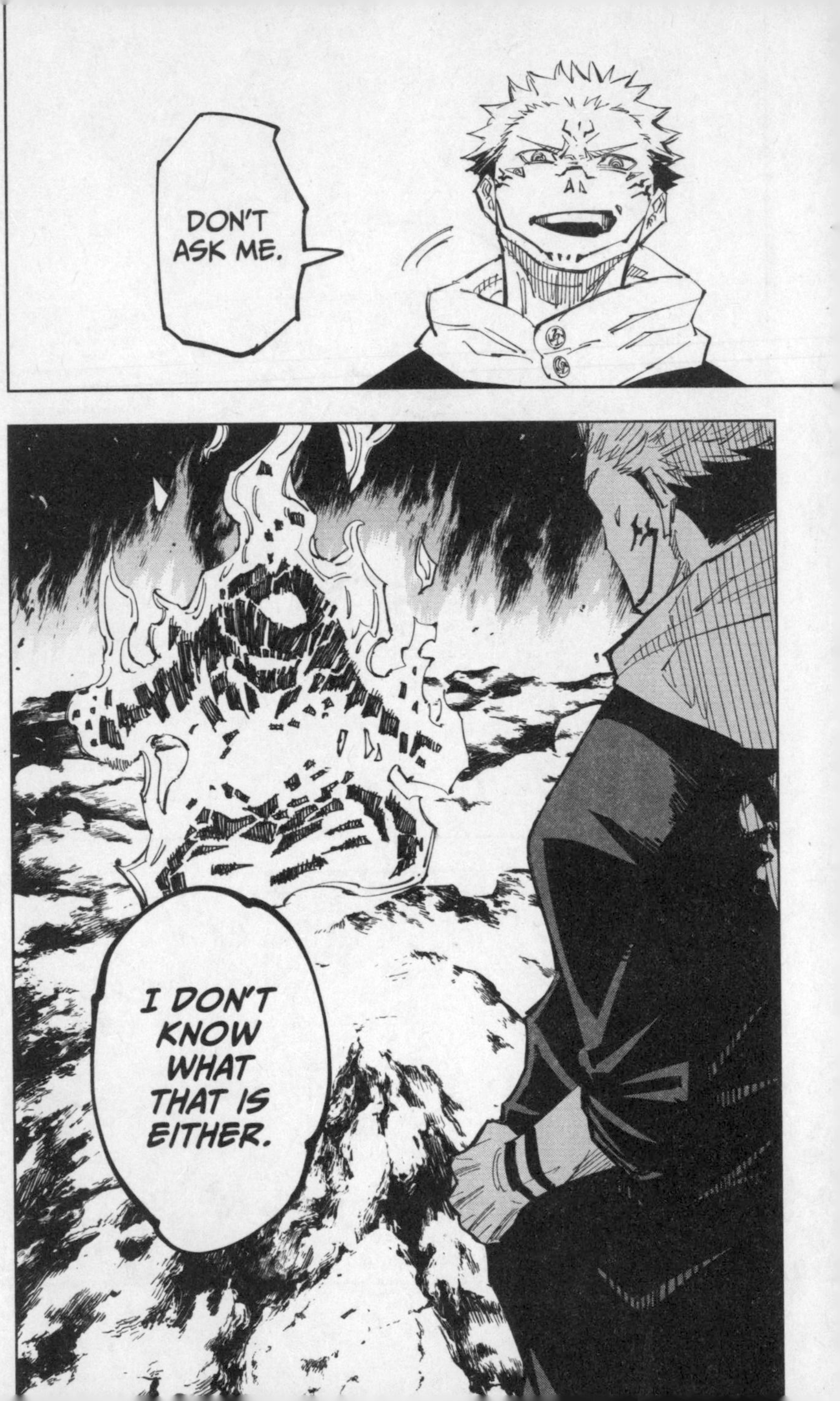
DON'T ASK ME.
I DON'T KNOW WHAT THAT IS EITHER.

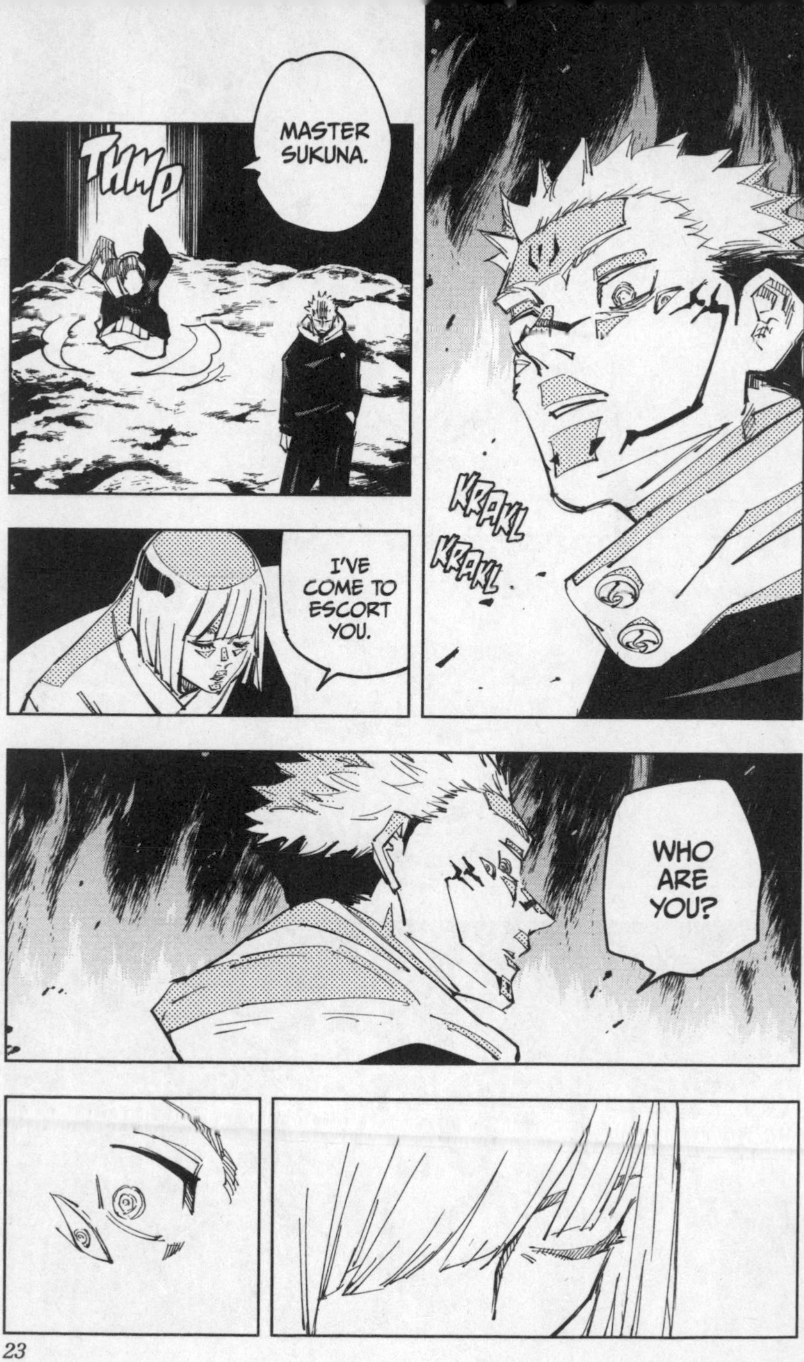
KRAKL
KRAKL
THMP
MASTER SUKUNA.
I'VE COME TO ESCORT YOU.
WHO ARE YOU?

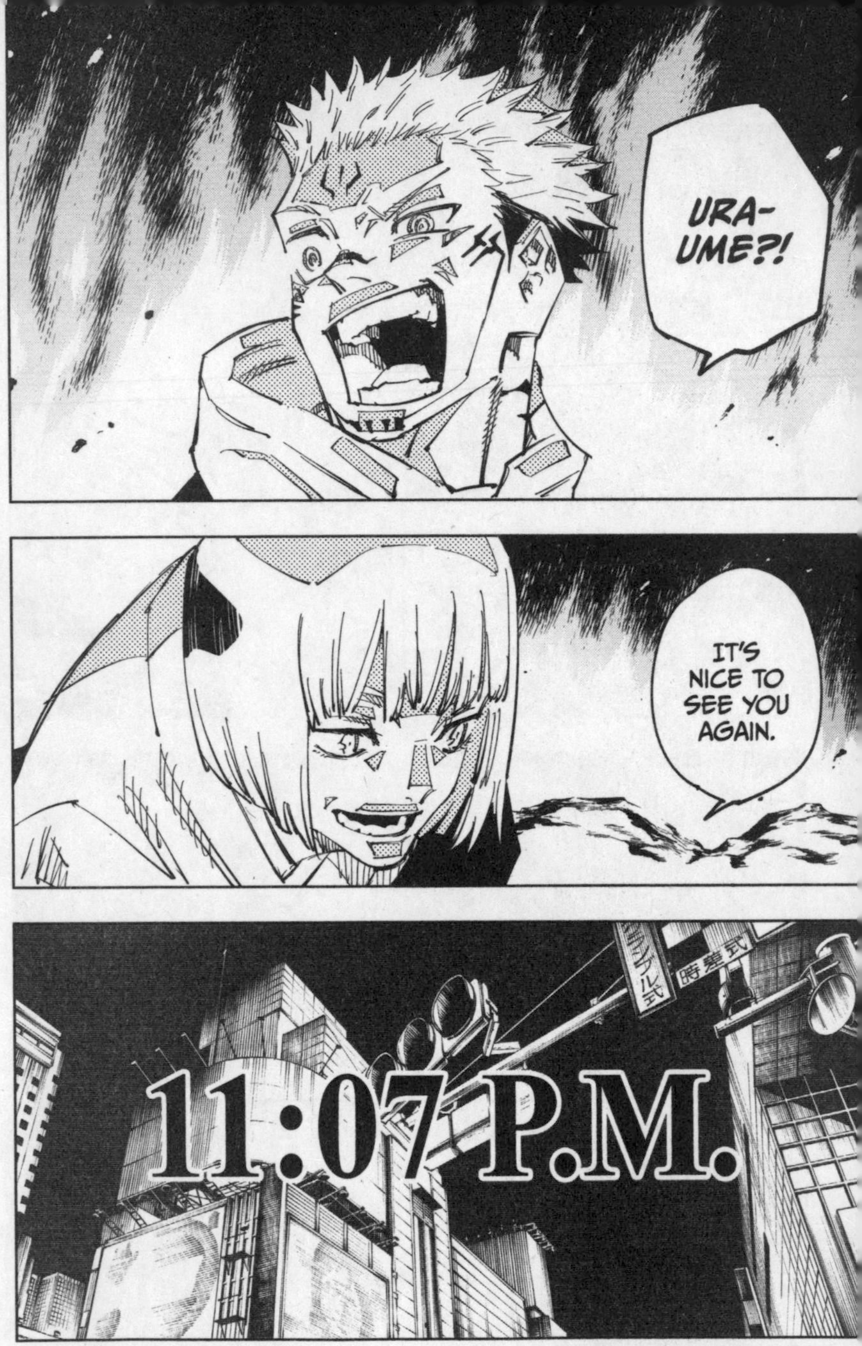
URA-UME?!
IT'S NICE TO SEE YOU AGAIN.
11:07 P.M.

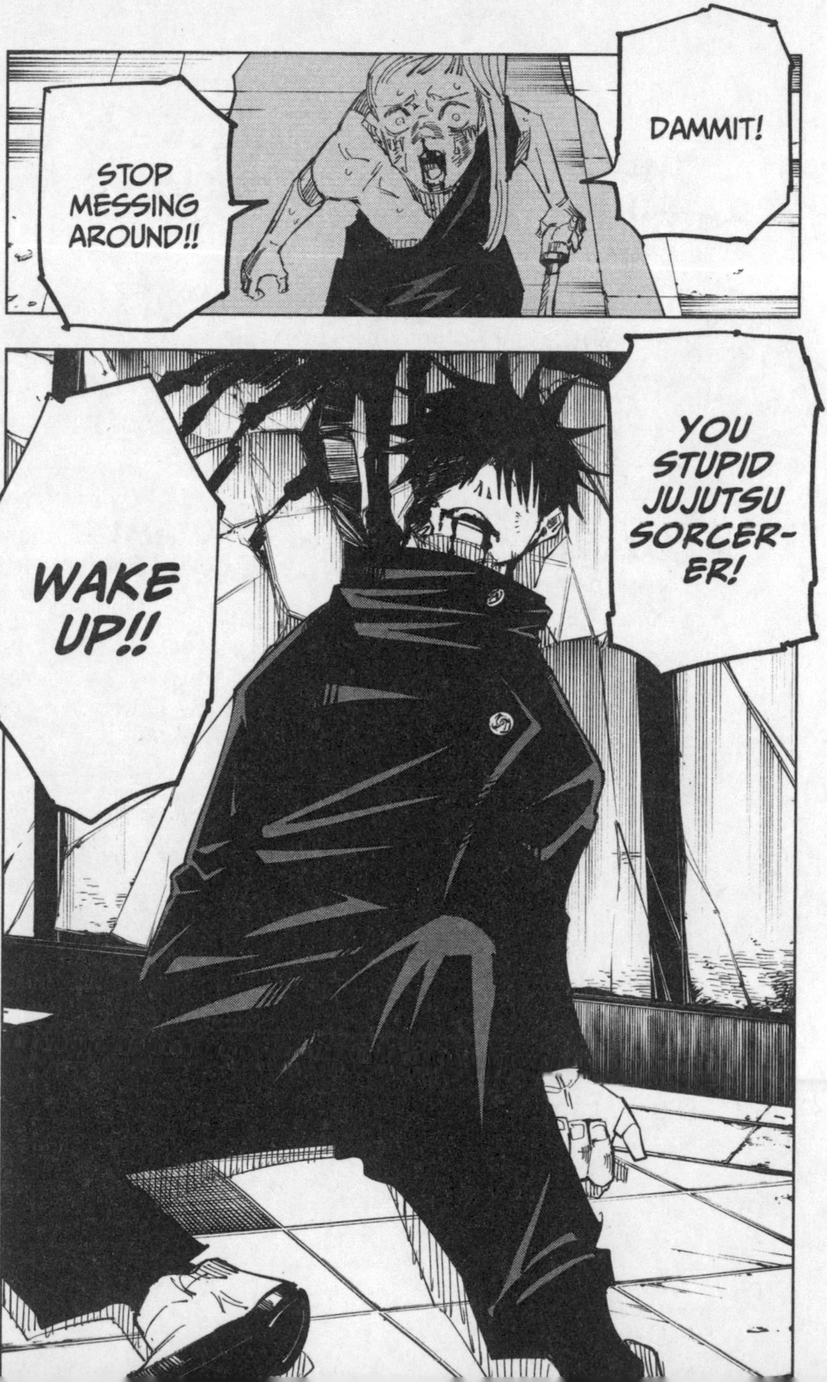
DAMMIT!
STOP MESSING AROUND!!
YOU STUPID JUJUTSU SORCER-ER!
WAKE UP!!

THE 2020 VALENTINES RANKINGS THAT I SERIOUSLY ALMOST FORGOT

PROBABLY RIGHT AROUND WHEN THE PAST ARC ENDED.

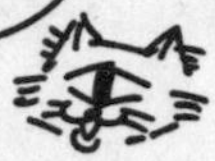

RANKINGS (VALENTINES RECEIVED)	CHARACTER	AKUTAMI'S COMMENT
1 (54)	GOJO	OKAY, I GET IT ALREADY...
2 (30)	GETO	NOT TOO BAD.
3 (23)	FUSHIGURO	YOU NEED TO TRY A LITTLE HARDER.
4 (22)	ITADORI	SQUEAKING BY AS THE MAIN CHARACTER.

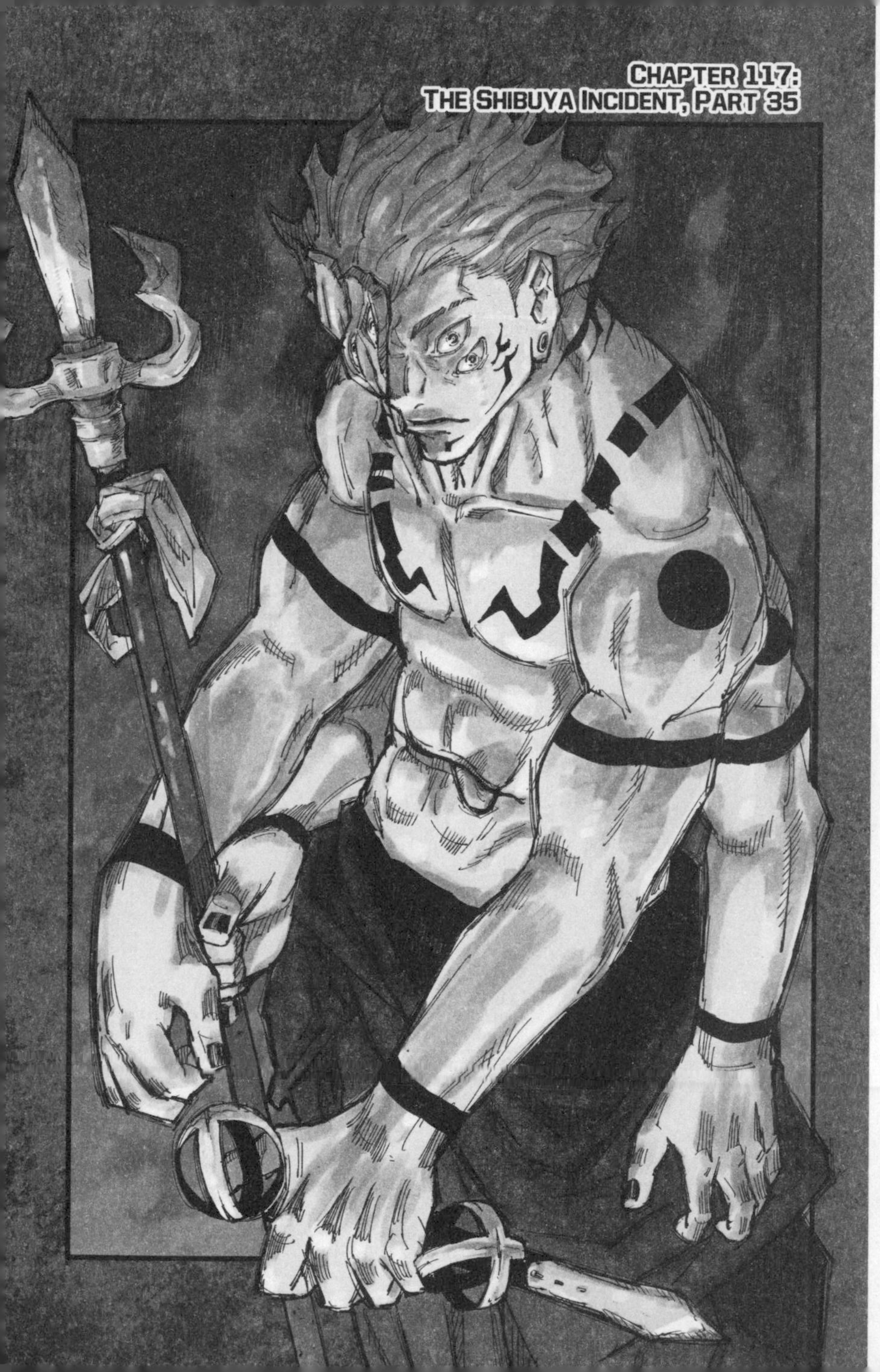
CHAPTER 117:
THE SHIBUYA INCIDENT, PART 35

JUJUTSU KAISEN

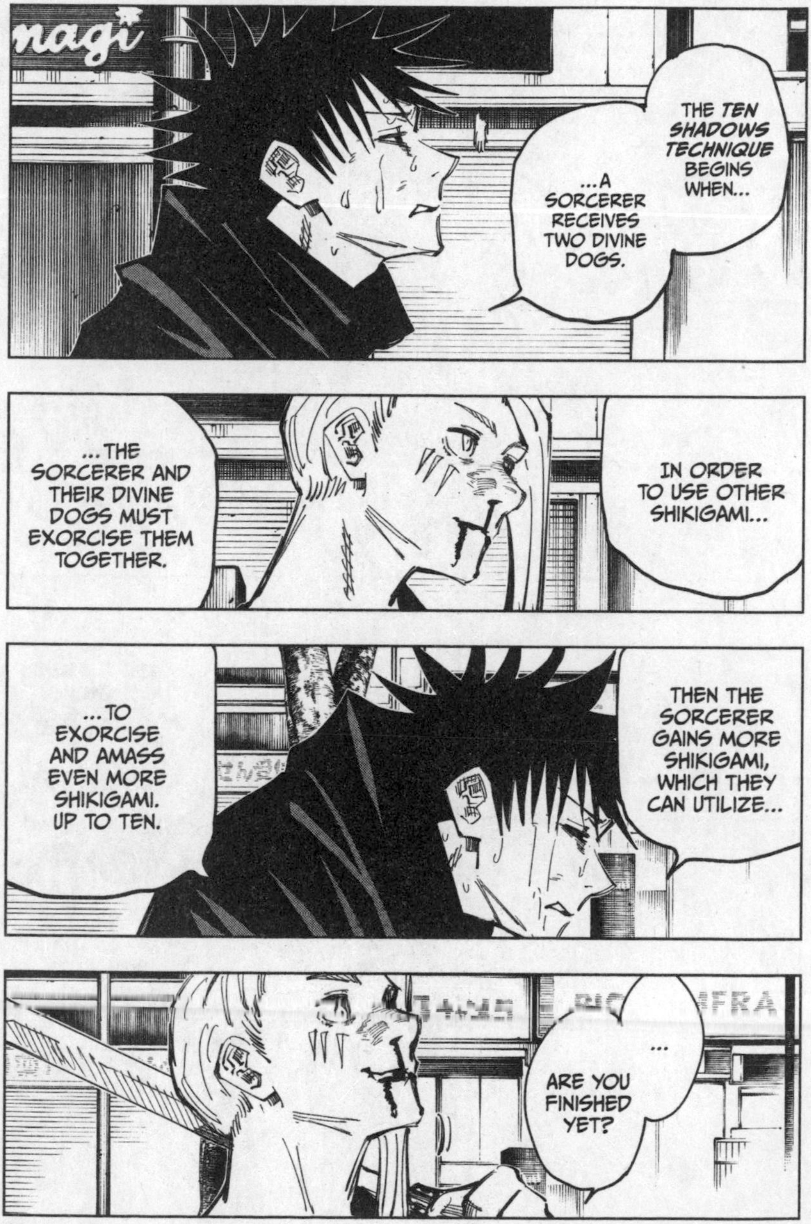
nagi
THE *TEN SHADOWS TECHNIQUE* BEGINS WHEN...
...A SORCERER RECEIVES TWO DIVINE DOGS.
IN ORDER TO USE OTHER SHIKIGAMI...
...THE SORCERER AND THEIR DIVINE DOGS MUST EXORCISE THEM TOGETHER.
THEN THE SORCERER GAINS MORE SHIKIGAMI, WHICH THEY CAN UTILIZE...
...TO EXORCISE AND AMASS EVEN MORE SHIKIGAMI. UP TO TEN.
... ARE YOU FINISHED YET?

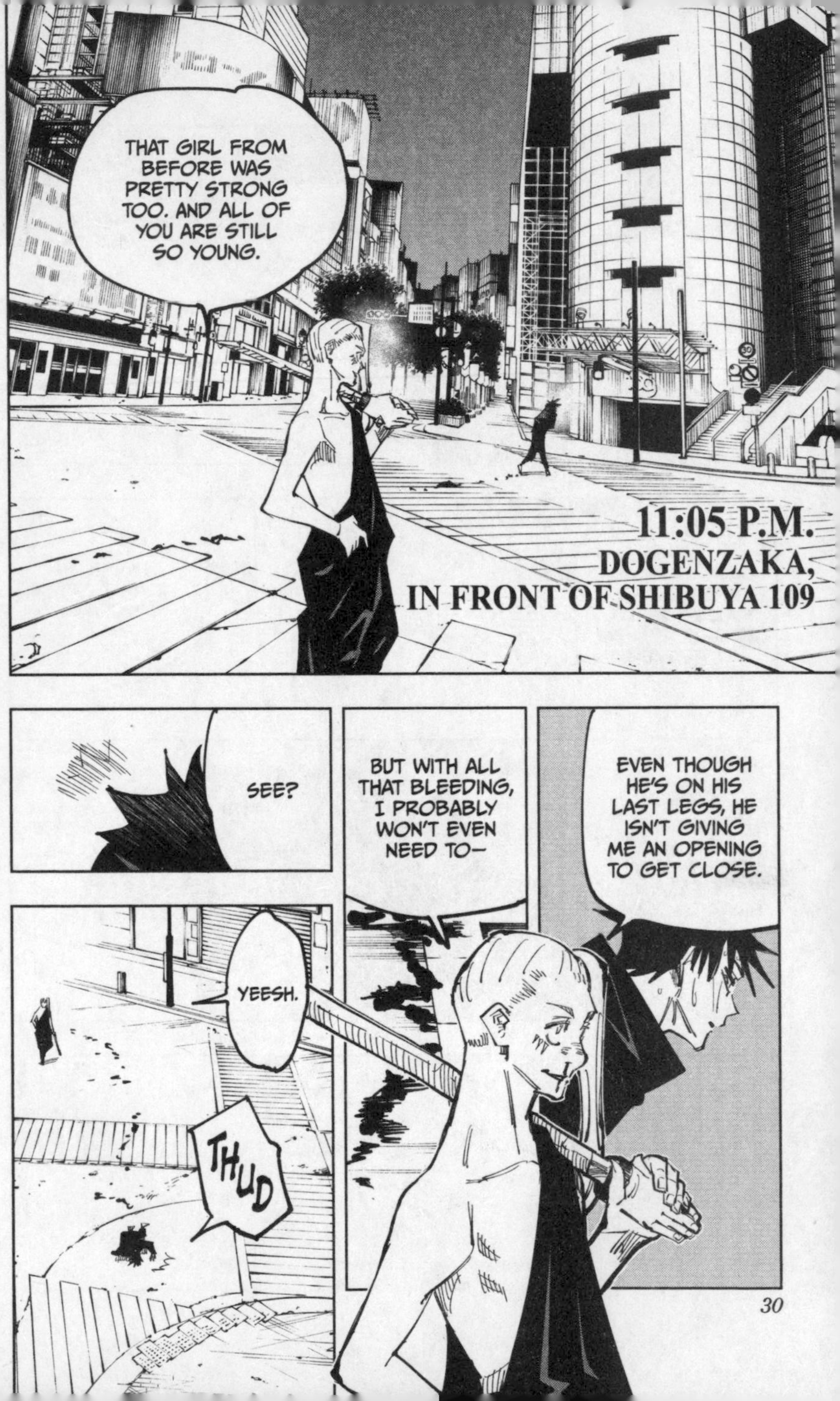
THAT GIRL FROM BEFORE WAS PRETTY STRONG TOO. AND ALL OF YOU ARE STILL SO YOUNG.
11:05 P.M.
DOGENZAKA, IN FRONT OF SHIBUYA 109
EVEN THOUGH HE'S ON HIS LAST LEGS, HE ISN'T GIVING ME AN OPENING TO GET CLOSE.
BUT WITH ALL THAT BLEEDING, I PROBABLY WON'T EVEN NEED TO—
SEE?
YEESH.
THUD

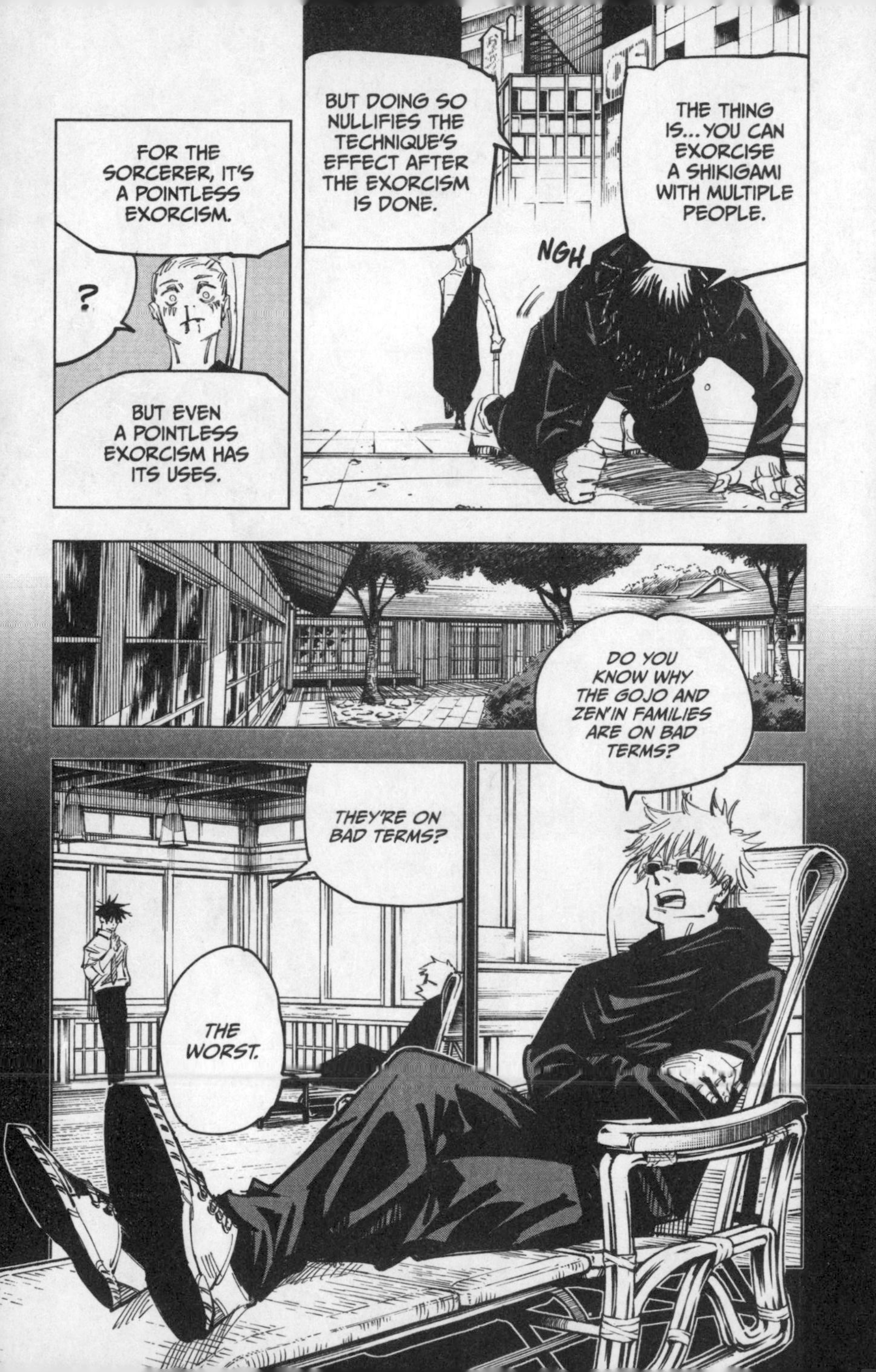
THE THING IS... YOU CAN EXORCISE A SHIKIGAMI WITH MULTIPLE PEOPLE.
BUT DOING SO NULLIFIES THE TECHNIQUE'S EFFECT AFTER THE EXORCISM IS DONE.
NGH
FOR THE SORCERER, IT'S A POINTLESS EXORCISM.
?
BUT EVEN A POINTLESS EXORCISM HAS ITS USES.
DO YOU KNOW WHY THE GOJO AND ZEN'IN FAMILIES ARE ON BAD TERMS?
THEY'RE ON BAD TERMS?
THE WORST.

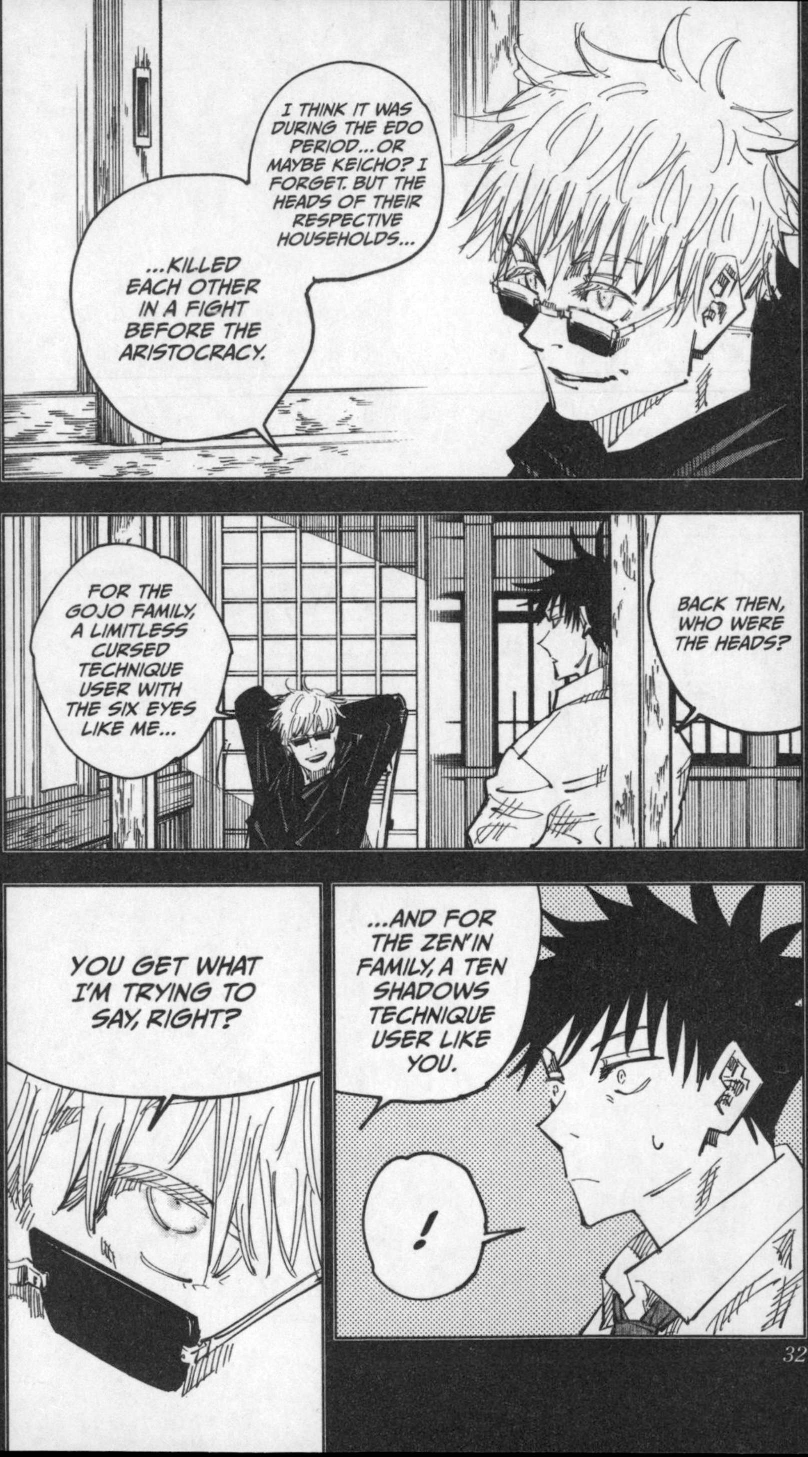
I THINK IT WAS DURING THE EDO PERIOD...OR MAYBE KEICHO? I FORGET. BUT THE HEADS OF THEIR RESPECTIVE HOUSEHOLDS...
...KILLED EACH OTHER IN A FIGHT BEFORE THE ARISTOCRACY.
BACK THEN, WHO WERE THE HEADS?
FOR THE GOJO FAMILY, A LIMITLESS CURSED TECHNIQUE USER WITH THE SIX EYES LIKE ME...
...AND FOR THE ZEN'IN FAMILY, A TEN SHADOWS TECHNIQUE USER LIKE YOU.
!
YOU GET WHAT I'M TRYING TO SAY, RIGHT?

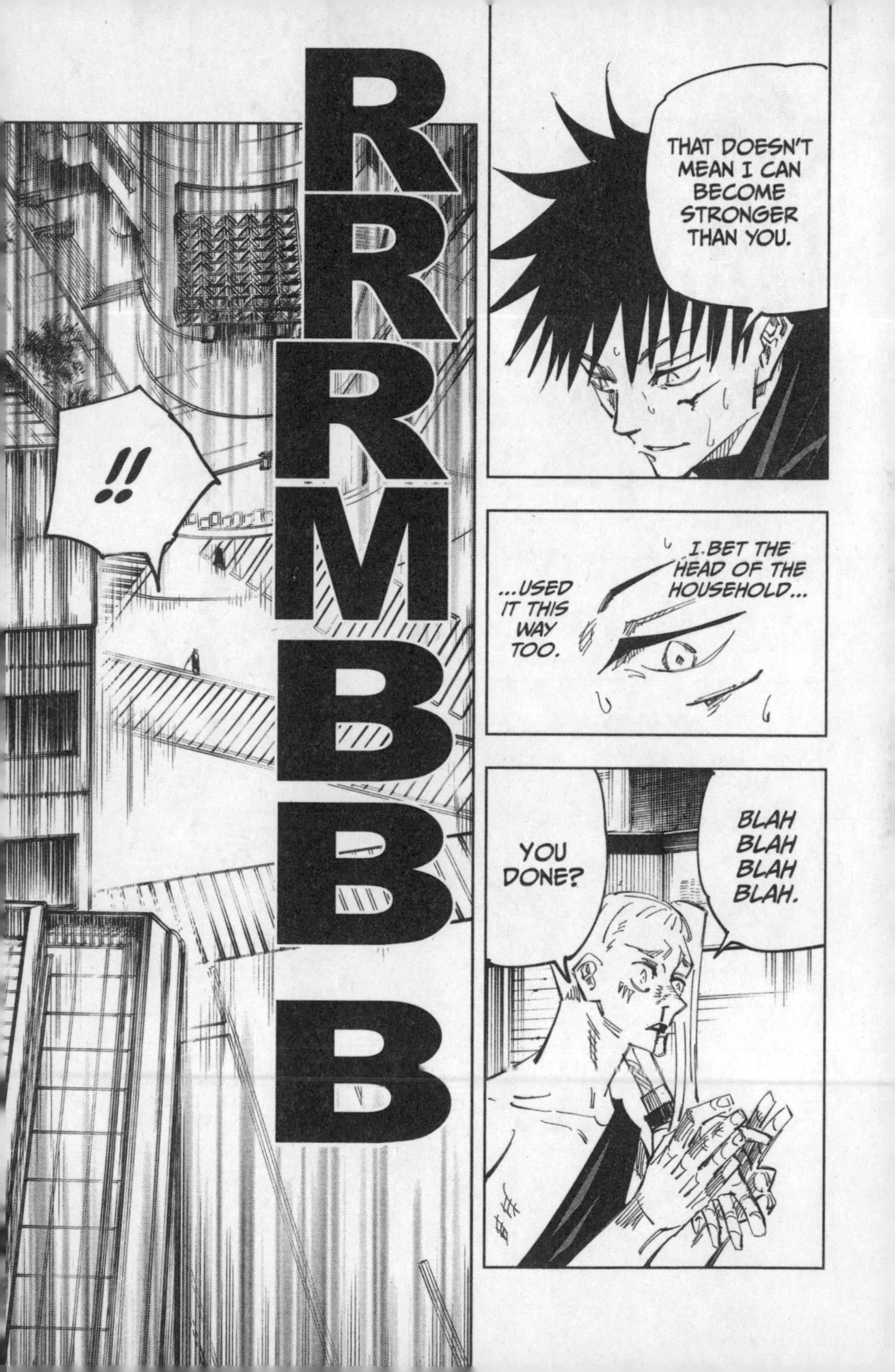
THAT DOESN'T MEAN I CAN BECOME STRONGER THAN YOU.
I BET THE HEAD OF THE HOUSEHOLD...
...USED IT THIS WAY TOO.
BLAH BLAH BLAH BLAH.
YOU DONE?
RRMBBB
!!

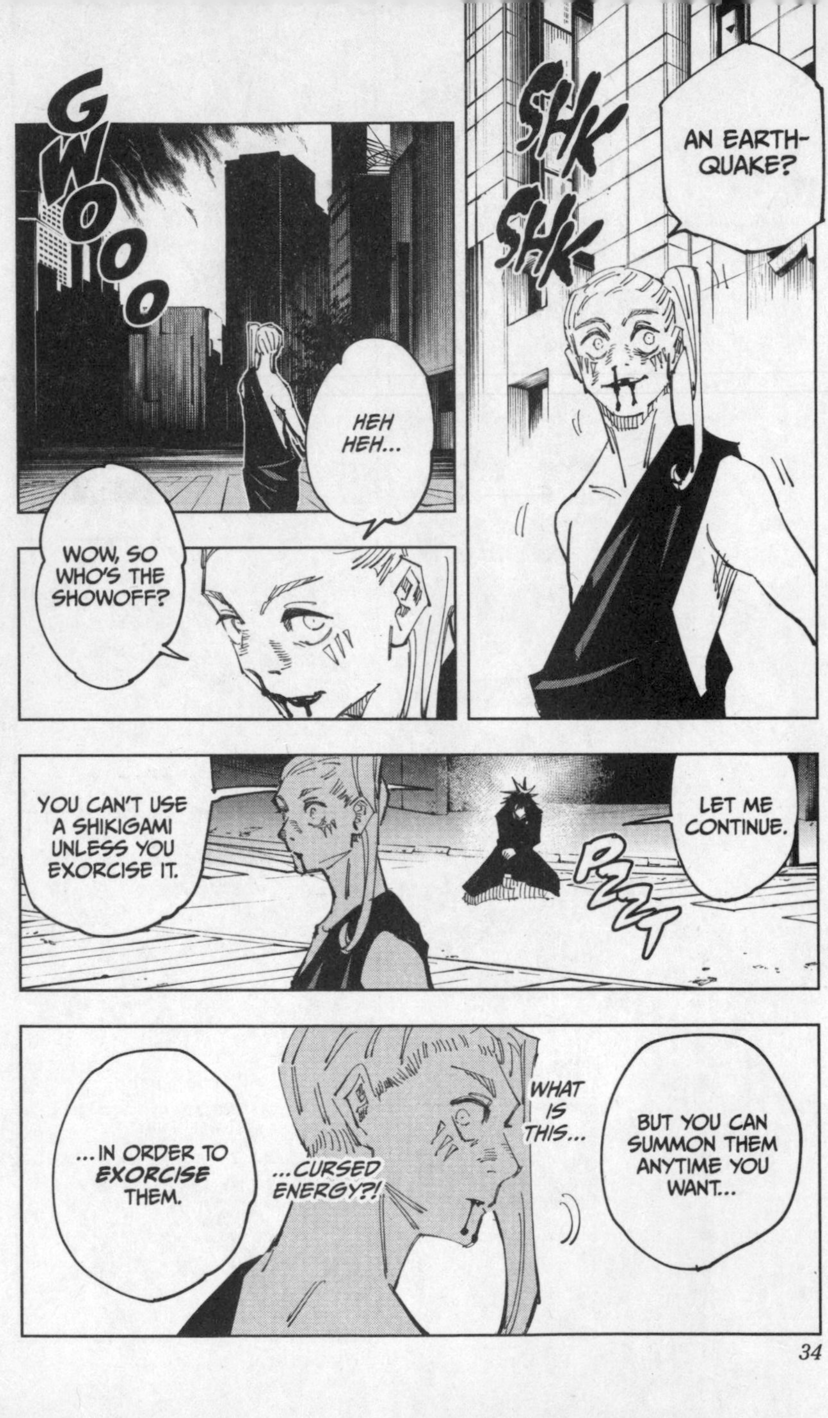
SHK SHK
AN EARTHQUAKE?
GWOOO
HEH HEH...
WOW, SO WHO'S THE SHOWOFF?
LET ME CONTINUE.
PZZT
YOU CAN'T USE A SHIKIGAMI UNLESS YOU EXORCISE IT.
BUT YOU CAN SUMMON THEM ANYTIME YOU WANT...
WHAT IS THIS...
...CURSED ENERGY?!
...IN ORDER TO EXORCISE THEM.

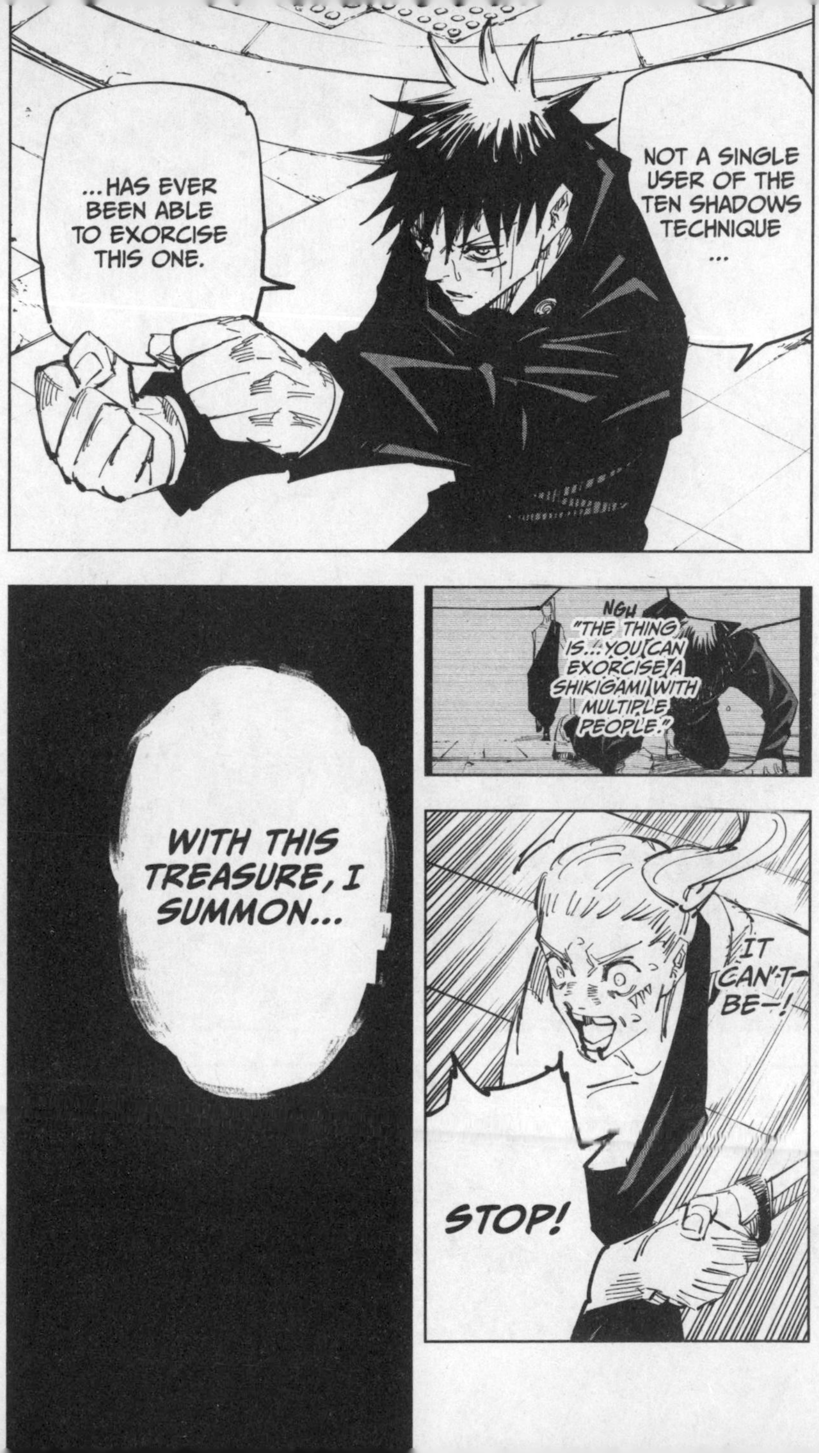
NOT A SINGLE USER OF THE TEN SHADOWS TECHNIQUE ...
...HAS EVER BEEN ABLE TO EXORCISE THIS ONE.
NGH
"THE THING IS... YOU CAN EXORCISE A SHIKIGAMI WITH MULTIPLE PEOPLE."
IT CAN'T BE—!
STOP!
WITH THIS TREASURE, I SUMMON...

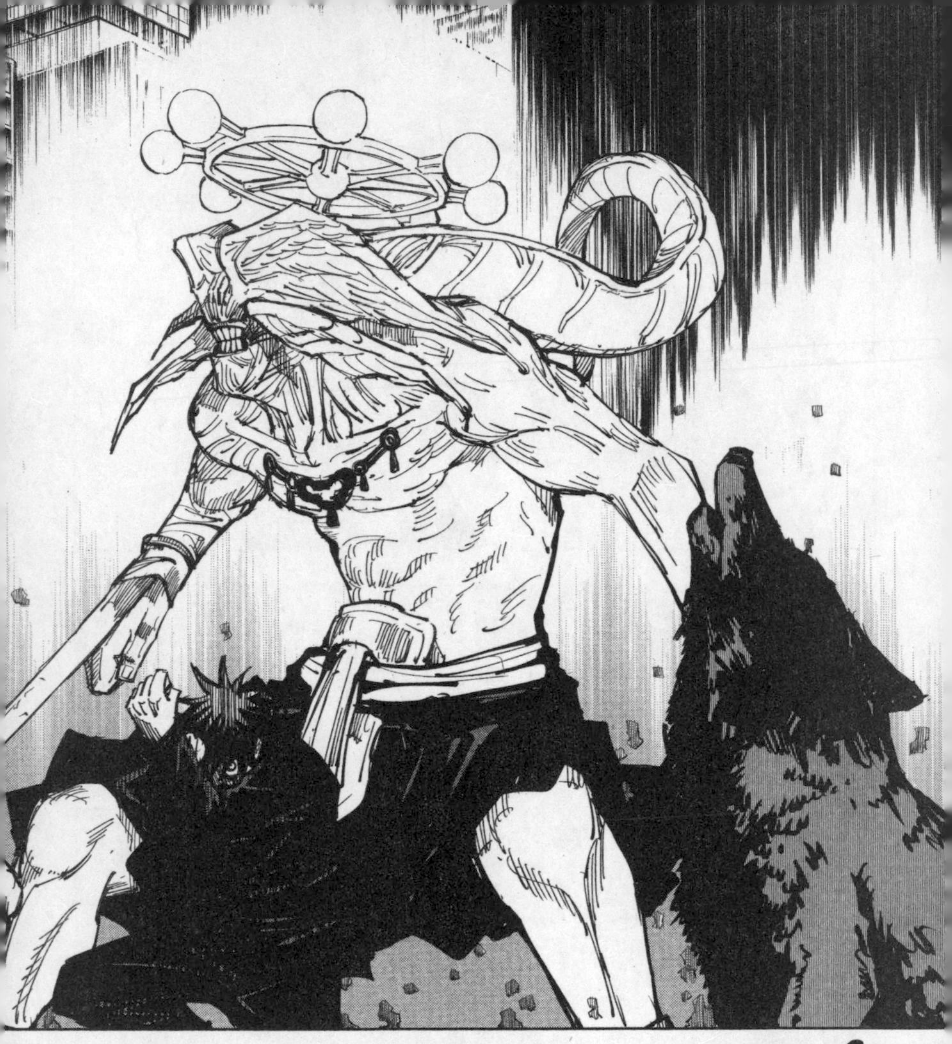

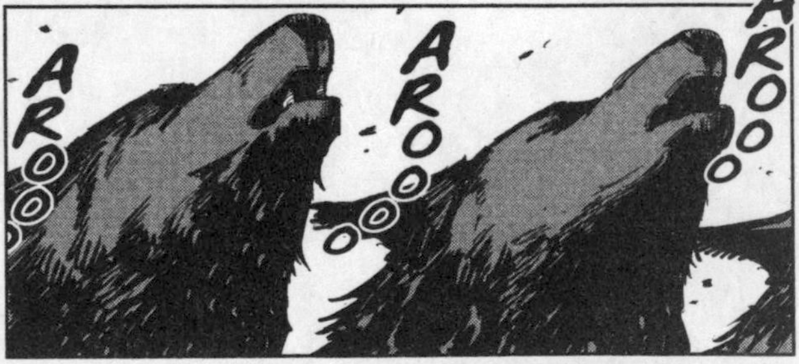
AROOOO
AROOOO
AROOOO

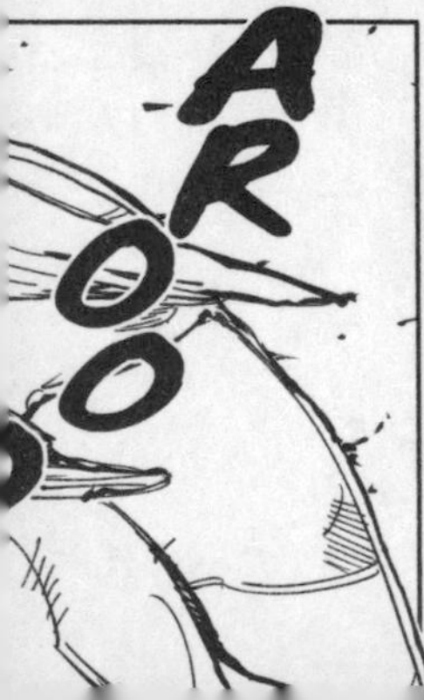
AROO

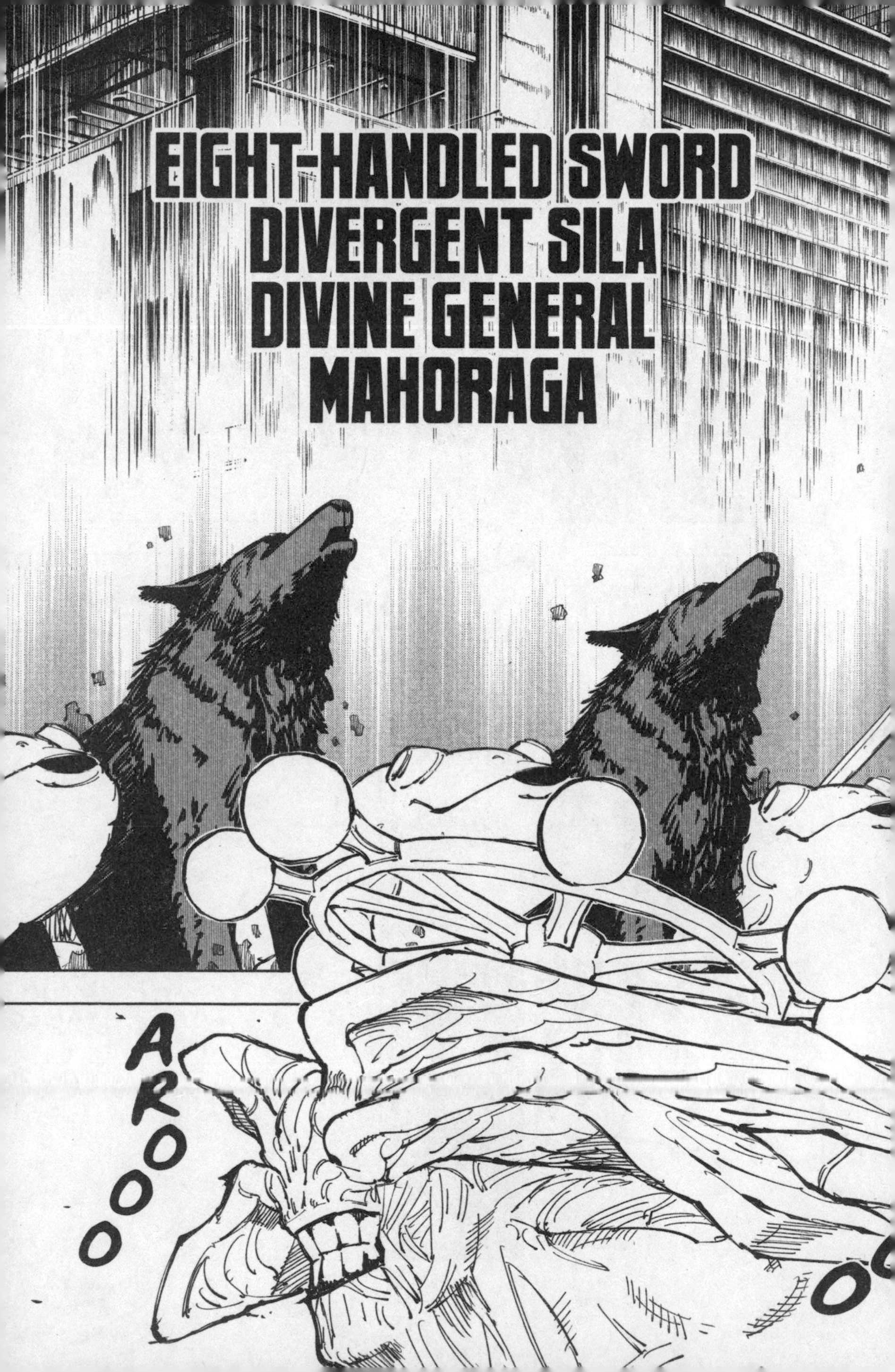
EIGHT-HANDLED SWORD DIVERGENT SILA DIVINE GENERAL MAHORAGA
AROOOO
OO

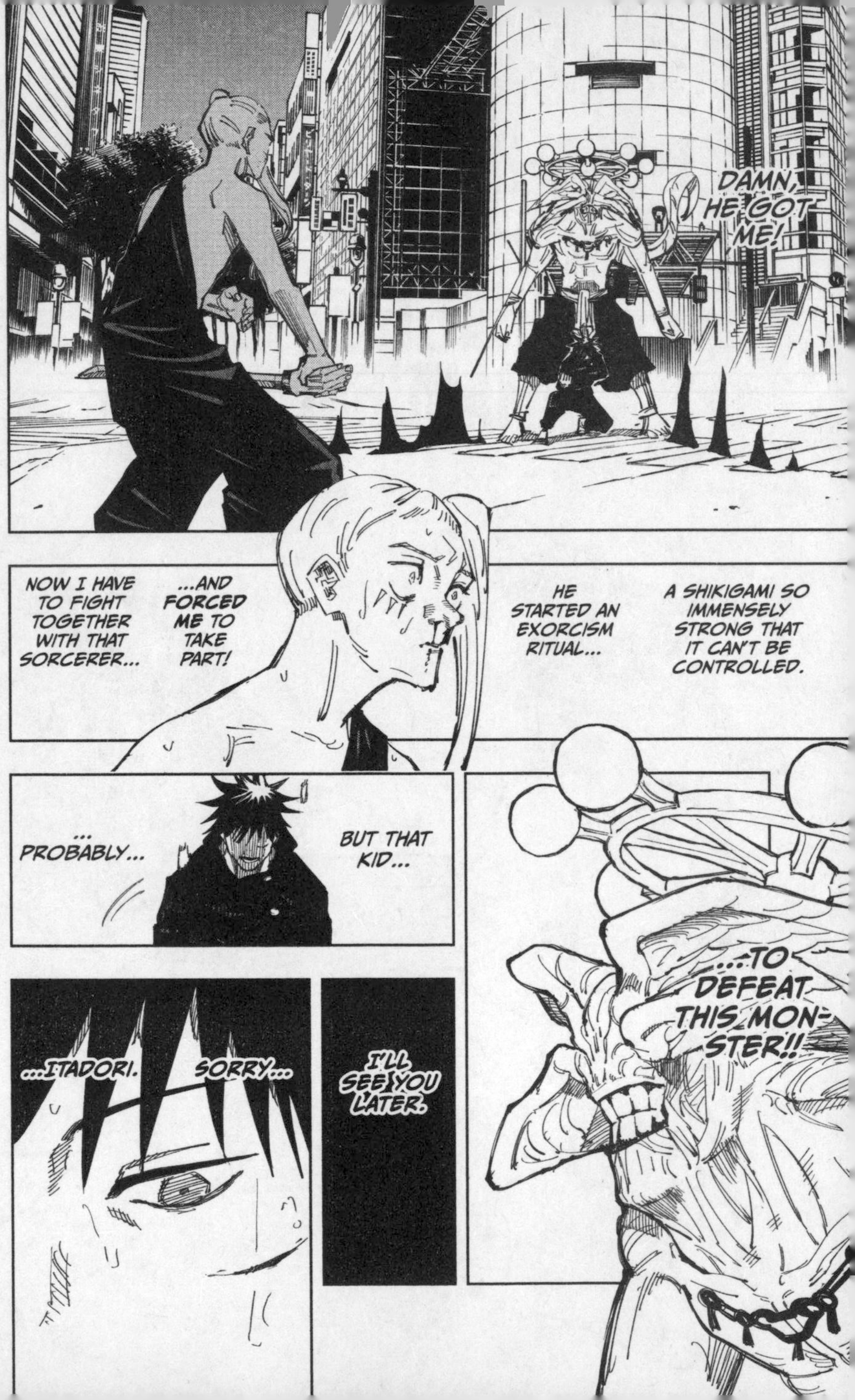
DAMN, HE GOT ME!
A SHIKIGAMI SO IMMENSELY STRONG THAT IT CAN'T BE CONTROLLED.
HE STARTED AN EXORCISM RITUAL...
...AND FORCED ME TO TAKE PART!
NOW I HAVE TO FIGHT TOGETHER WITH THAT SORCERER...
...TO DEFEAT THIS MON-STER!!
BUT THAT KID...
... PROBABLY...
I'LL SEE YOU LATER.
SORRY...
...ITADORI.

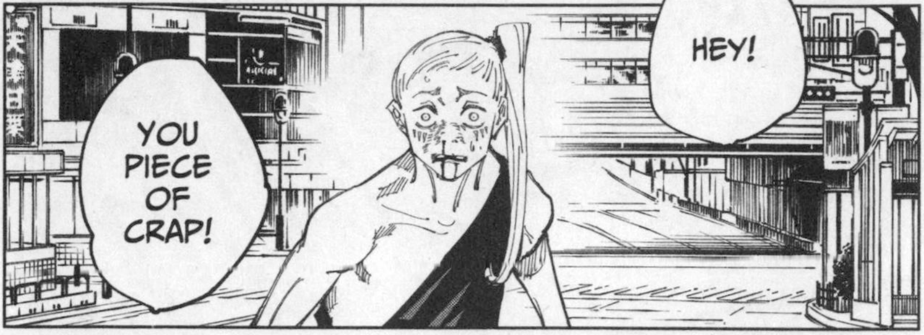
HEY!
YOU PIECE OF CRAP!
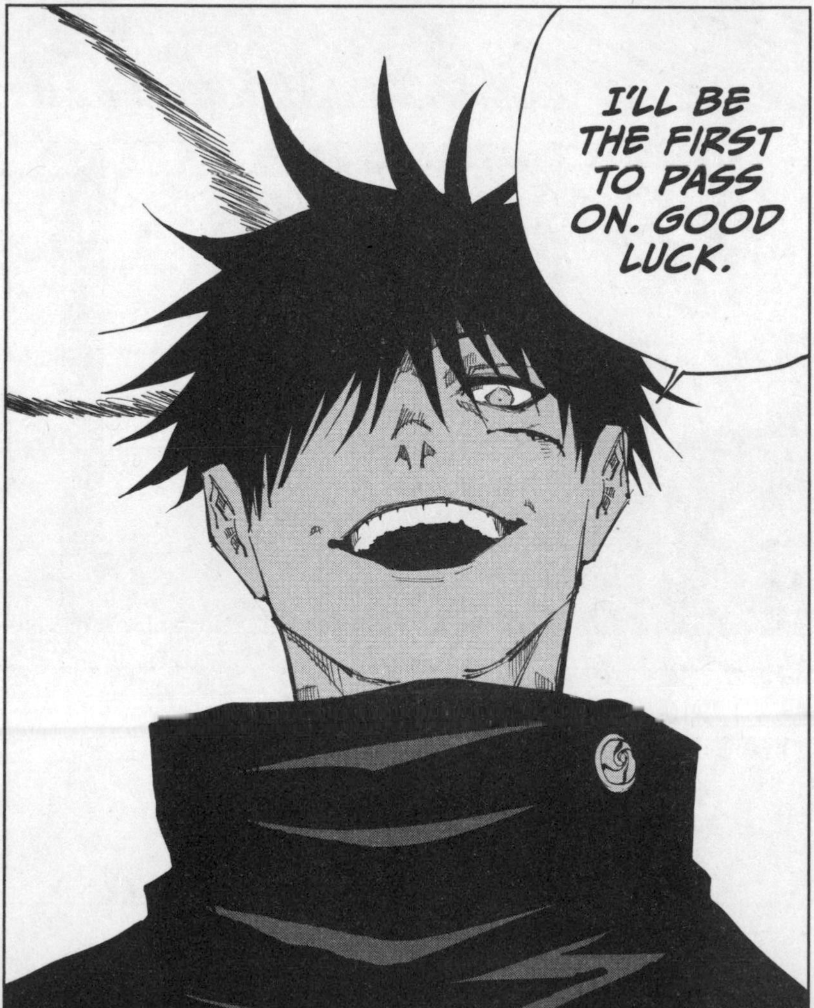
I'LL BE THE FIRST TO PASS ON. GOOD LUCK.

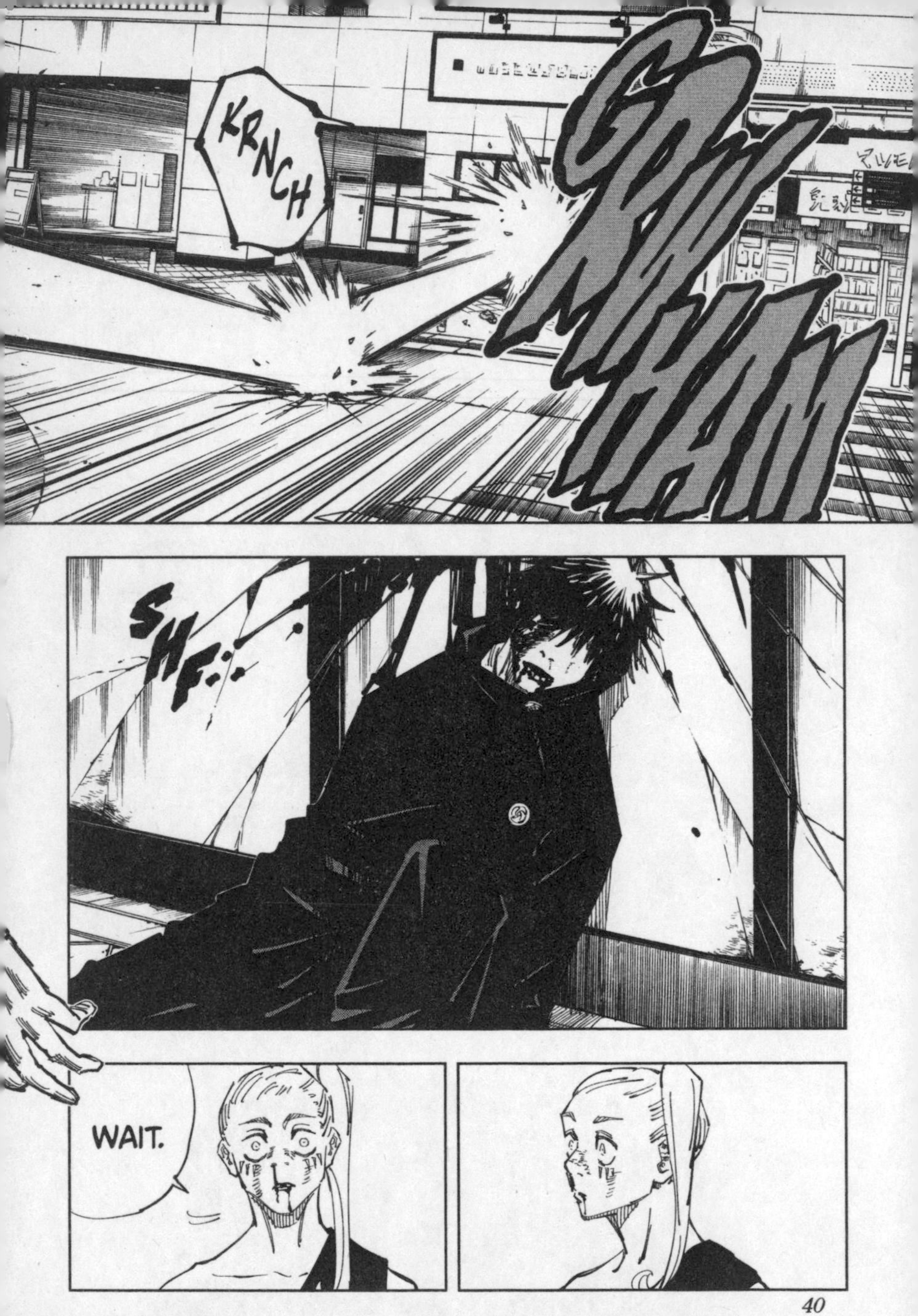
KRNCH
GRAK
WHAM
SHF...
WAIT.

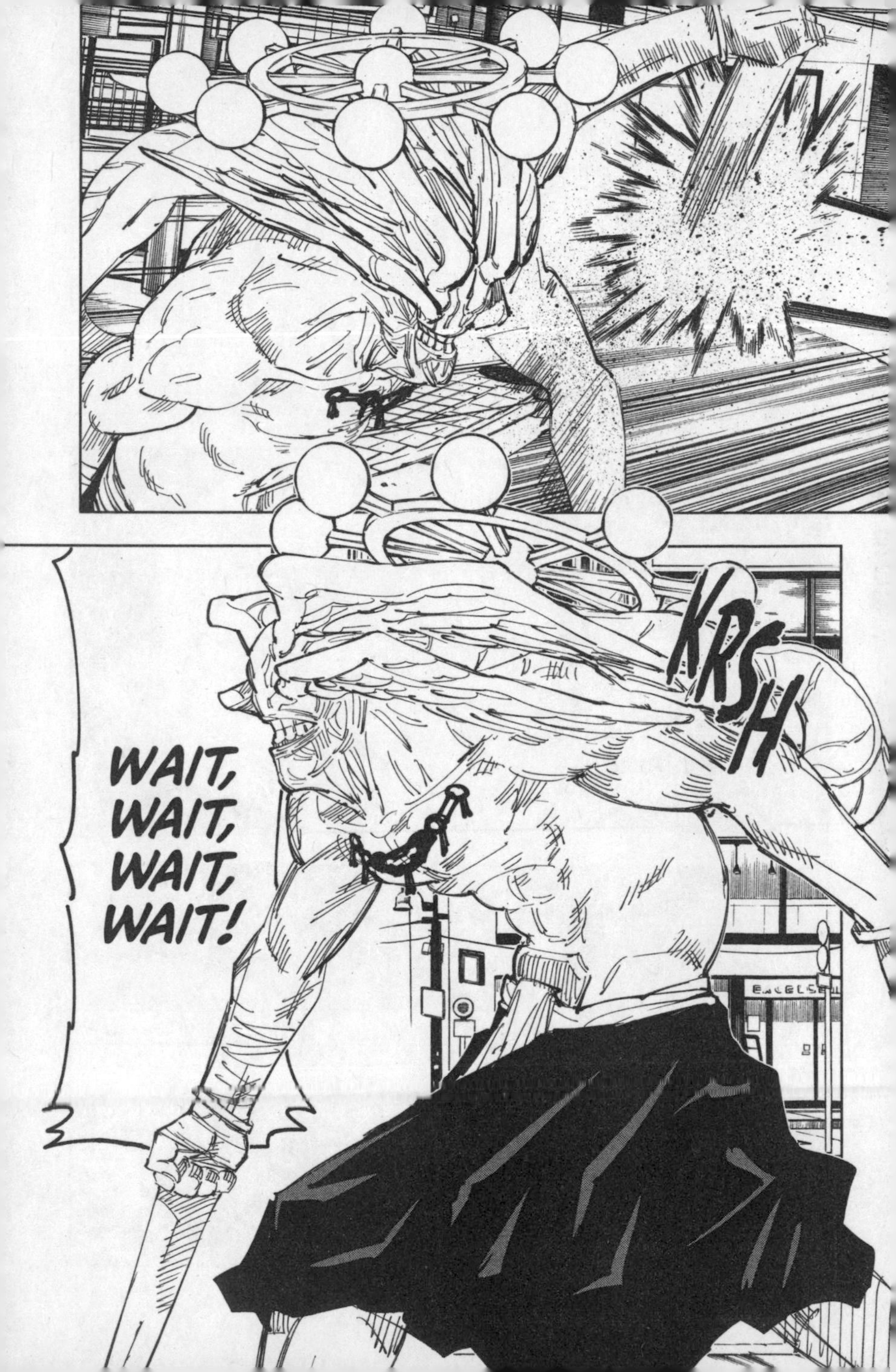
KRSH
WAIT, WAIT, WAIT, WAIT!

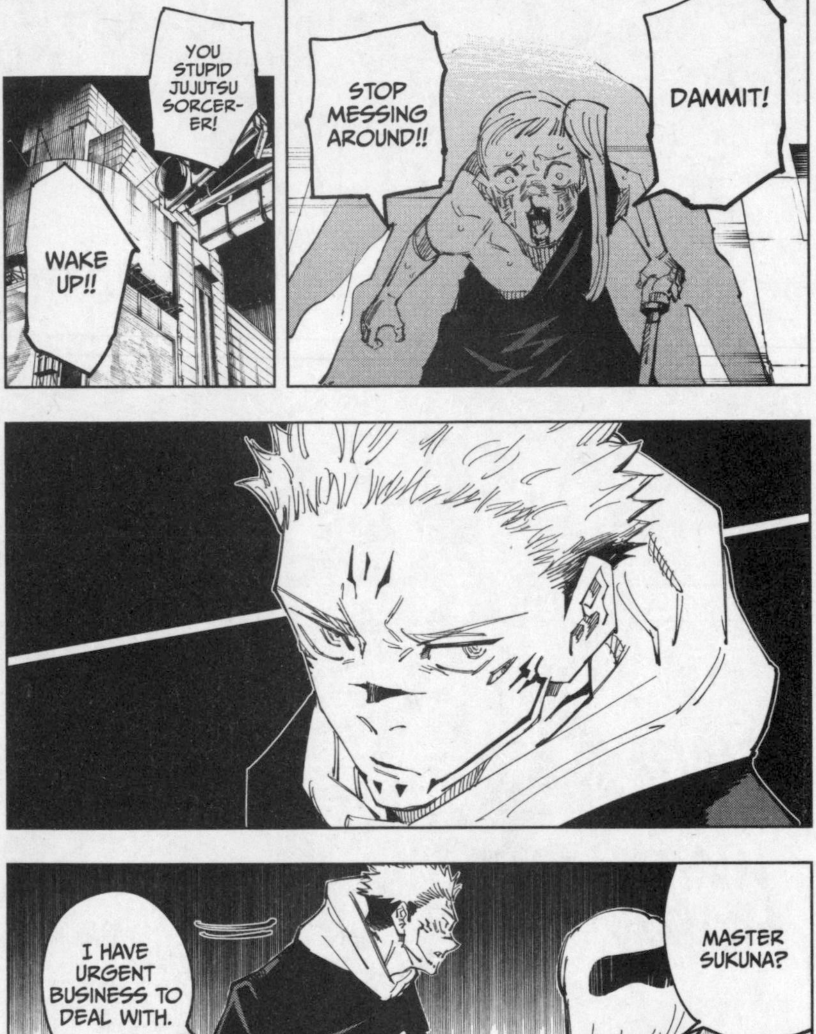
DAMMIT!
STOP MESSING AROUND!!
YOU STUPID JUJUTSU SORCERER!
WAKE UP!!
MASTER SUKUNA?
I HAVE URGENT BUSINESS TO DEAL WITH.

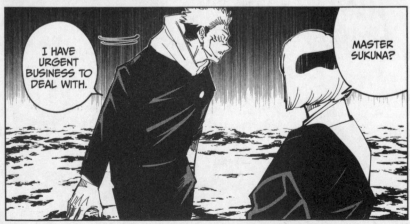

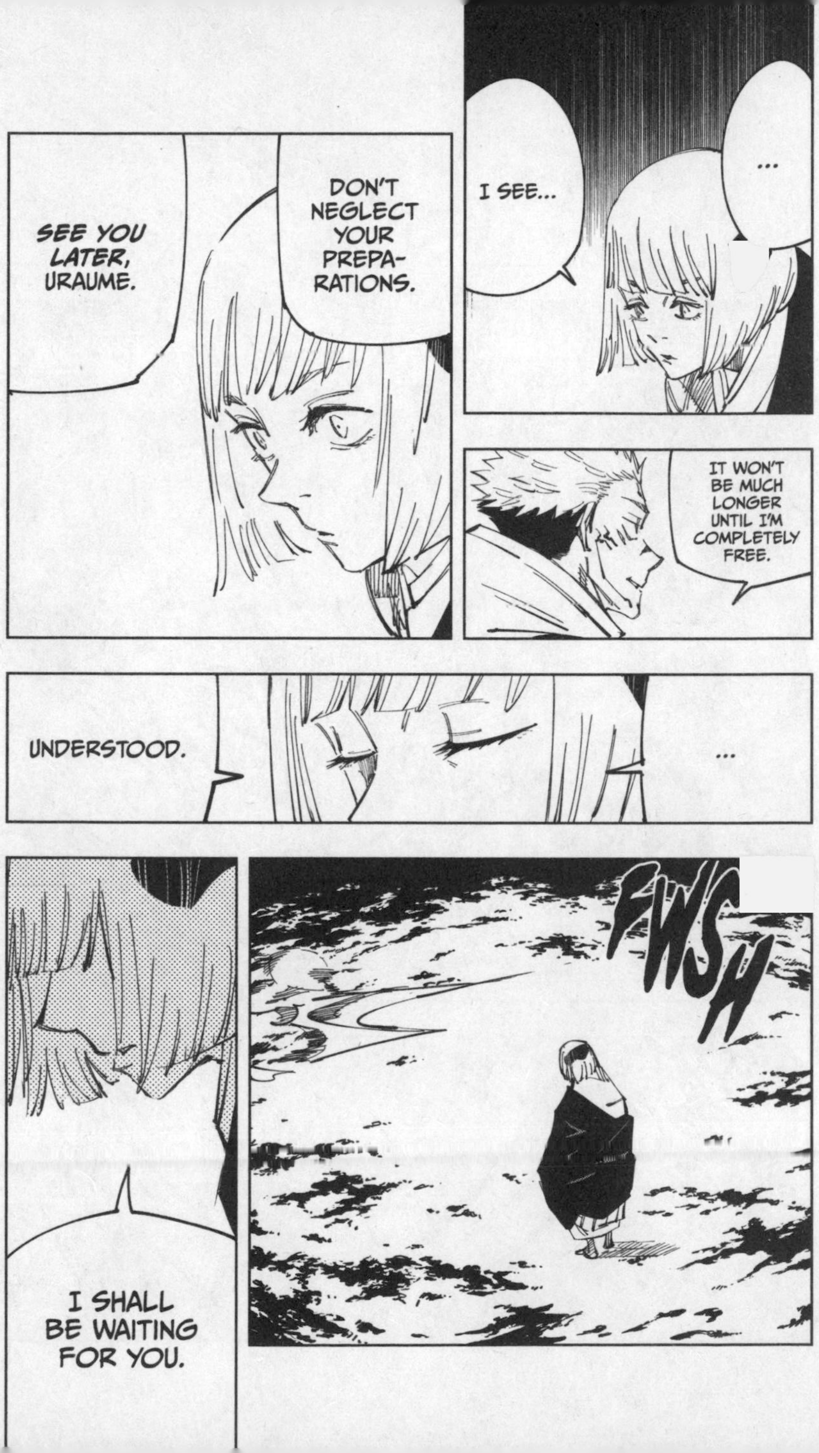
...
I SEE...
DON'T NEGLECT YOUR PREPARATIONS.
SEE YOU LATER, URAUME.
IT WON'T BE MUCH LONGER UNTIL I'M COMPLETELY FREE.
...
UNDERSTOOD.
FWSH
I SHALL BE WAITING FOR YOU.

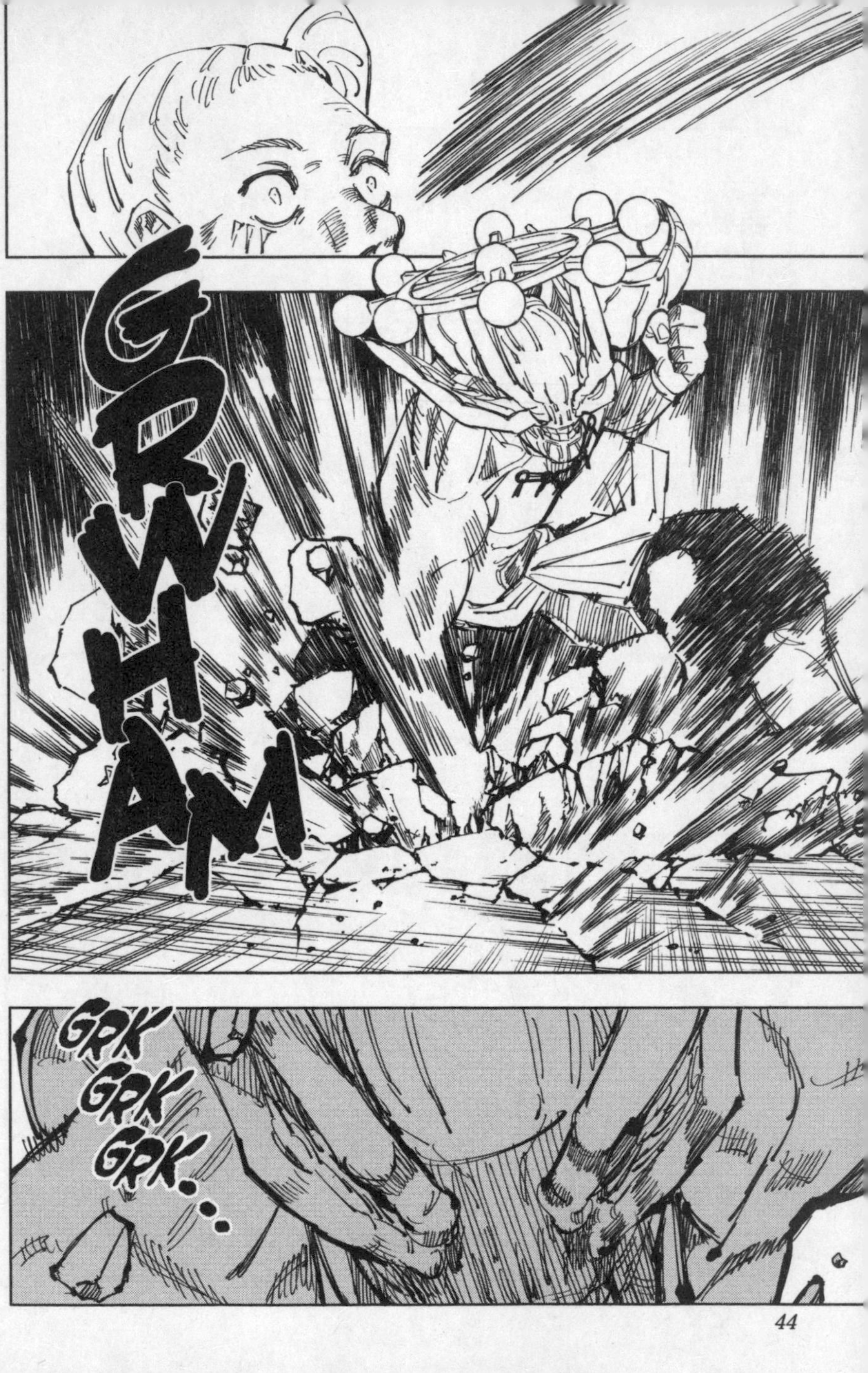
GRWHAM
GRK GRK GRK...

A STATE OF SUSPENDED DEATH!

IF THIS TRASH IS KILLED, THAT'S THE END OF THE RITUAL. MEGUMI FUSHIGURO WILL DIE AS WELL.

HE WAS MOST LIKELY DRAGGED INTO THE EXORCISM RITUAL.

I KNEW IT WAS A GOOD IDEA TO SAVE THIS PIECE OF TRASH.

I SEE...

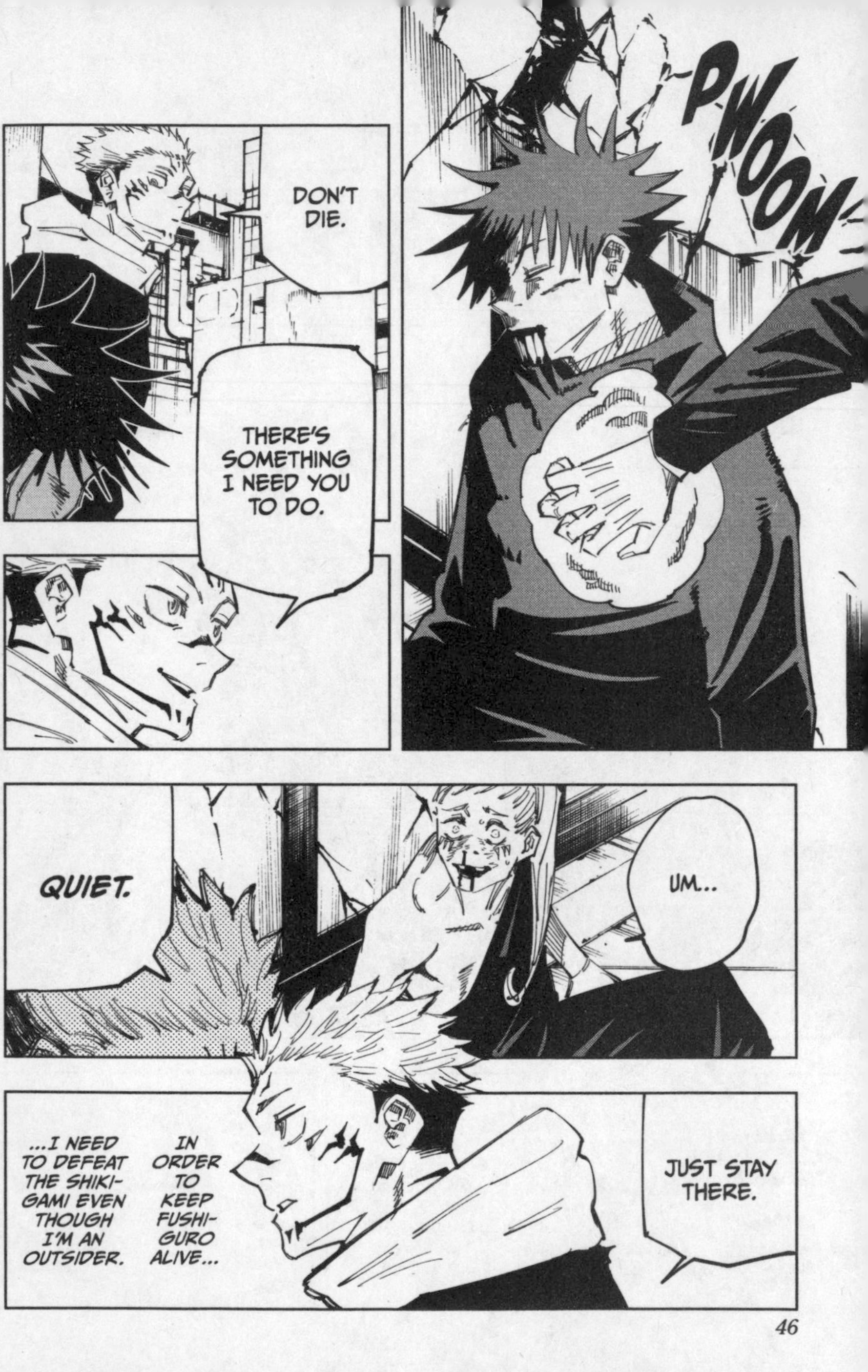
PWOOM
DON'T DIE.
THERE'S SOMETHING I NEED YOU TO DO.
UM...
QUIET.
JUST STAY THERE.
IN ORDER TO KEEP FUSHIGURO ALIVE...
...I NEED TO DEFEAT THE SHIKIGAMI EVEN THOUGH I'M AN OUTSIDER.

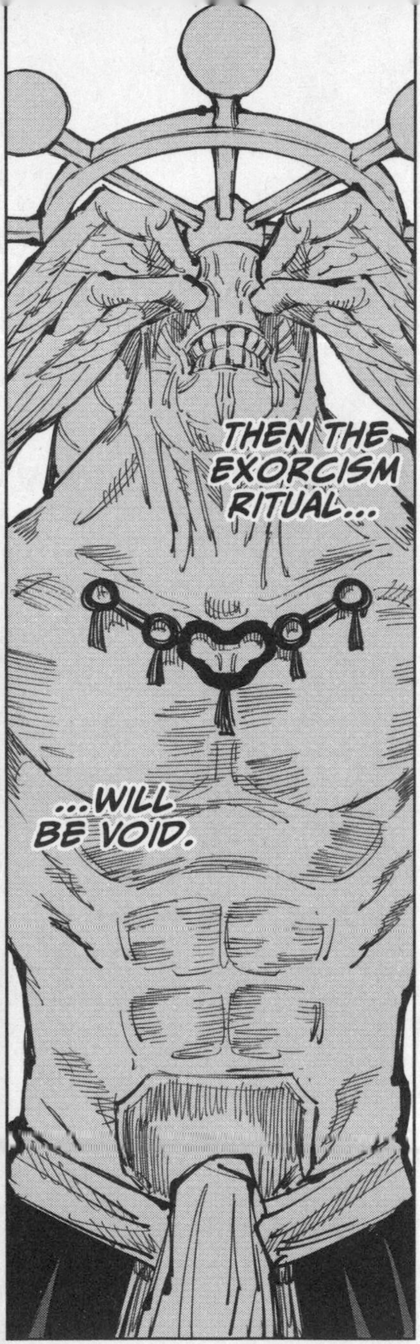
THEN THE EXORCISM RITUAL...
...WILL BE VOID.
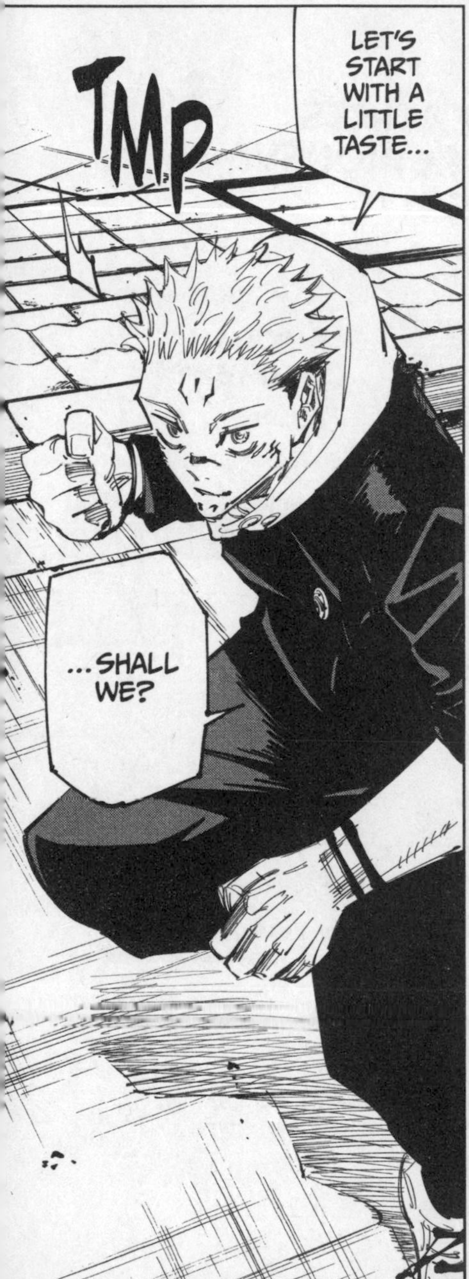
LET'S START WITH A LITTLE TASTE...
TMP
...SHALL WE?

THE 2020 VALENTINES RANKINGS THAT I SERIOUSLY ALMOST FORGOT

RANKINGS (VALENTINES RECEIVED)	CHARACTER	AKUTAMI'S COMMENT
5 (19)	NANAMI	FIFTH IS FIRST.
6 (13)	KUGISAKI	NICE!
7 (7)	CHOSO	HE HASN'T BEEN SHOWING UP MUCH, HAS HE?
8 (6)	INUMAKI	EVEN THOUGH I'VE BARELY EXPLORED HIM...
9 (5)	MAKI	MAYBE I'LL CHANGE HER HAIRSTYLE...

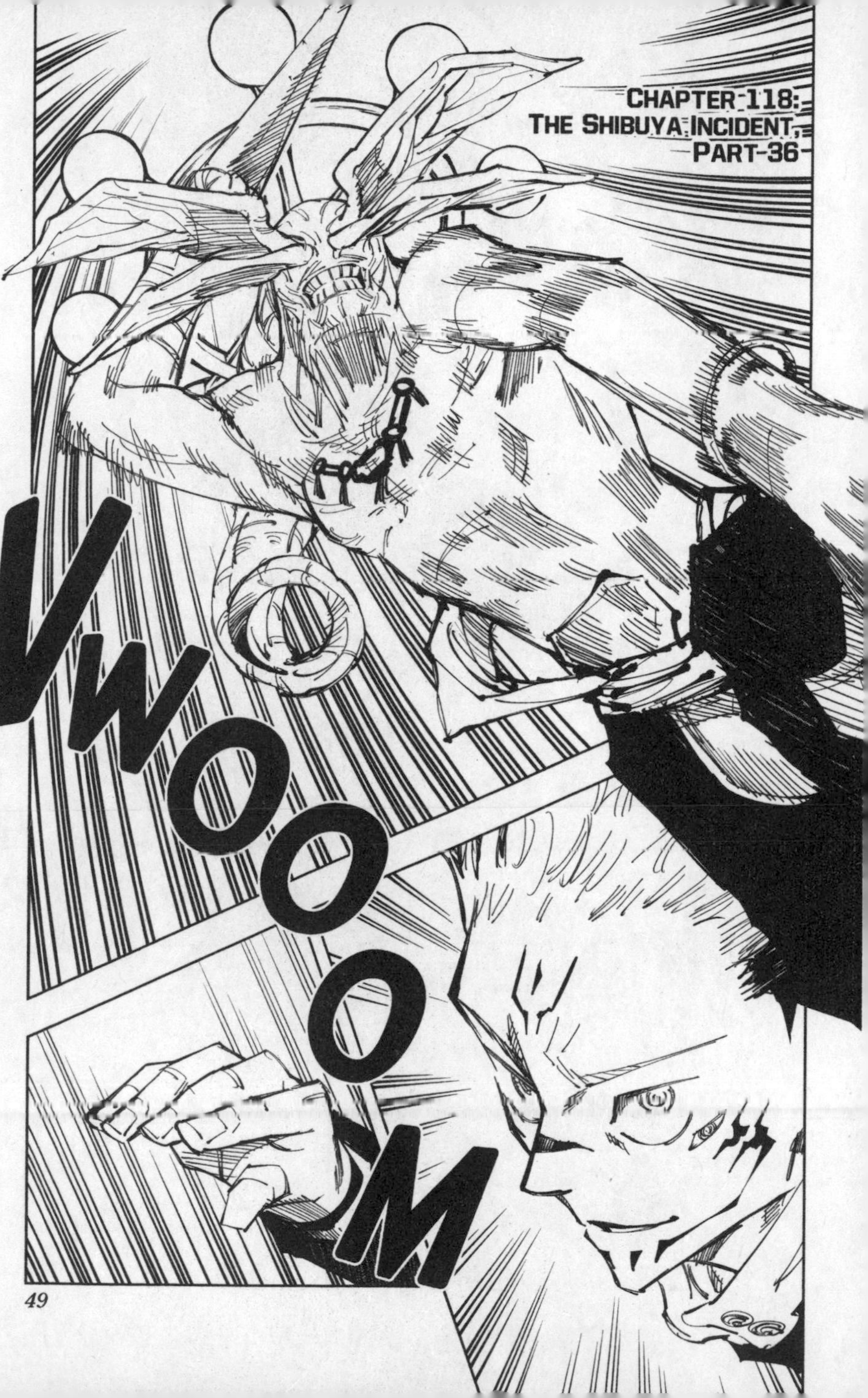

Chapter 118:
The Shibuya Incident,
Part 36
VWOOOOM

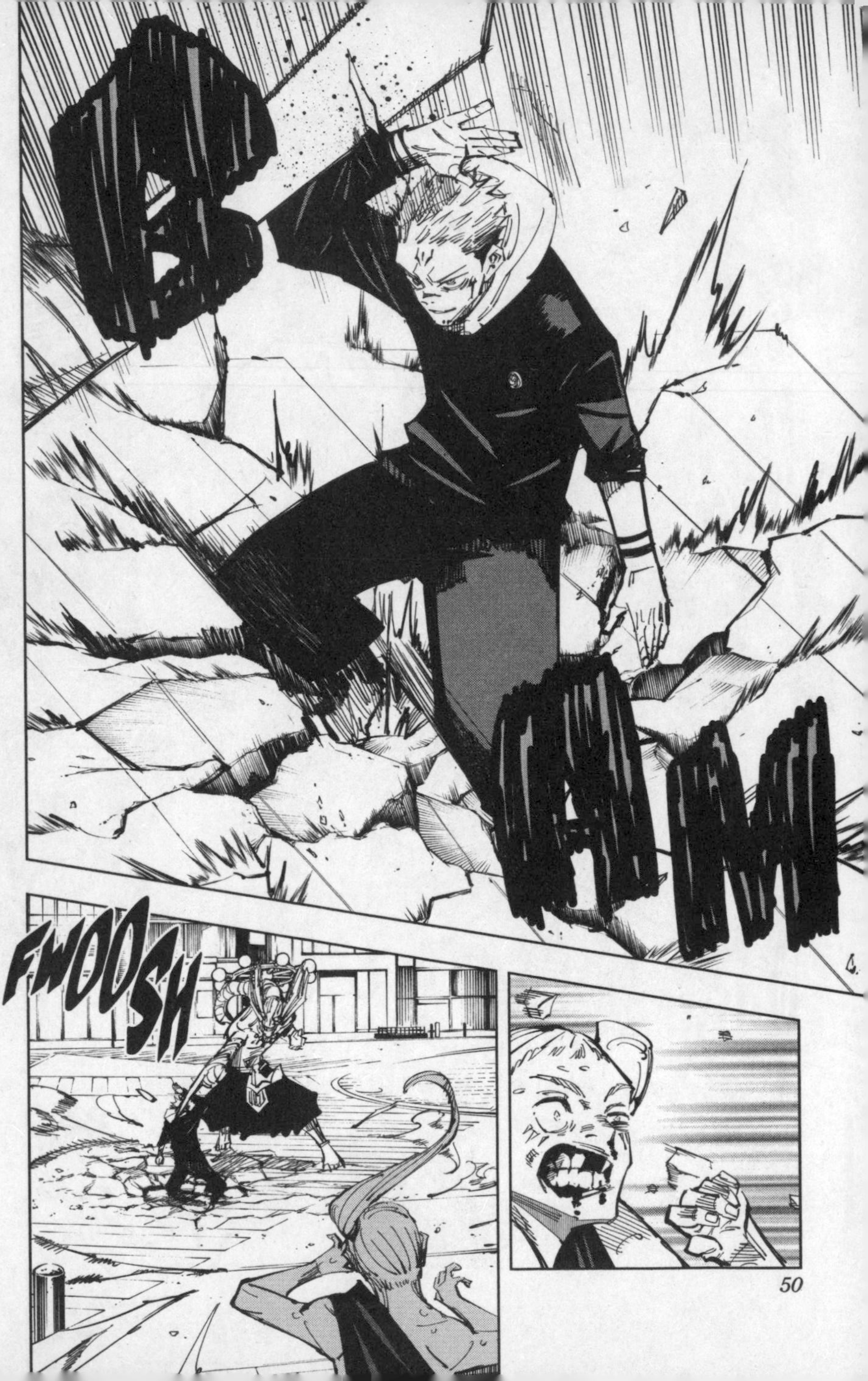
BAM
FWOOSH

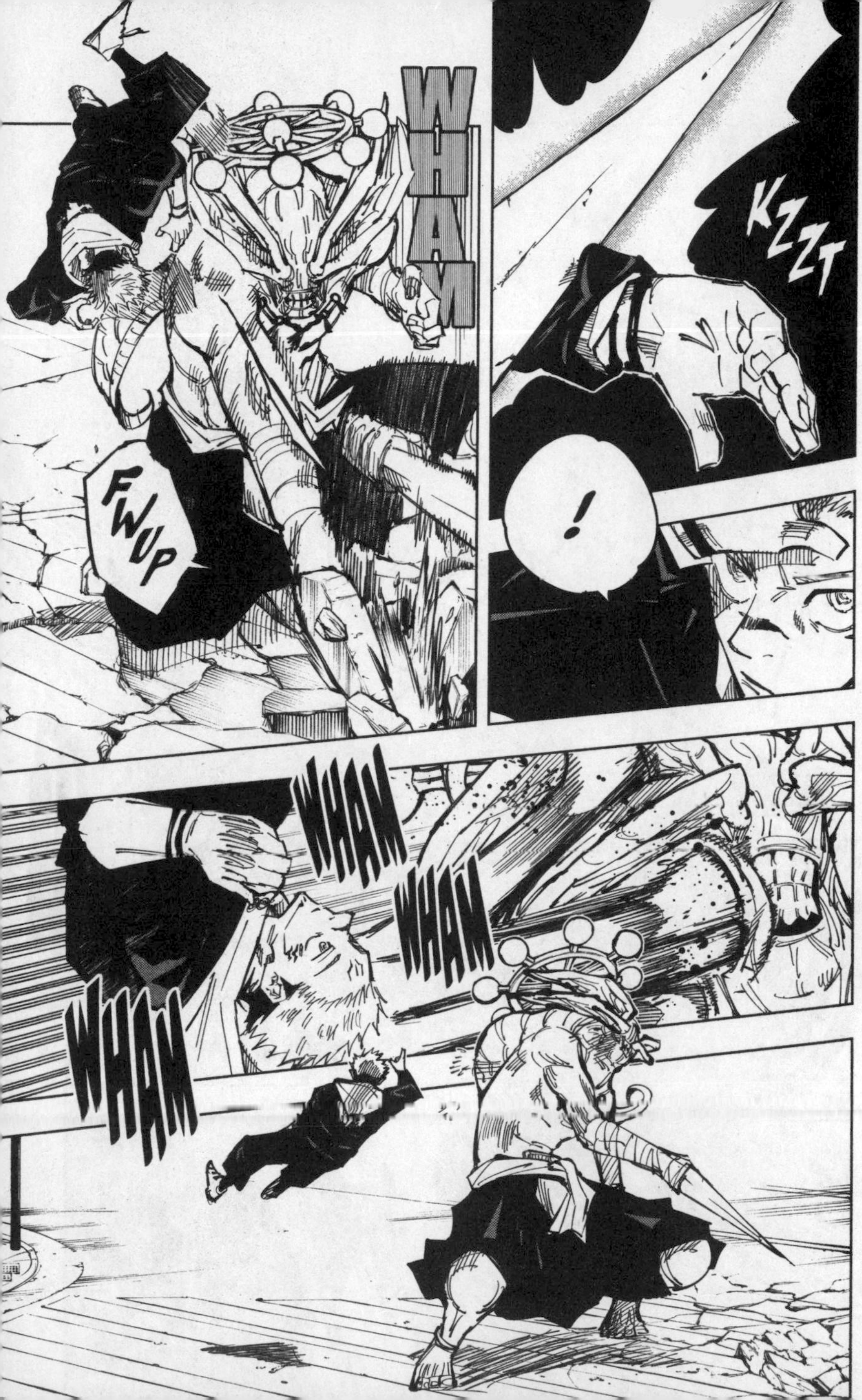
KZZT
!
WHAM
FWUP
WHAM
WHAM
WHAM

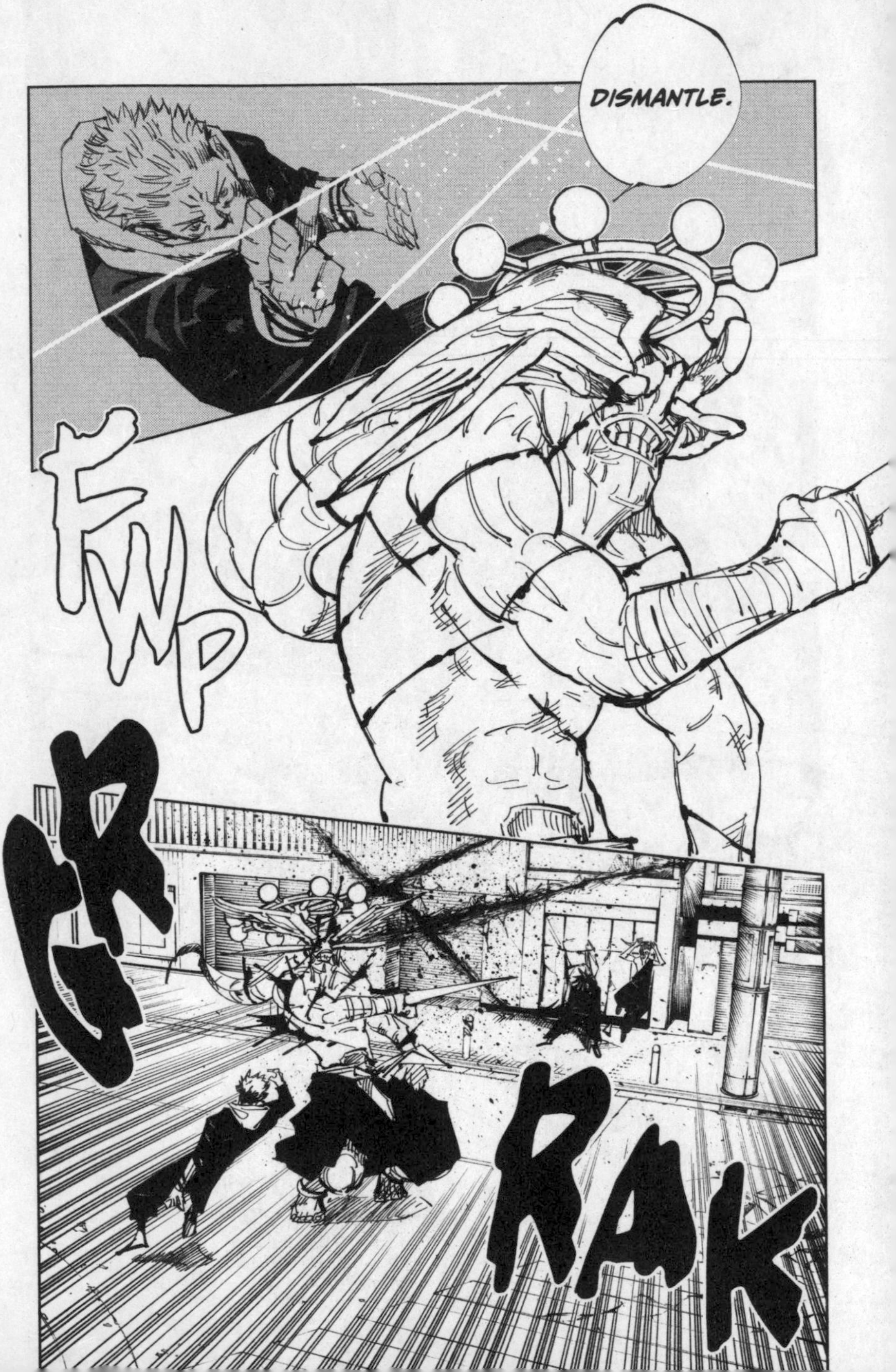
DISMANTLE.
FWP
CRRAK

THAT'S A SPECIALIZED BLADE FOR CURSED SPIRITS. THE SWORD OF EXTERMINATION.

THUNK

IT'S ENVELOPED IN POSITIVE ENERGY, THAT IS SIMILAR TO REVERSE CURSED ENERGY.

KZZT

IF I WAS A CURSED SPIRIT, I'D BE A GONER.

KTNK

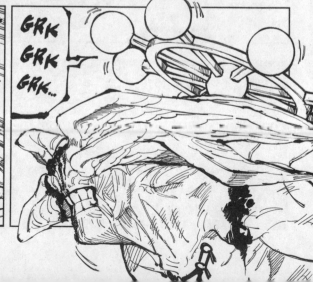

GRK GRK GRK...

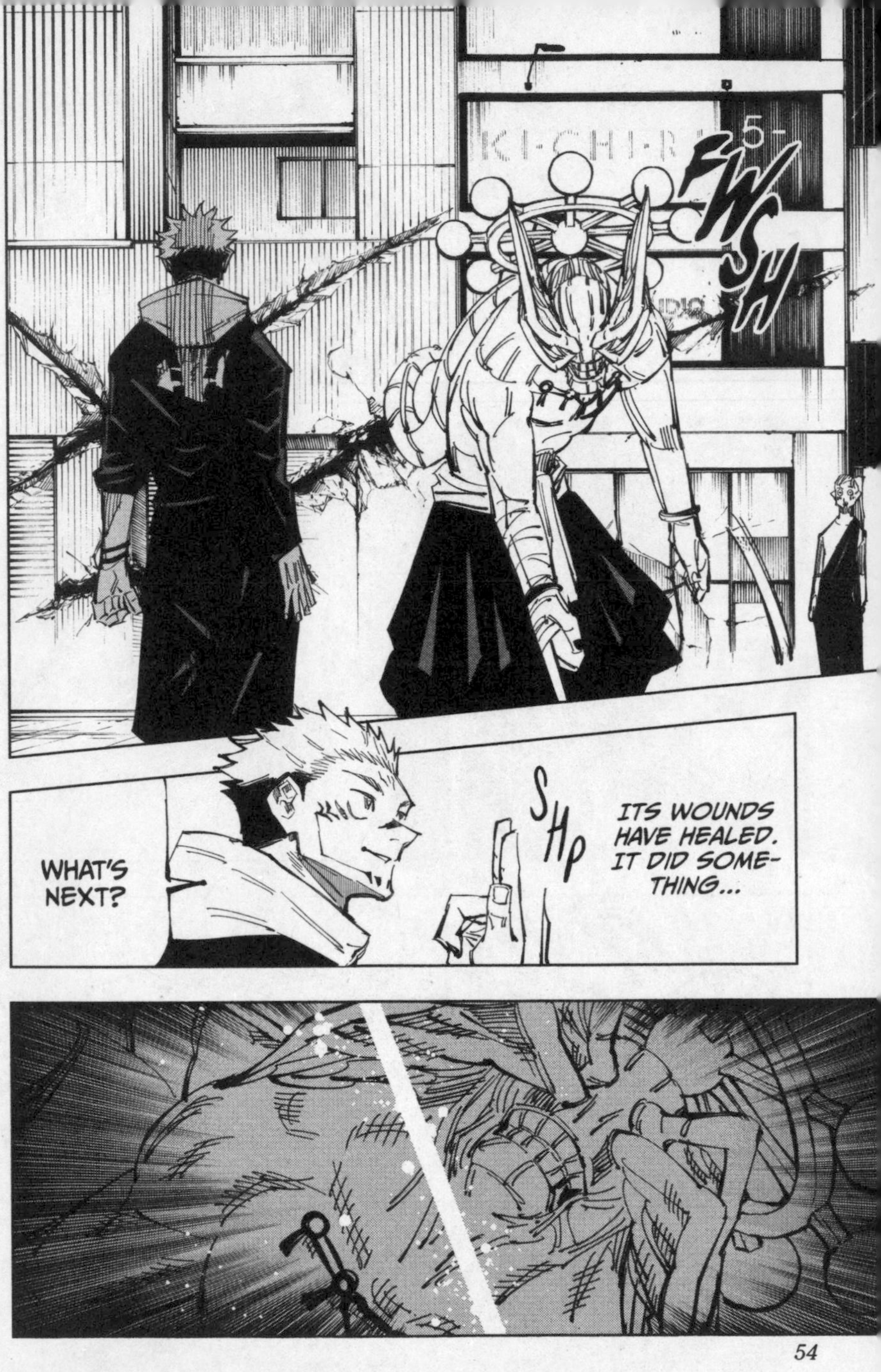
FWSH
SHP
ITS WOUNDS HAVE HEALED. IT DID SOME-THING...
WHAT'S NEXT?

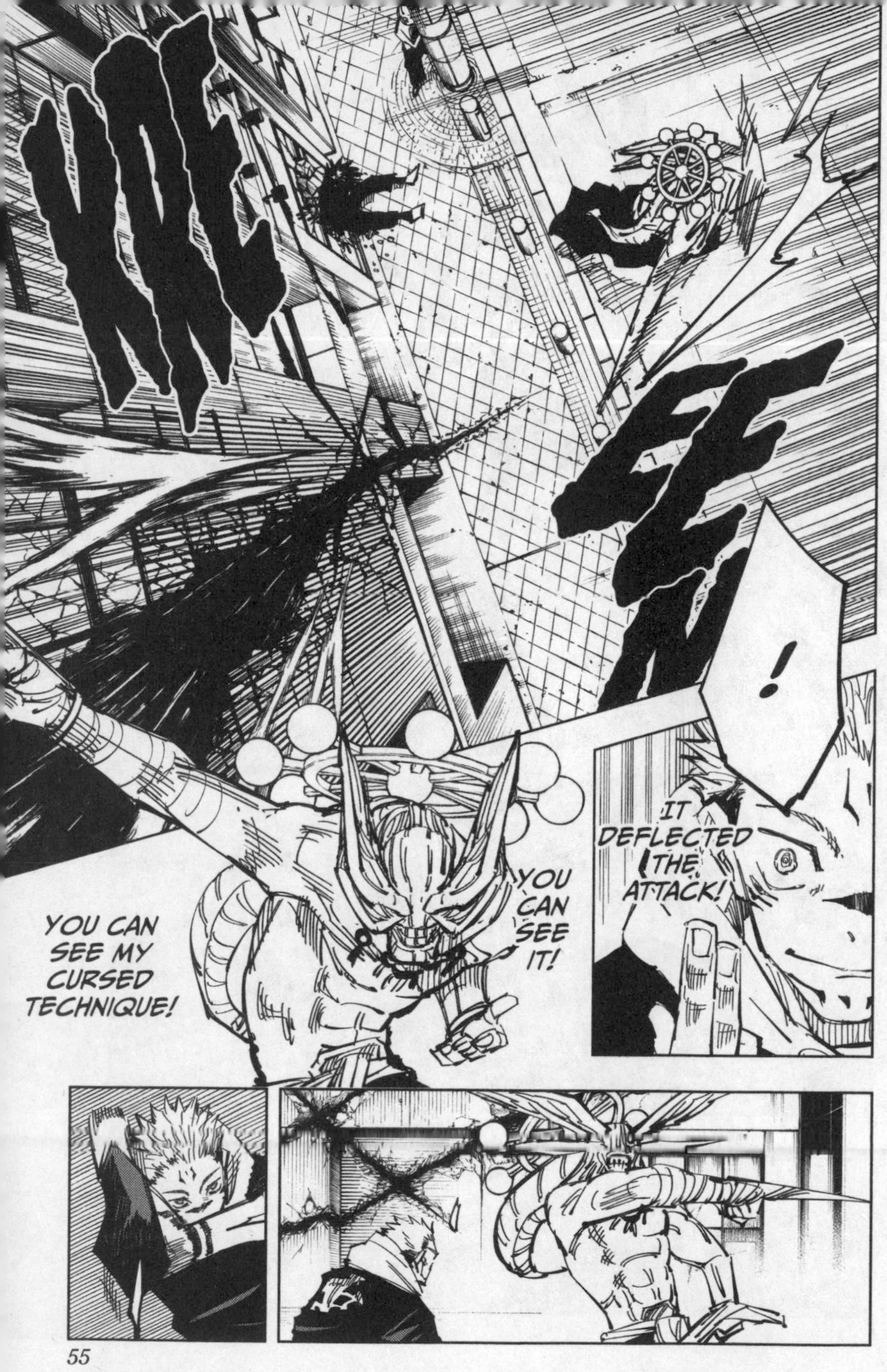
!
IT DEFLECTED THE ATTACK!
YOU CAN SEE IT!
YOU CAN SEE MY CURSED TECHNIQUE!

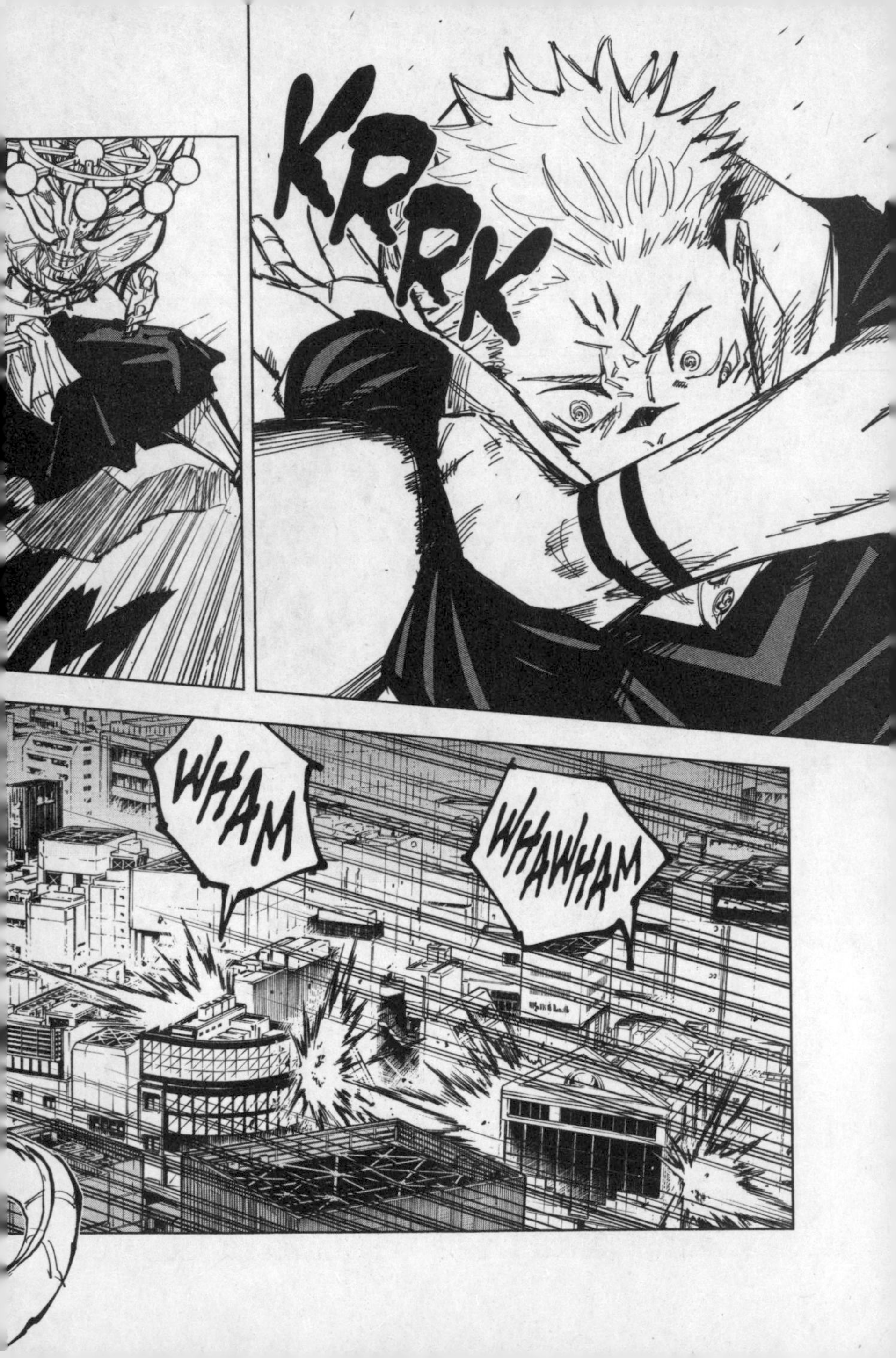
KRRK
WHAM
WHAWHAM

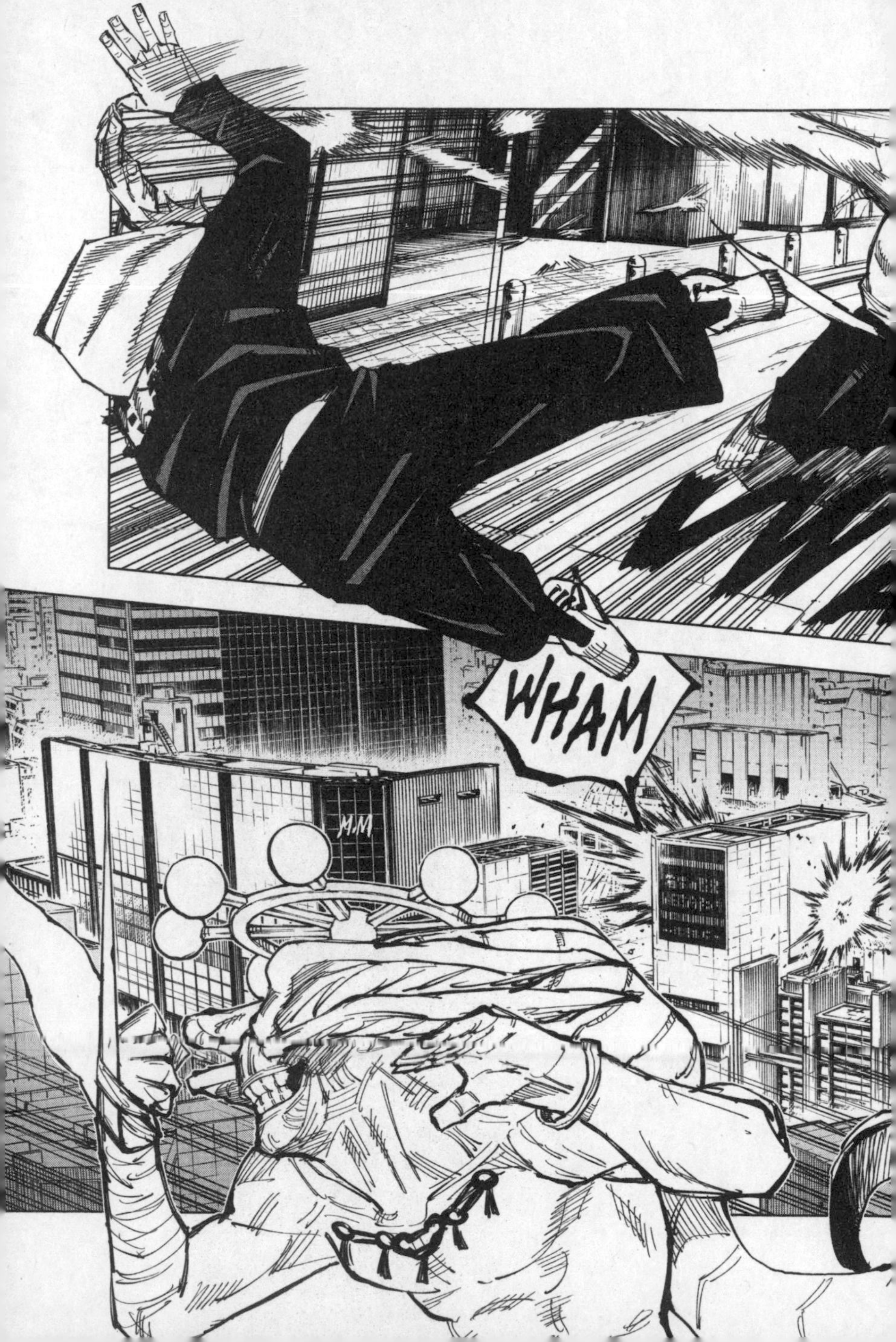
WHAM
M.M

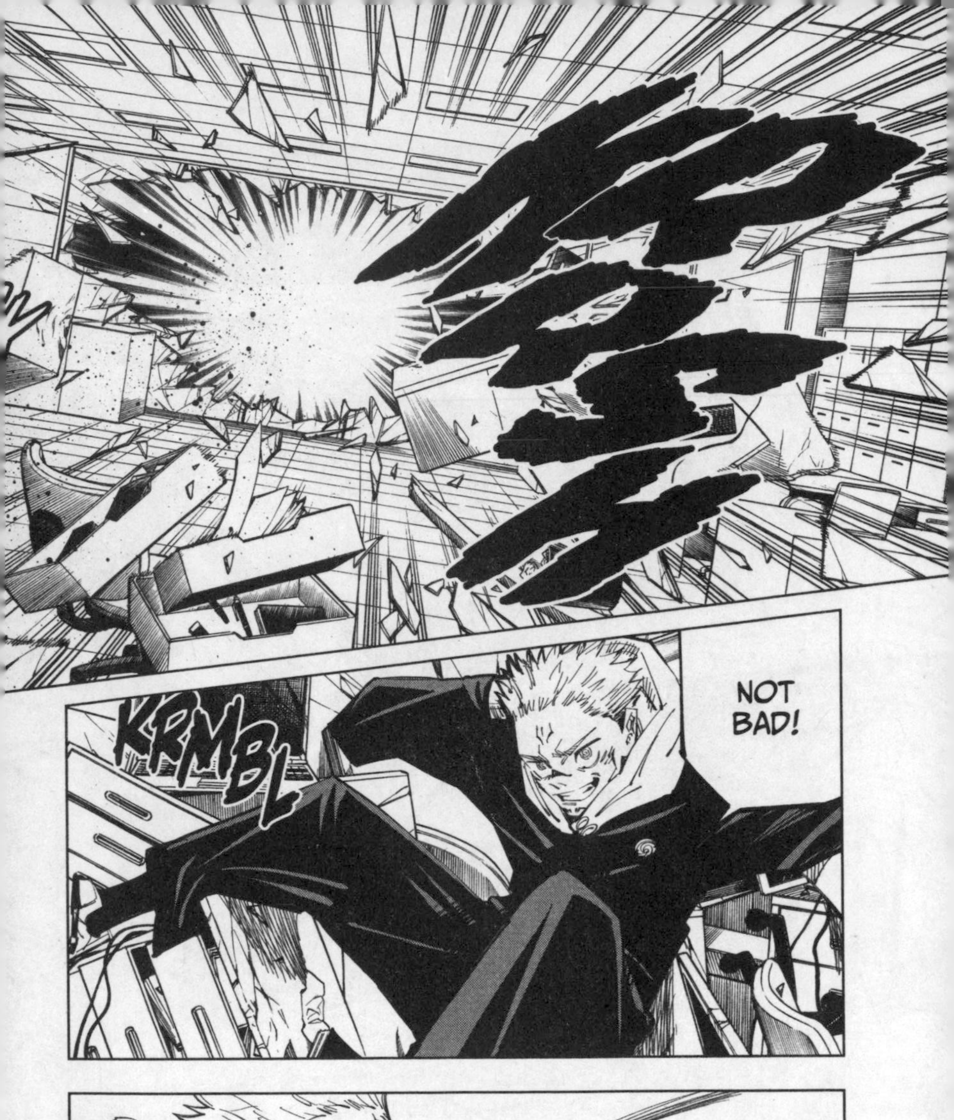
NOT BAD!
KRMBL

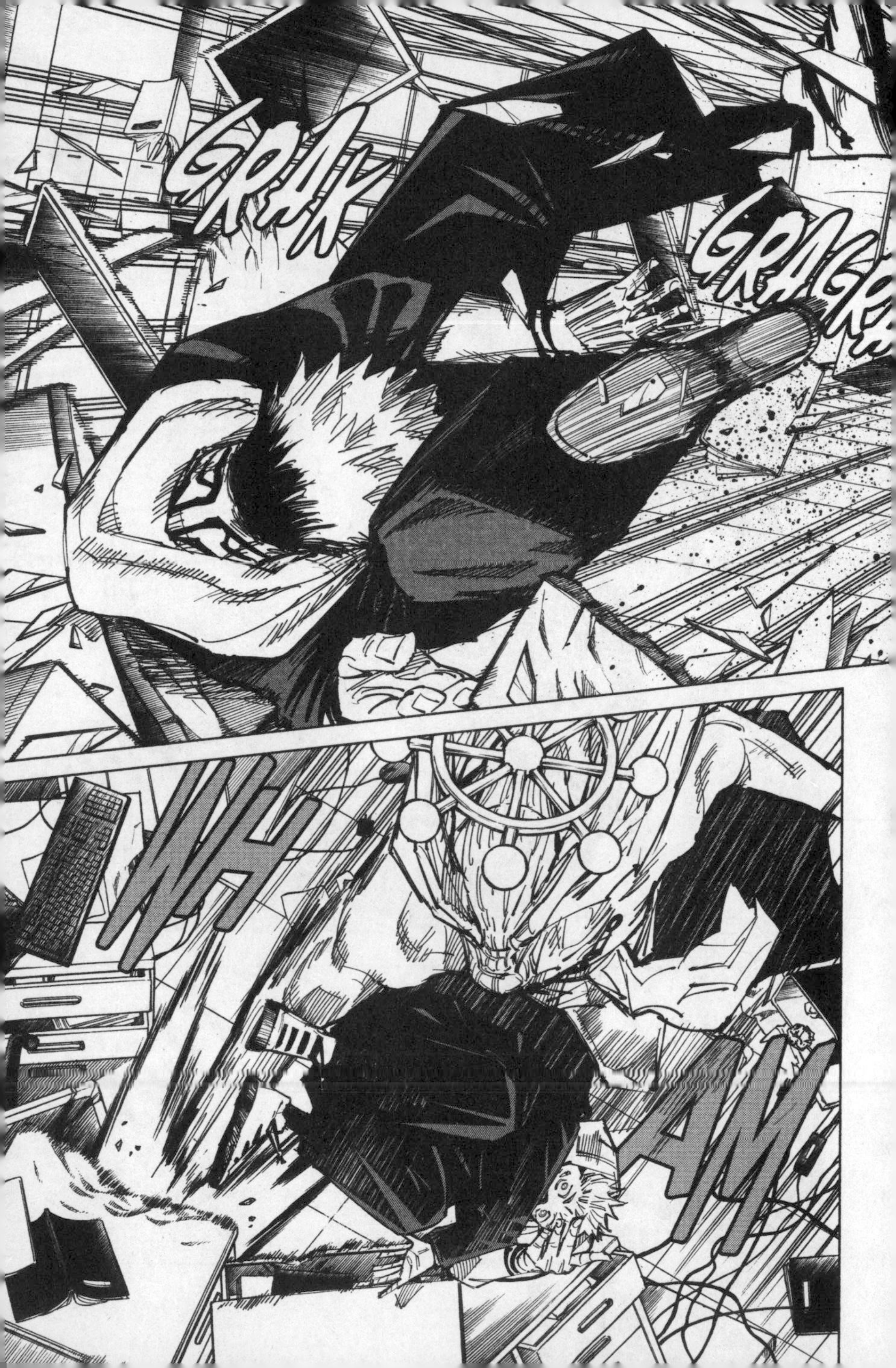
GRACK
GRAK
WHAM

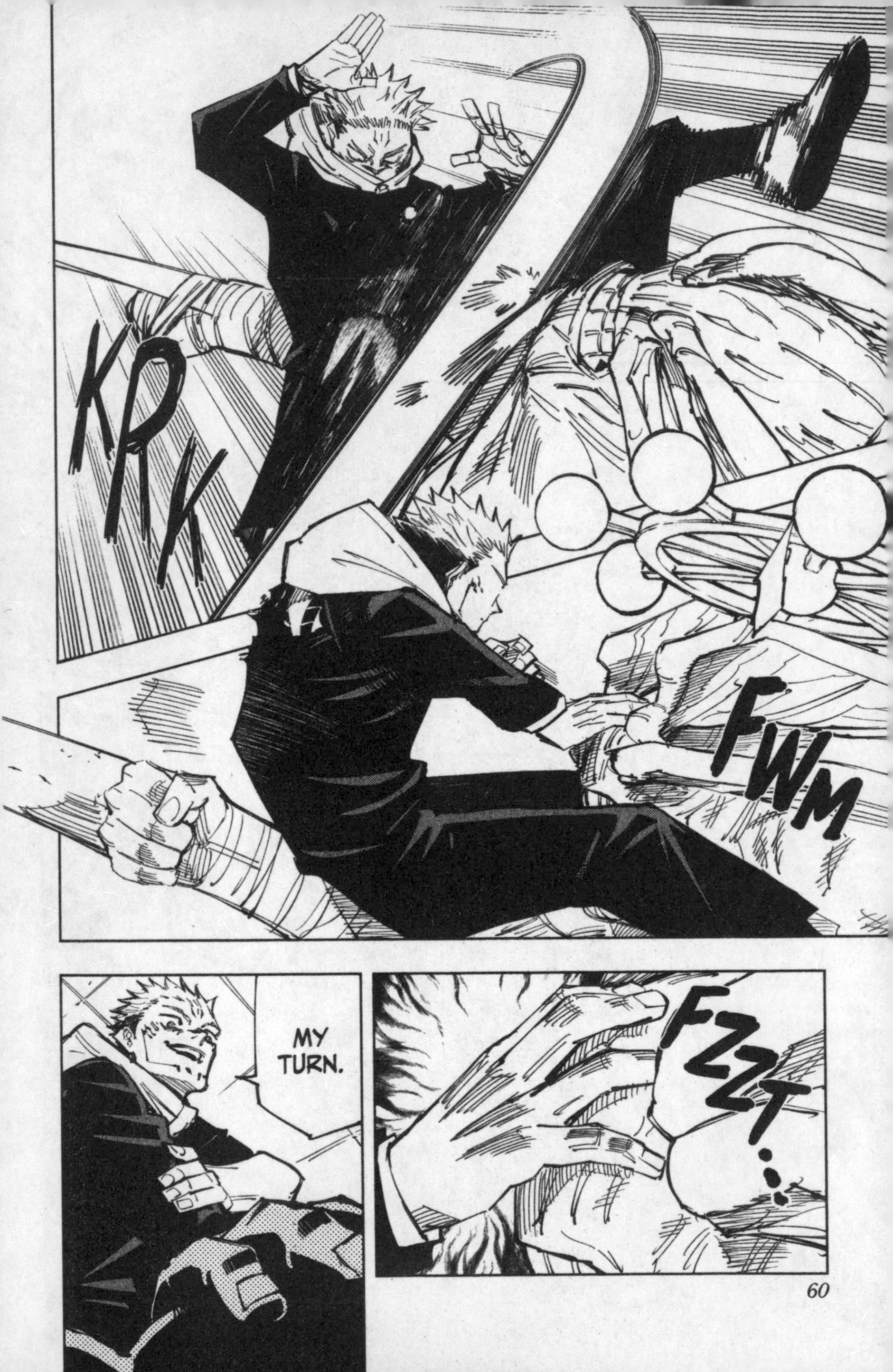
KRK
FWM
FZZT...
MY TURN.

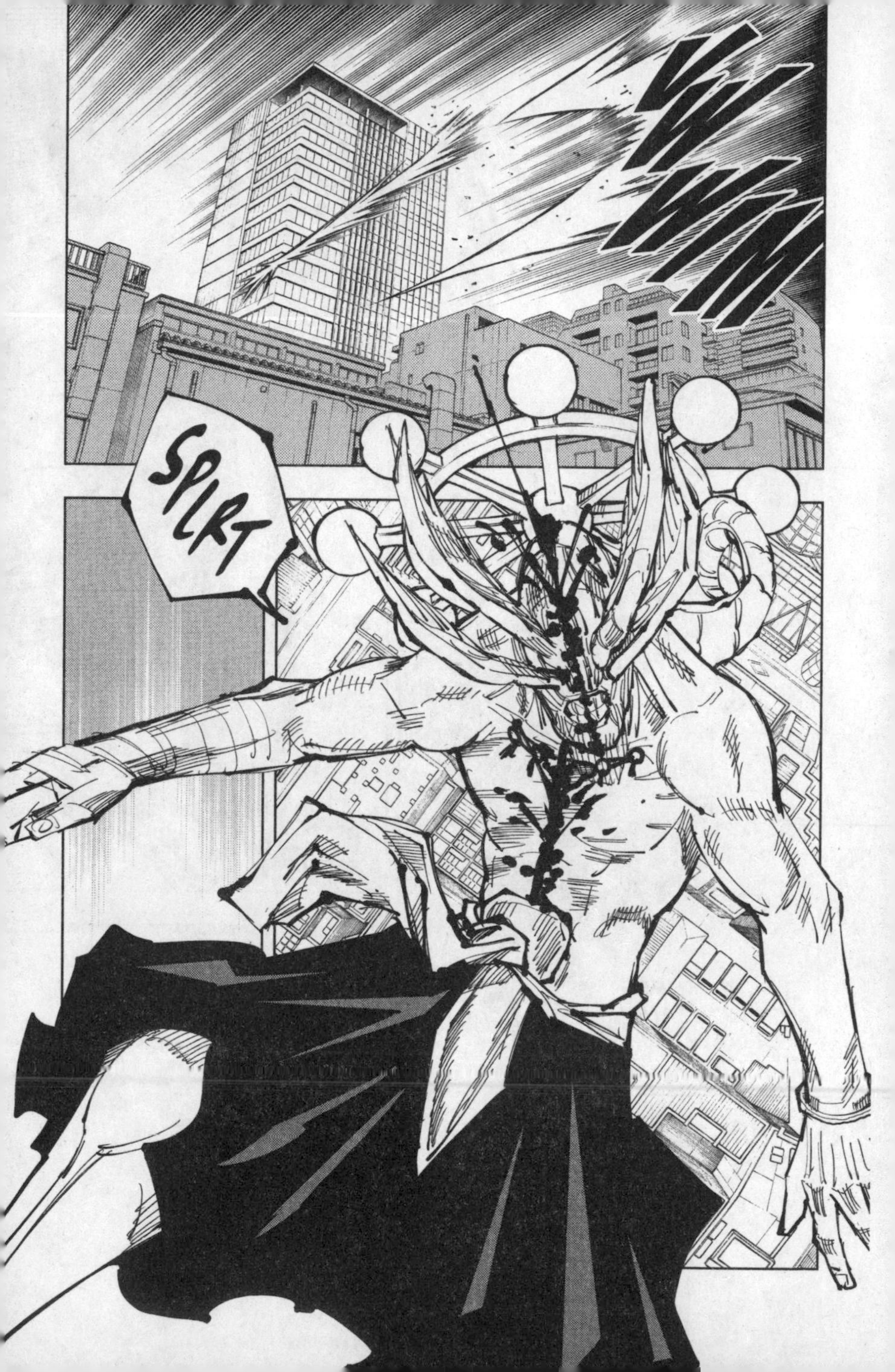
SPLRT

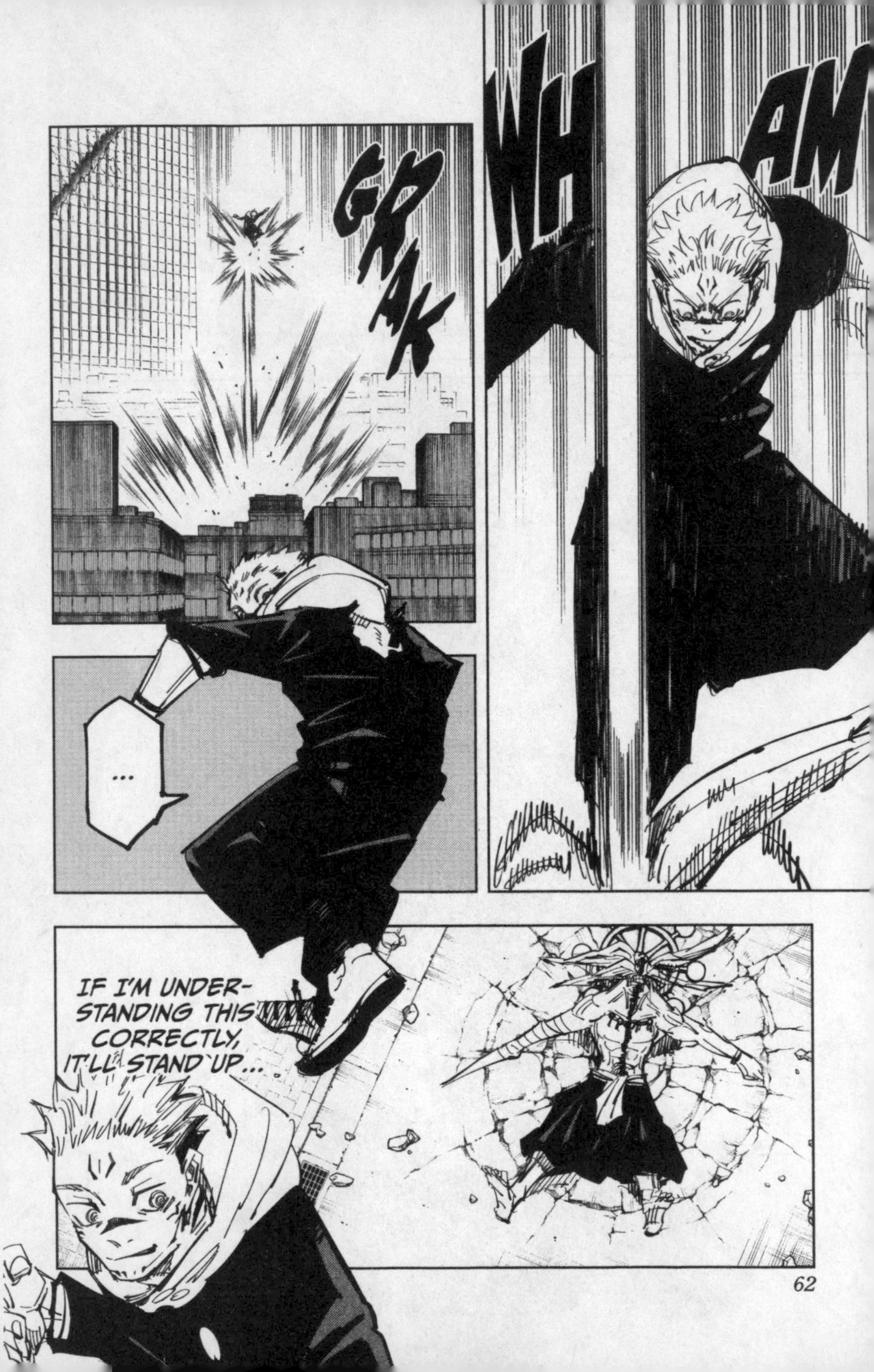
WHAM
GRAK
...
IF I'M UNDERSTANDING THIS CORRECTLY, IT'LL STAND UP...

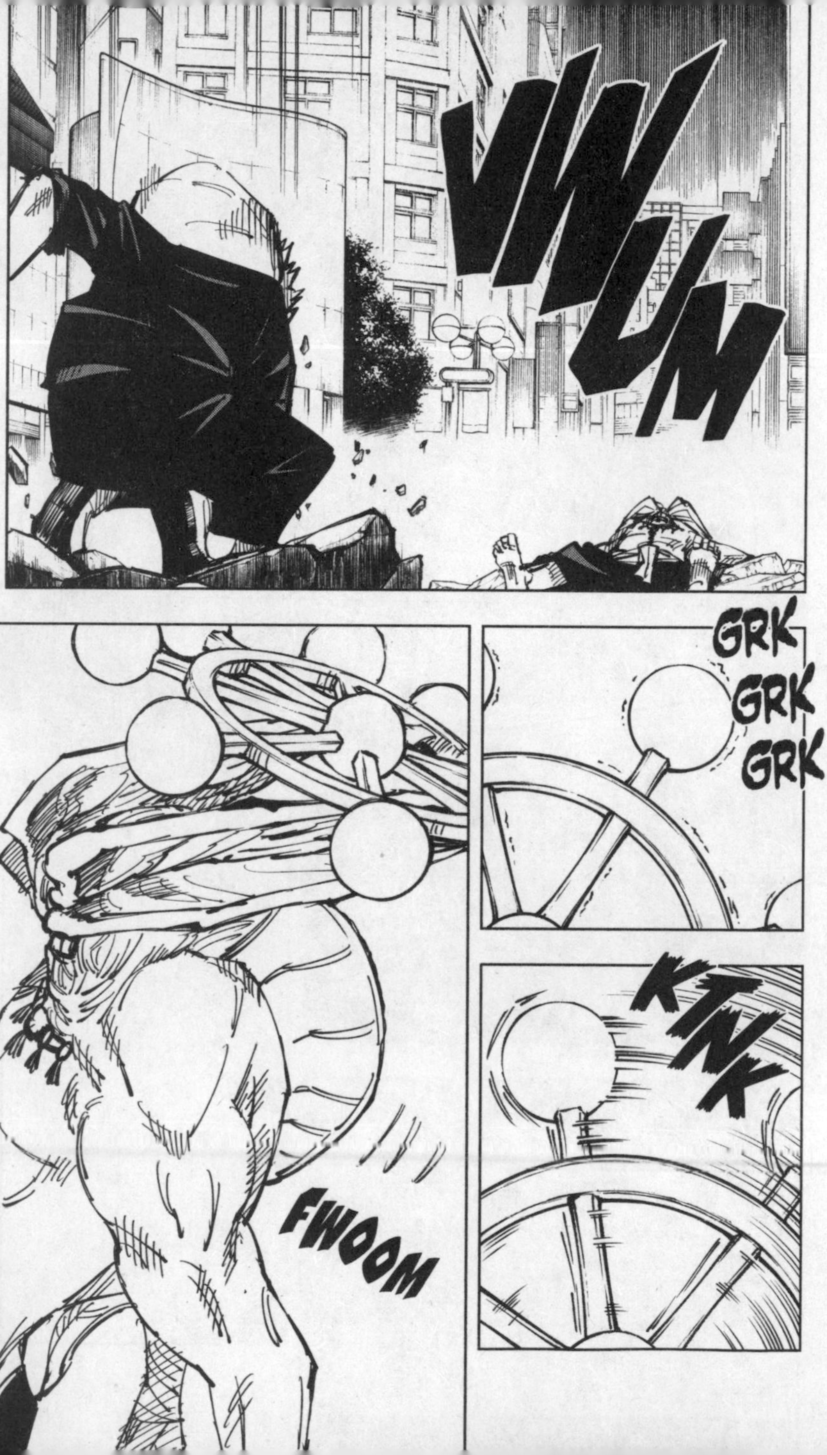
VWUM
GRK
GRK
GRK
KTNK
FWOOM

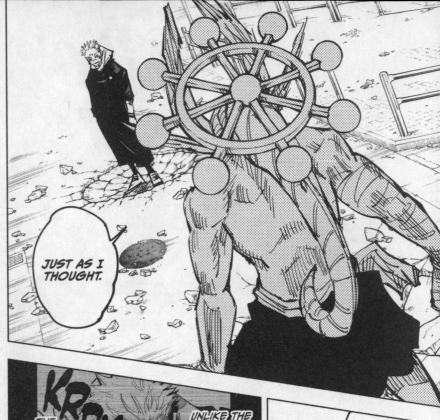

JUST AS I THOUGHT.

KRRK

...THE SECOND WAS IMBUED WITH CURSED ENERGY.

UNLIKE THE FIRST ATTACK, WHICH WAS IMBUED WITH POSITIVE ENERGY...

THAT SECOND ATTACK...

IT'S SIMILAR TO YAMATA NO OROCHI.

BOTH OCCURRED AFTER THAT WHEEL ON ITS BACK TURNED.

AS FOR MY ATTACK... IT WAS ABLE TO RECOGNIZE DISMANTLE.

64

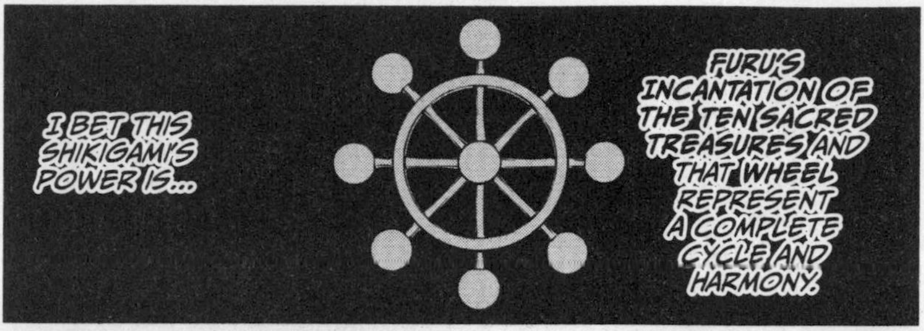
FURU'S INCANTATION OF THE TEN SACRED TREASURES AND THAT WHEEL REPRESENT A COMPLETE CYCLE AND HARMONY.
I BET THIS SHIKIGAMI'S POWER IS...
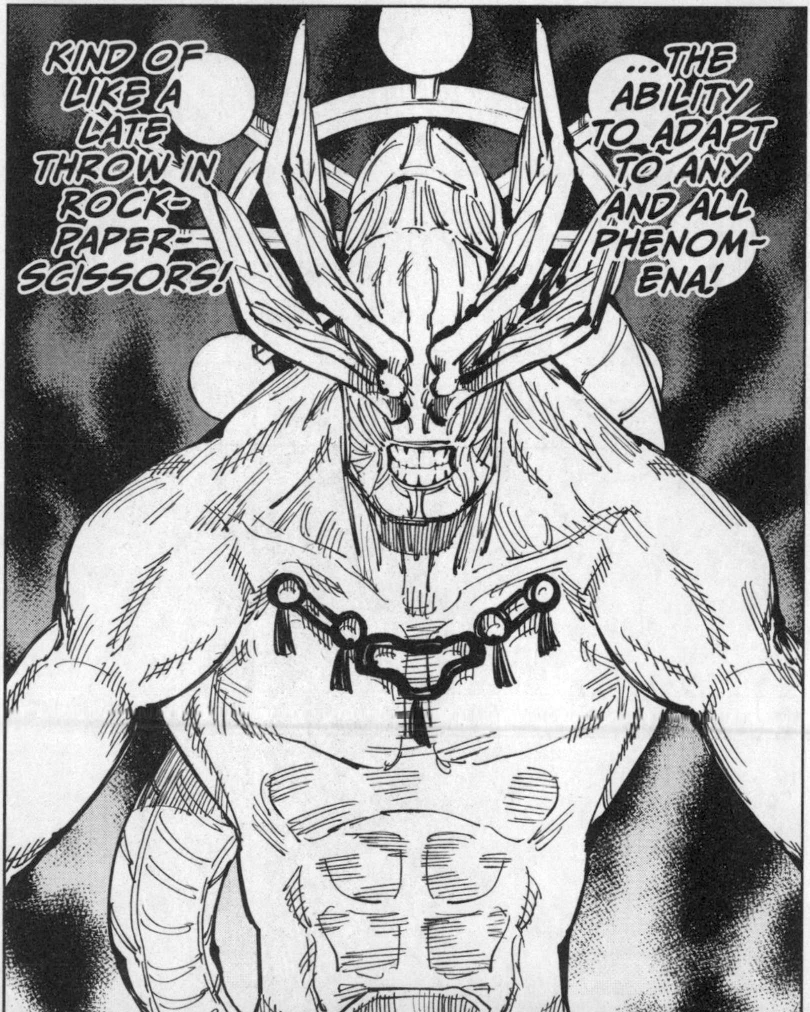
...THE ABILITY TO ADAPT TO ANY AND ALL PHENOM-ENA!
KIND OF LIKE A LATE THROW IN ROCK-PAPER-SCISSORS!

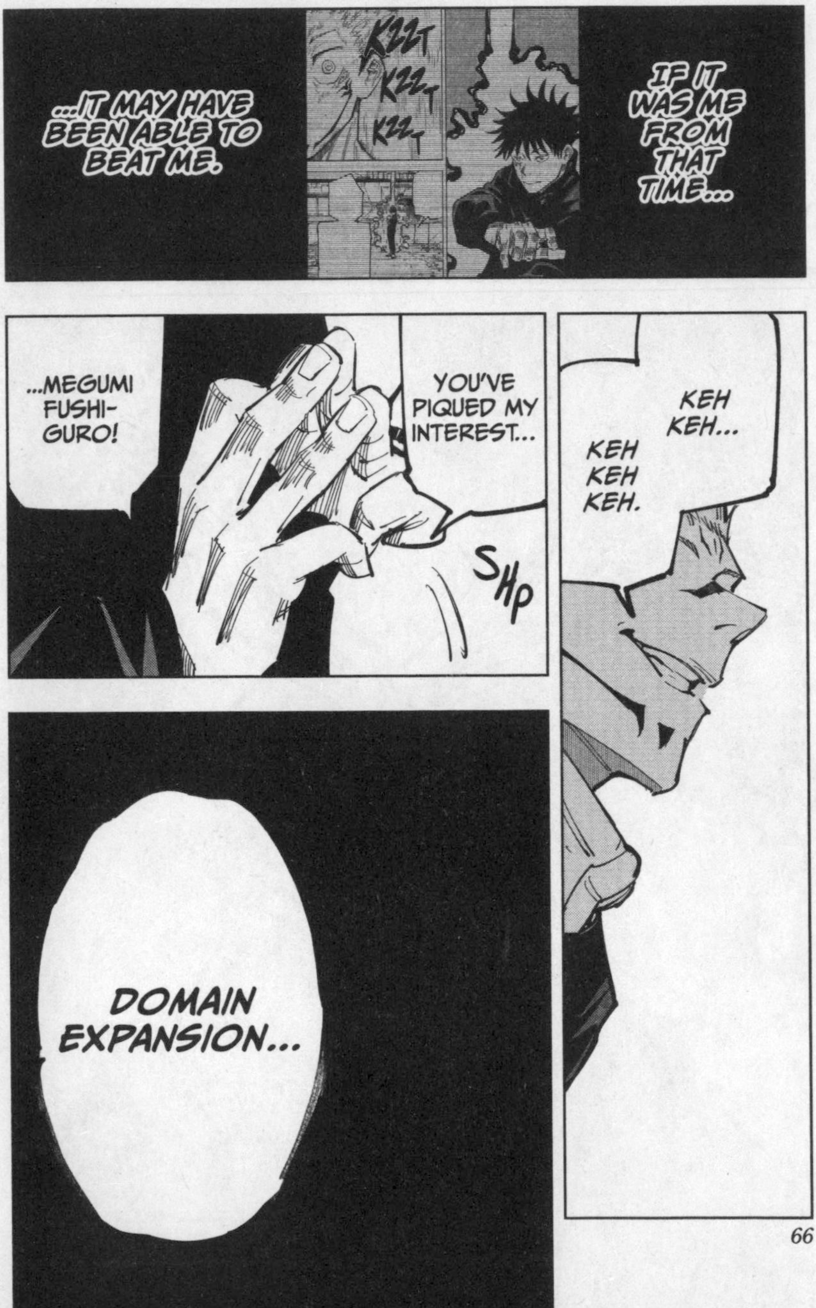
IF IT WAS ME FROM THAT TIME...
KZZT KZZT KZZT
...IT MAY HAVE BEEN ABLE TO BEAT ME.
KEH KEH...
KEH KEH KEH.
YOU'VE PIQUED MY INTEREST...
...MEGUMI FUSHIGURO!
SHP
DOMAIN EXPANSION...

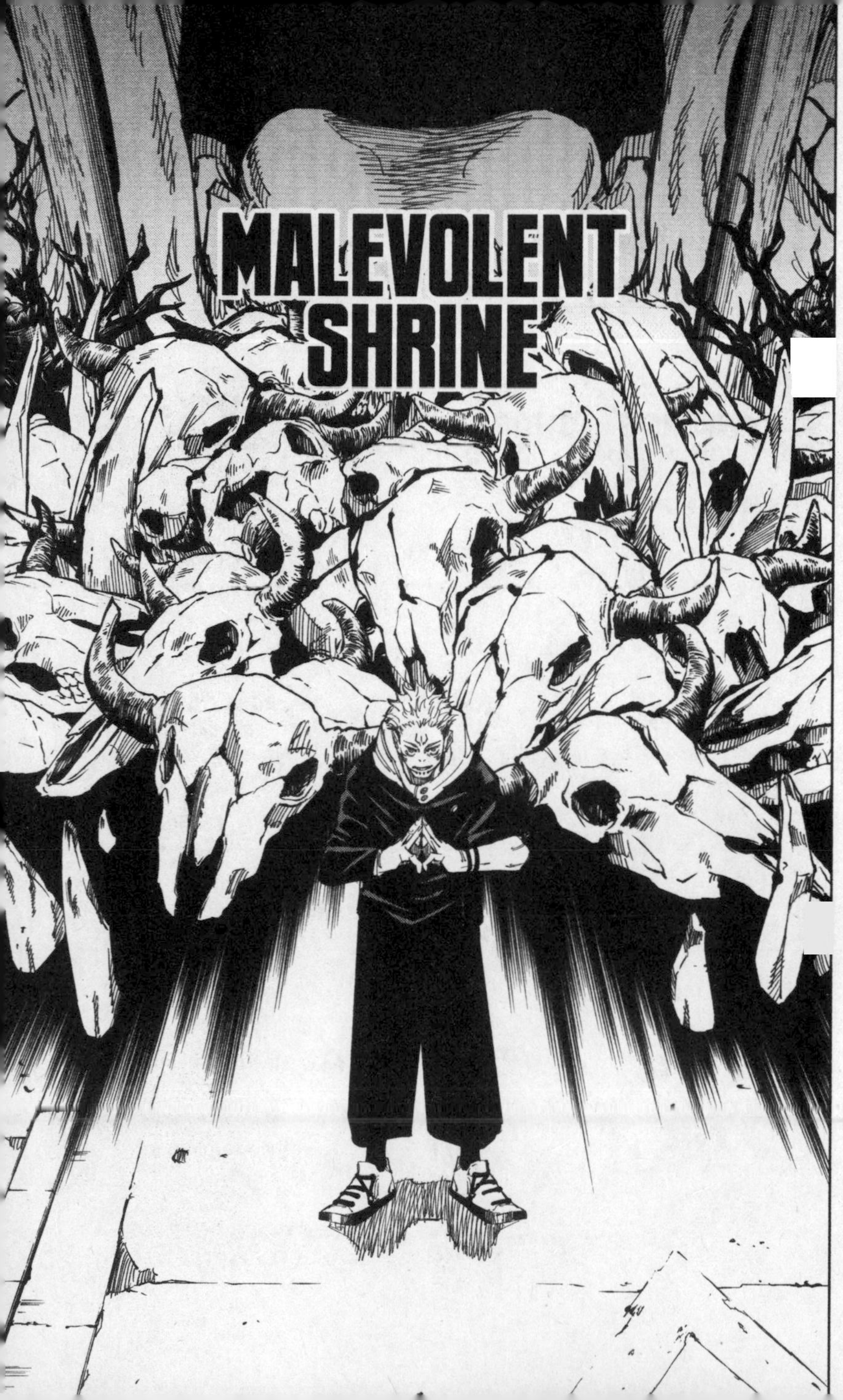
MALEVOLENT SHRINE

THE 2020 VALENTINES RANKINGS THAT I SERIOUSLY ALMOST FORGOT

RANKINGS (VALENTINES RECEIVED)	CHARACTER	AKUTAMI'S COMMENT
10 (4)	INO	MAYBE THE INCIDENT WAS STARTING ABOUT THAT TIME?
11 (3)	IEIRI	MACROSS F IN A SET WITH GOJO.
	IJICHI	COME ON, TETSUO!
	KAMO	HE LOST TO CHOSO... HA HA!
14 (2)	MEI MEI	AGE INDETERMINATE.
	MIWA	AFTER ALL, SHE'S CUTE!
	OZAWA	EVEN THOUGH SHE JUST BRIEFLY POPPED IN?

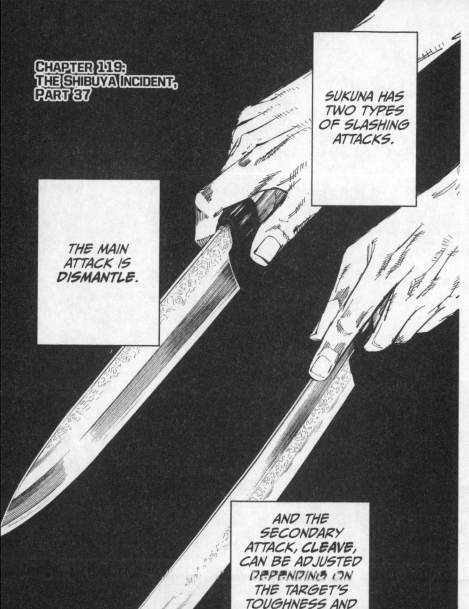

CHAPTER 119:
THE SHIBUYA INCIDENT,
PART 37

SUKUNA HAS
TWO TYPES
OF SLASHING
ATTACKS.

THE MAIN
ATTACK IS
DISMANTLE.

AND THE
SECONDARY
ATTACK, CLEAVE,
CAN BE ADJUSTED
DEPENDING ON
THE TARGET'S
TOUGHNESS AND
CURSED ENERGY
LEVEL TO CUT
THEM DOWN
IN ONE FELL
SWOOP.

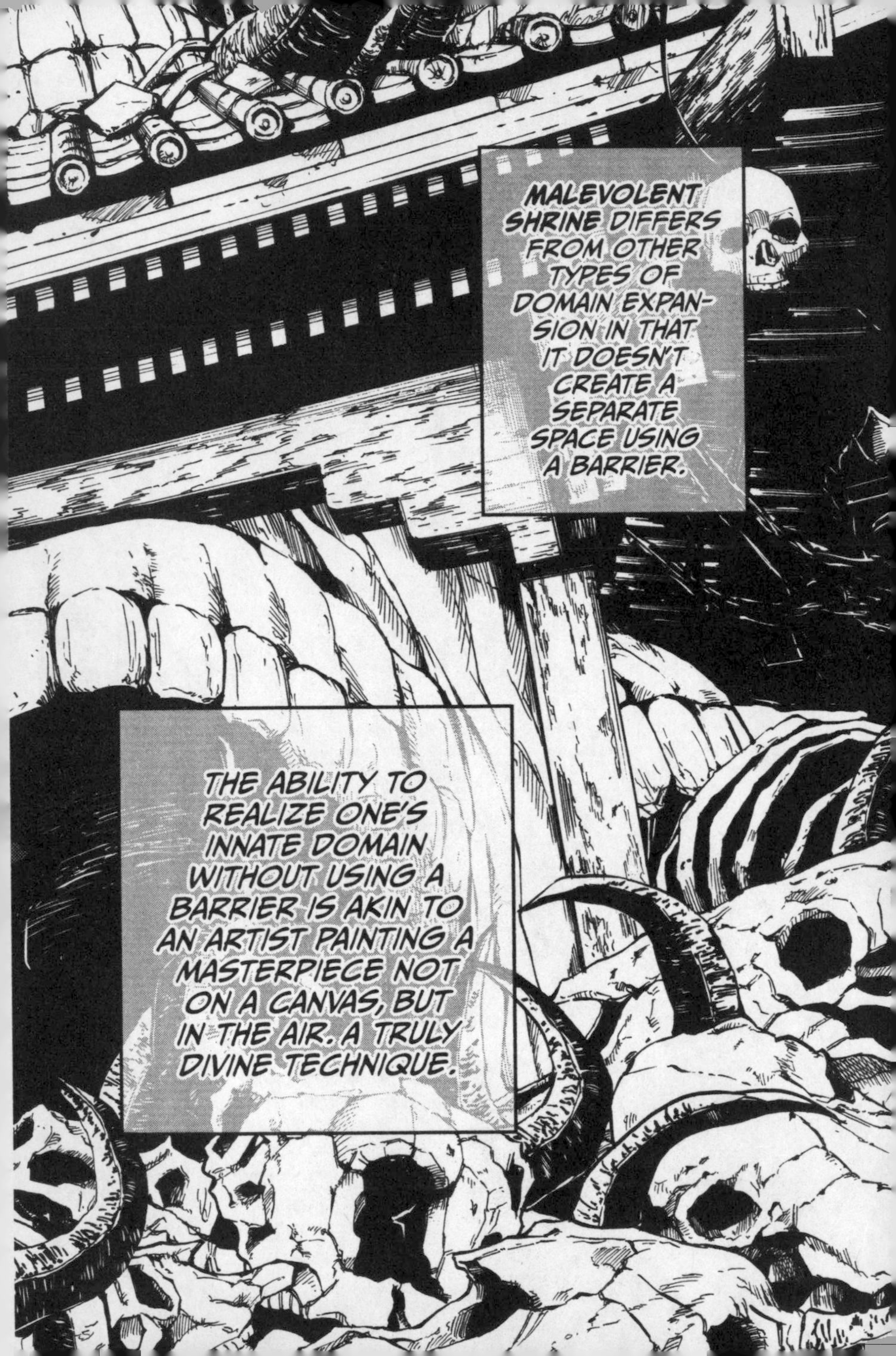
MALEVOLENT SHRINE DIFFERS FROM OTHER TYPES OF DOMAIN EXPANSION IN THAT IT DOESN'T CREATE A SEPARATE SPACE USING A BARRIER.
THE ABILITY TO REALIZE ONE'S INNATE DOMAIN WITHOUT USING A BARRIER IS AKIN TO AN ARTIST PAINTING A MASTERPIECE NOT ON A CANVAS, BUT IN THE AIR. A TRULY DIVINE TECHNIQUE.

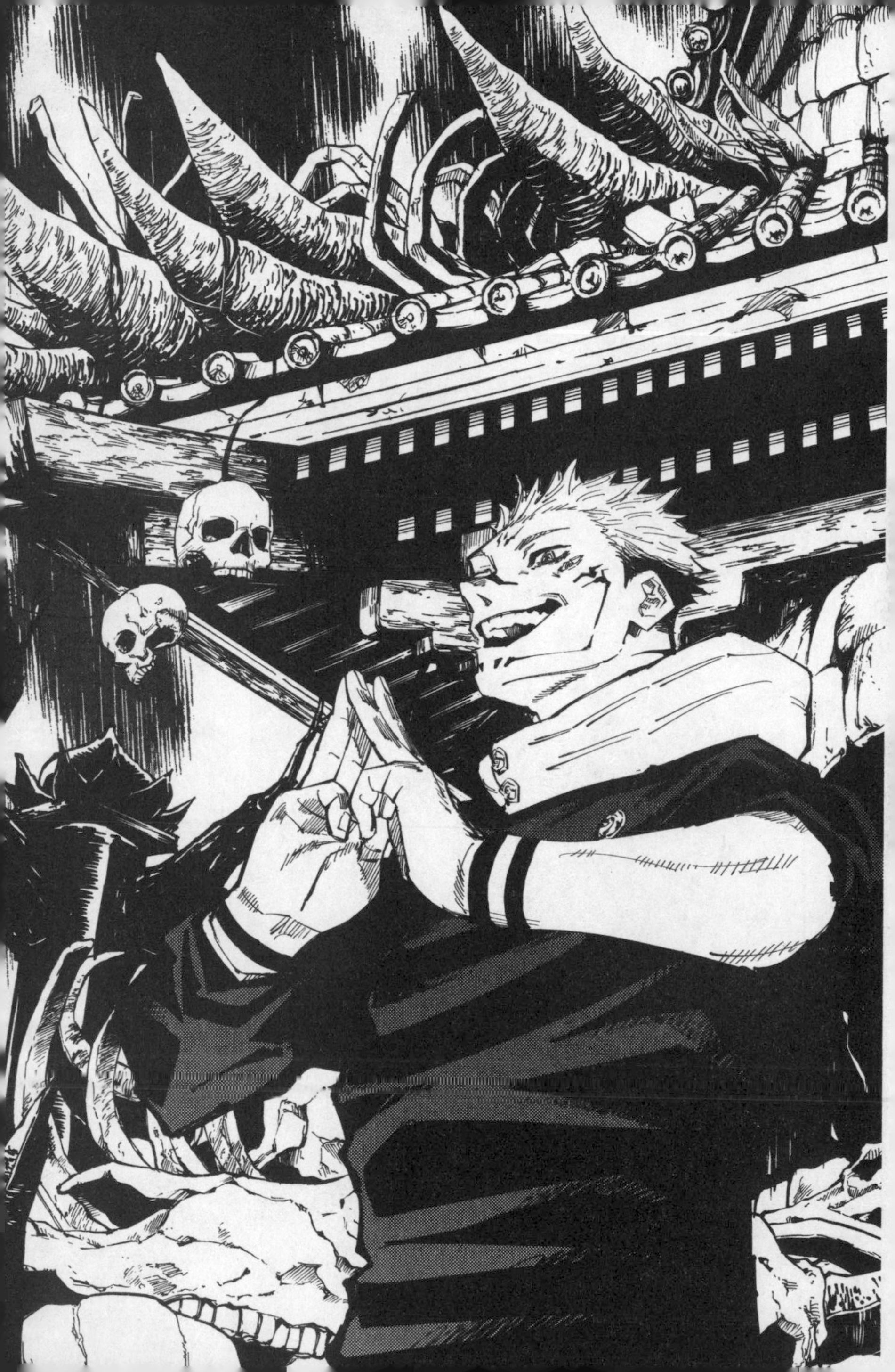

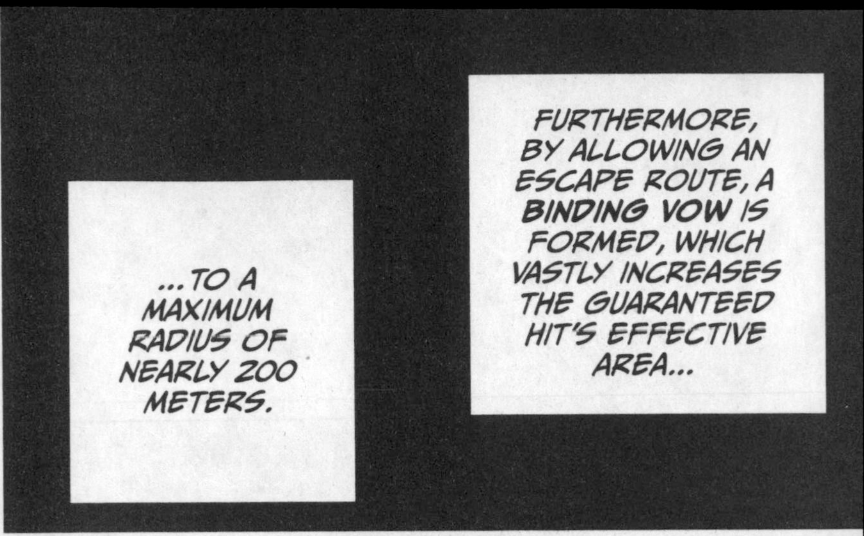
FURTHERMORE, BY ALLOWING AN ESCAPE ROUTE, A BINDING VOW IS FORMED, WHICH VASTLY INCREASES THE GUARANTEED HIT'S EFFECTIVE AREA...
...TO A MAXIMUM RADIUS OF NEARLY 200 METERS.

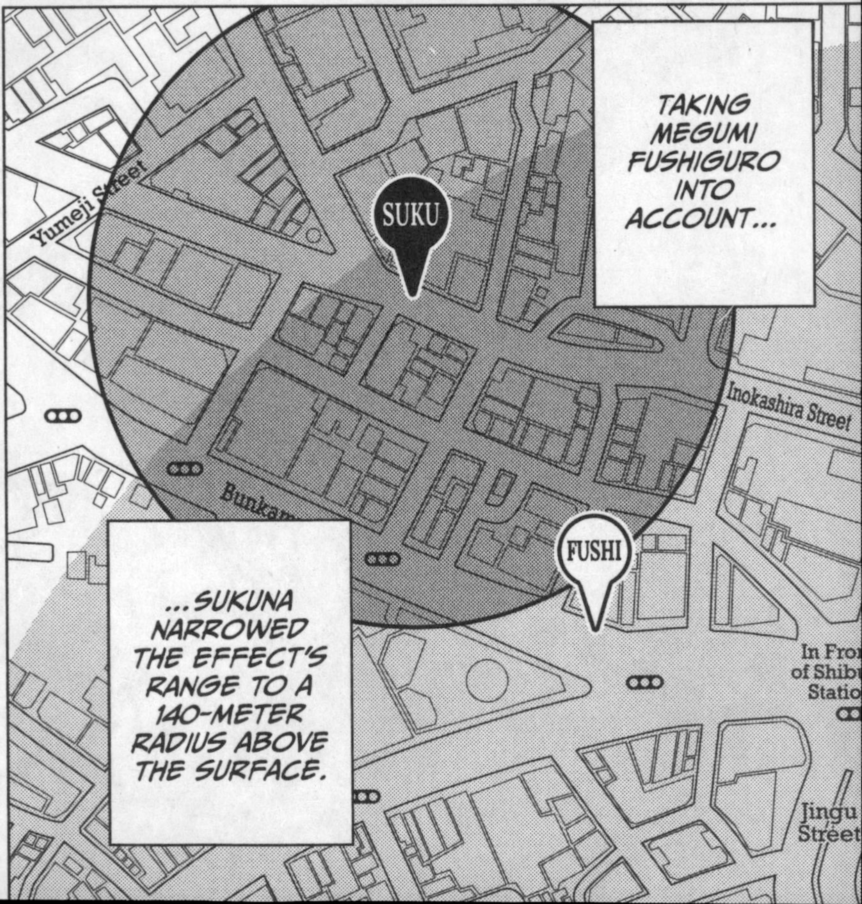
TAKING MEGUMI FUSHIGURO INTO ACCOUNT...
Yumeji Street
SUKU
Inokashira Street
FUSHI
Jingu Street
...SUKUNA NARROWED THE EFFECT'S RANGE TO A 140-METER RADIUS ABOVE THE SURFACE.

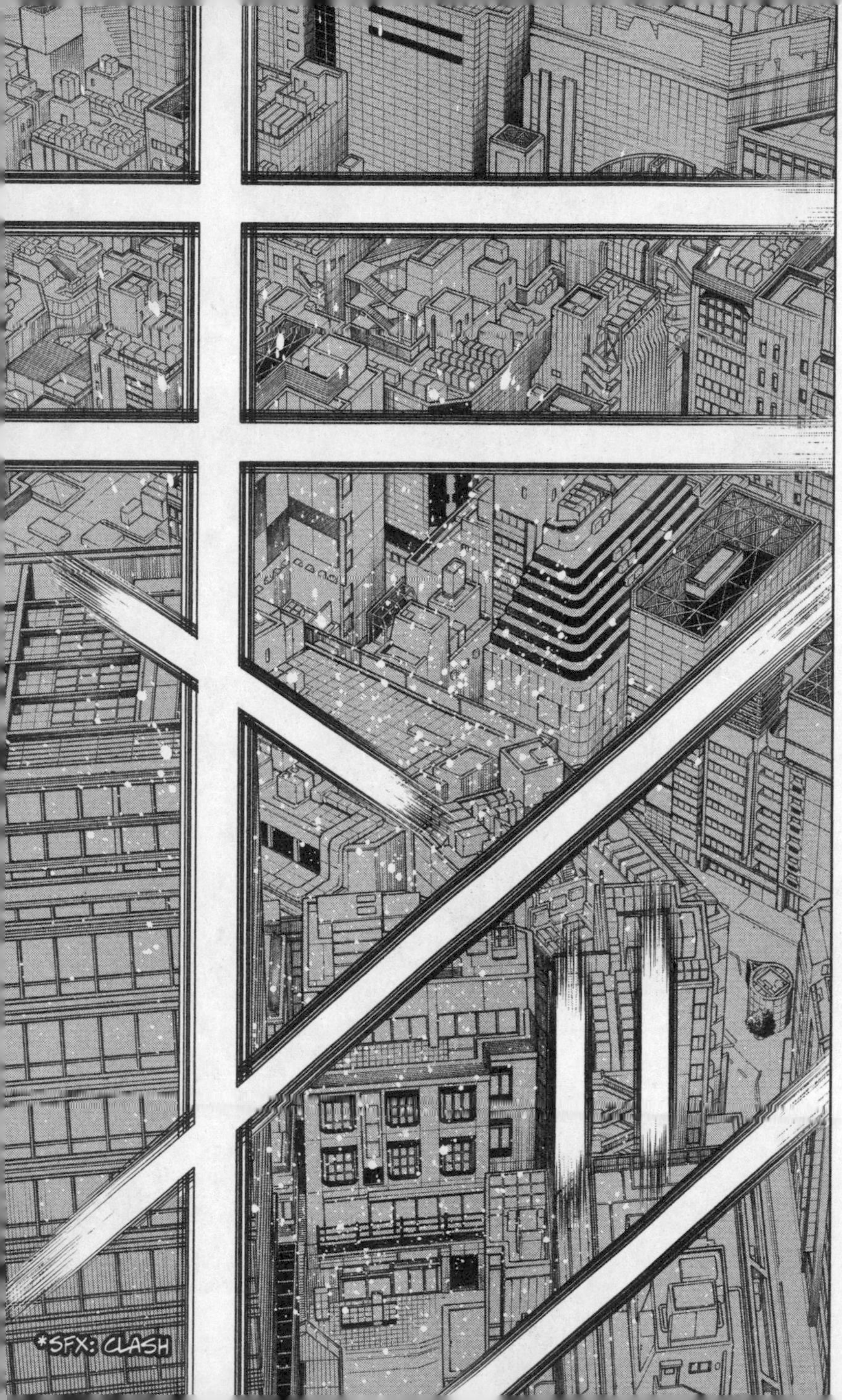
*SFX: CLASH

STILL NO RECEPTION.

HOW'S YOUR PHONE?

BUT...I DON'T THINK WE NEED TO WORRY ANYMORE.

HUH?

IT'D BE BAD IF BOTH OF OUR PHONES RAN OUT OF POWER.

DON'T USE YOURS TOO MUCH, KEIKO.

ME NEITHER ...

TRUE...

THAT MEGA-PHONE GUY IS HERE.

OH RIGHT, THAT G—

FOR INANIMATE OBJECTS— DISMANTLE.

FOR ANYTHING WITH CURSED ENERGY WITHIN RANGE—CLEAVE.

UNTIL MALEVOLENT SHRINE IS GONE...

...IT WILL RELENTLESLY ATTACK ALL TARGETS WITHIN THE EFFECTIVE RANGE OF ITS GUARANTEED HIT.

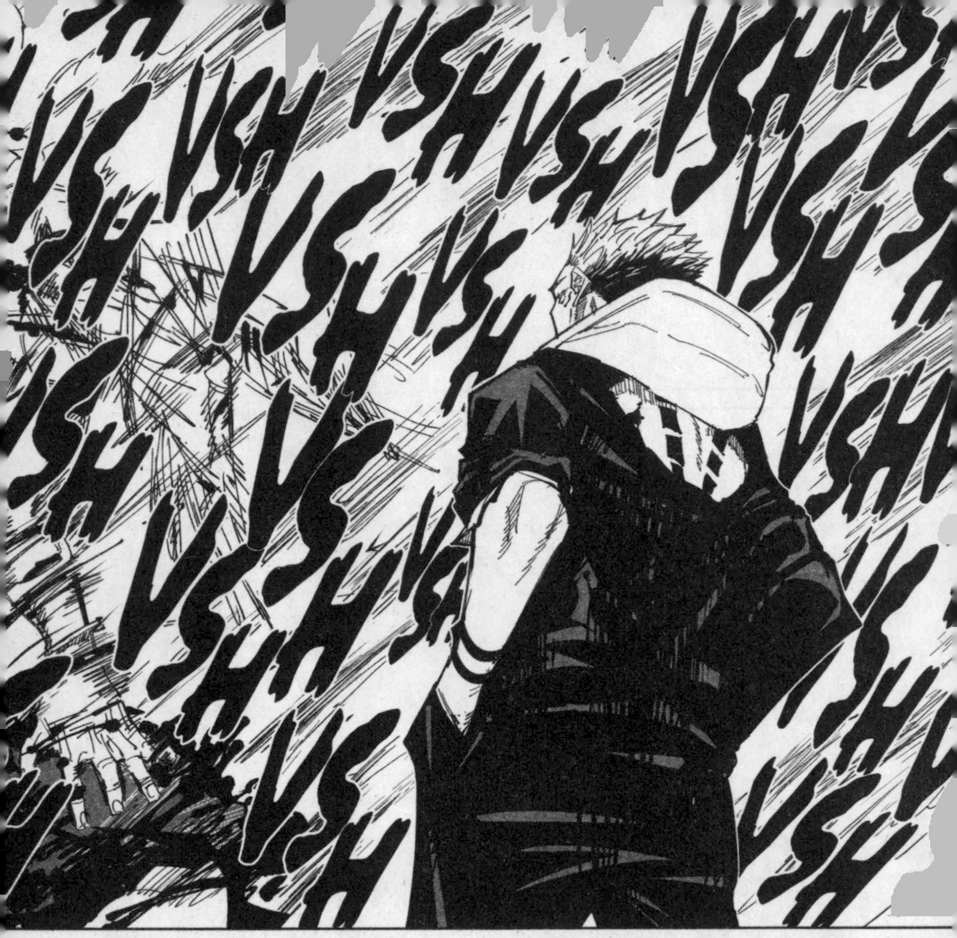
VSH
VSH
VSH
VSH
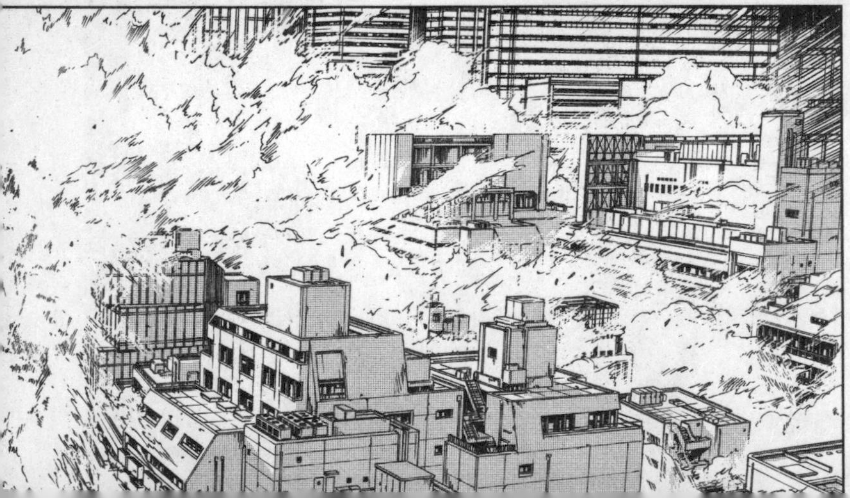

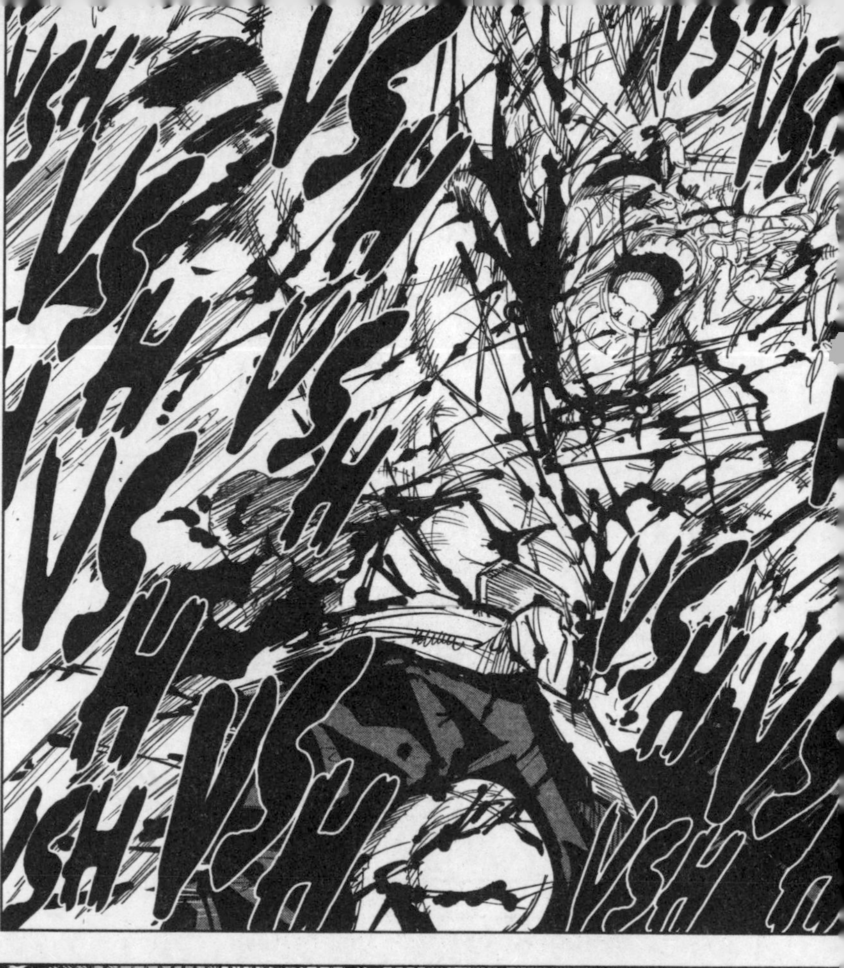
VSH
VSH
VSH
VSH
VSH
VSH
VSH
VSH
VSH
VSH
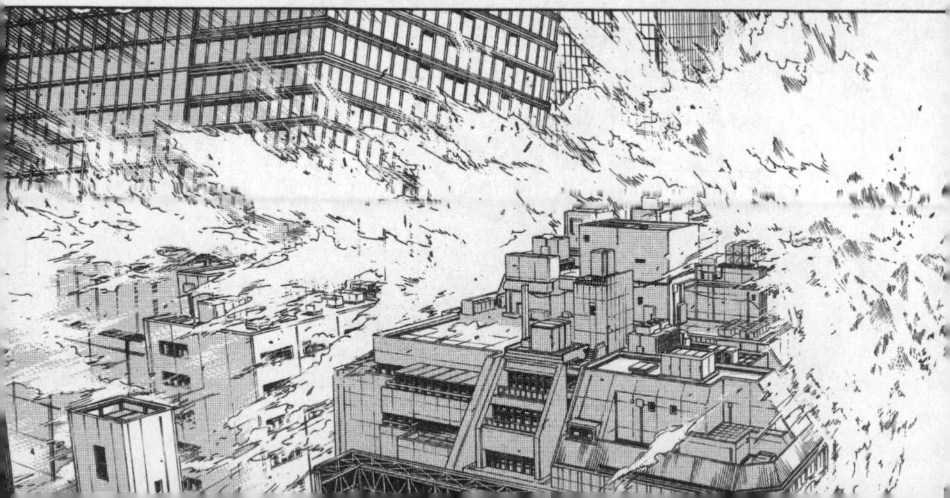

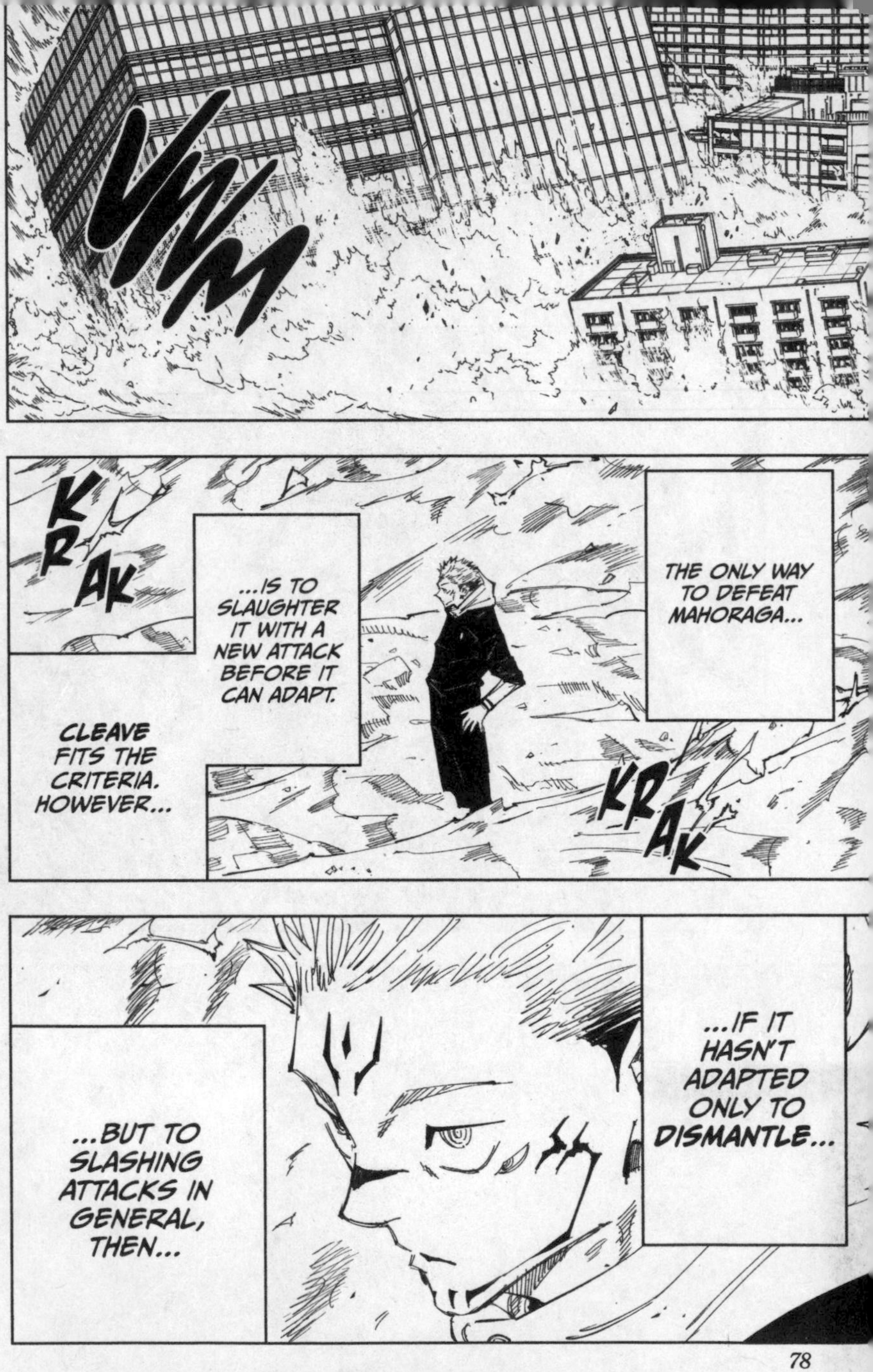
VWM
THE ONLY WAY TO DEFEAT MAHORAGA...
...IS TO SLAUGHTER IT WITH A NEW ATTACK BEFORE IT CAN ADAPT.
KRAK
KRAK
CLEAVE FITS THE CRITERIA. HOWEVER...
...IF IT HASN'T ADAPTED ONLY TO DISMANTLE...
...BUT TO SLASHING ATTACKS IN GENERAL, THEN...

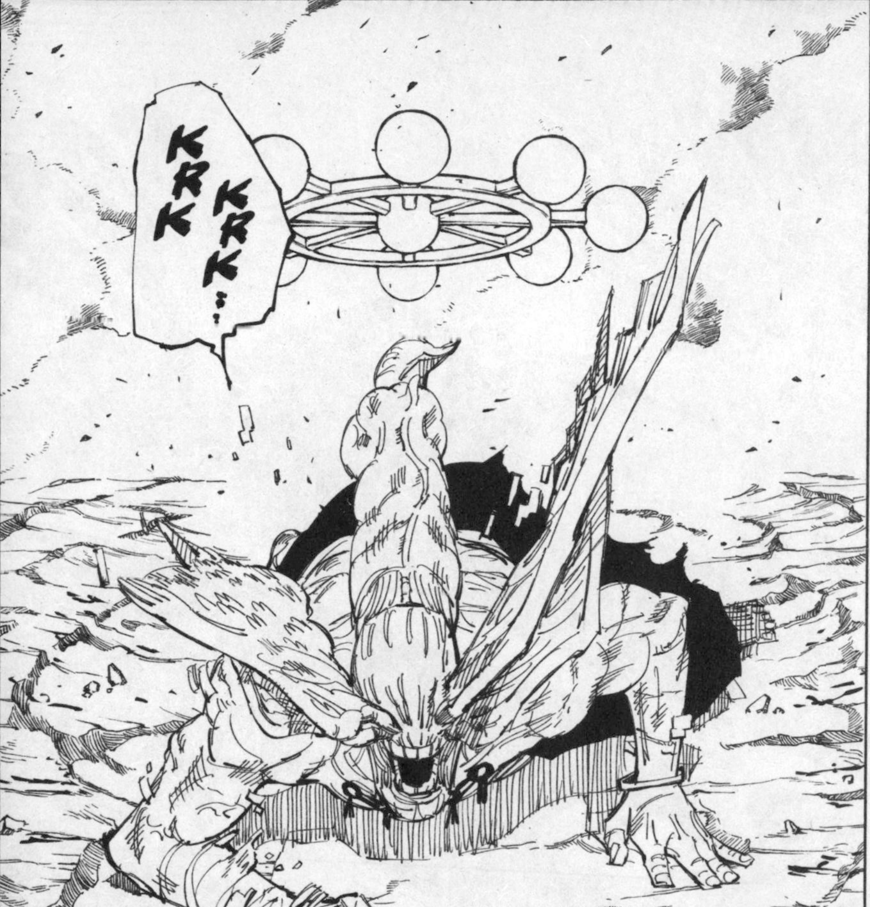
KRK KRK...
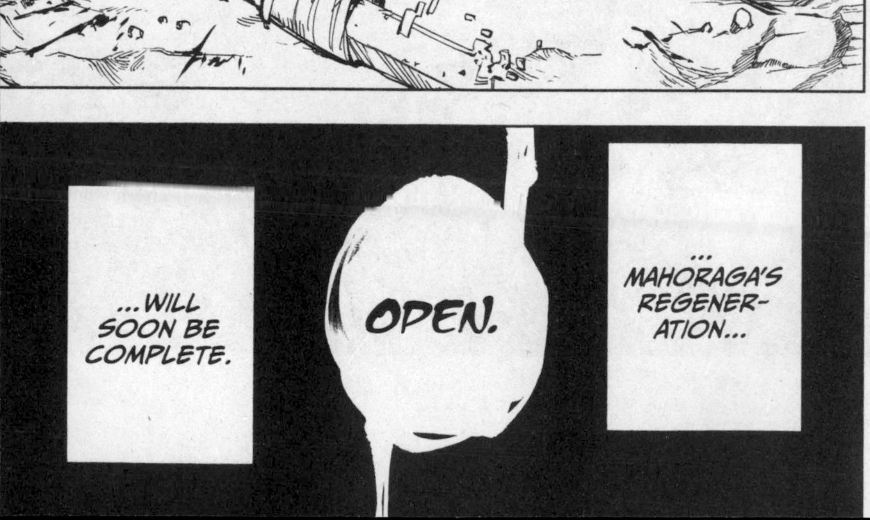
... MAHORAGA'S REGENER-ATION...
OPEN.
...WILL SOON BE COMPLETE.

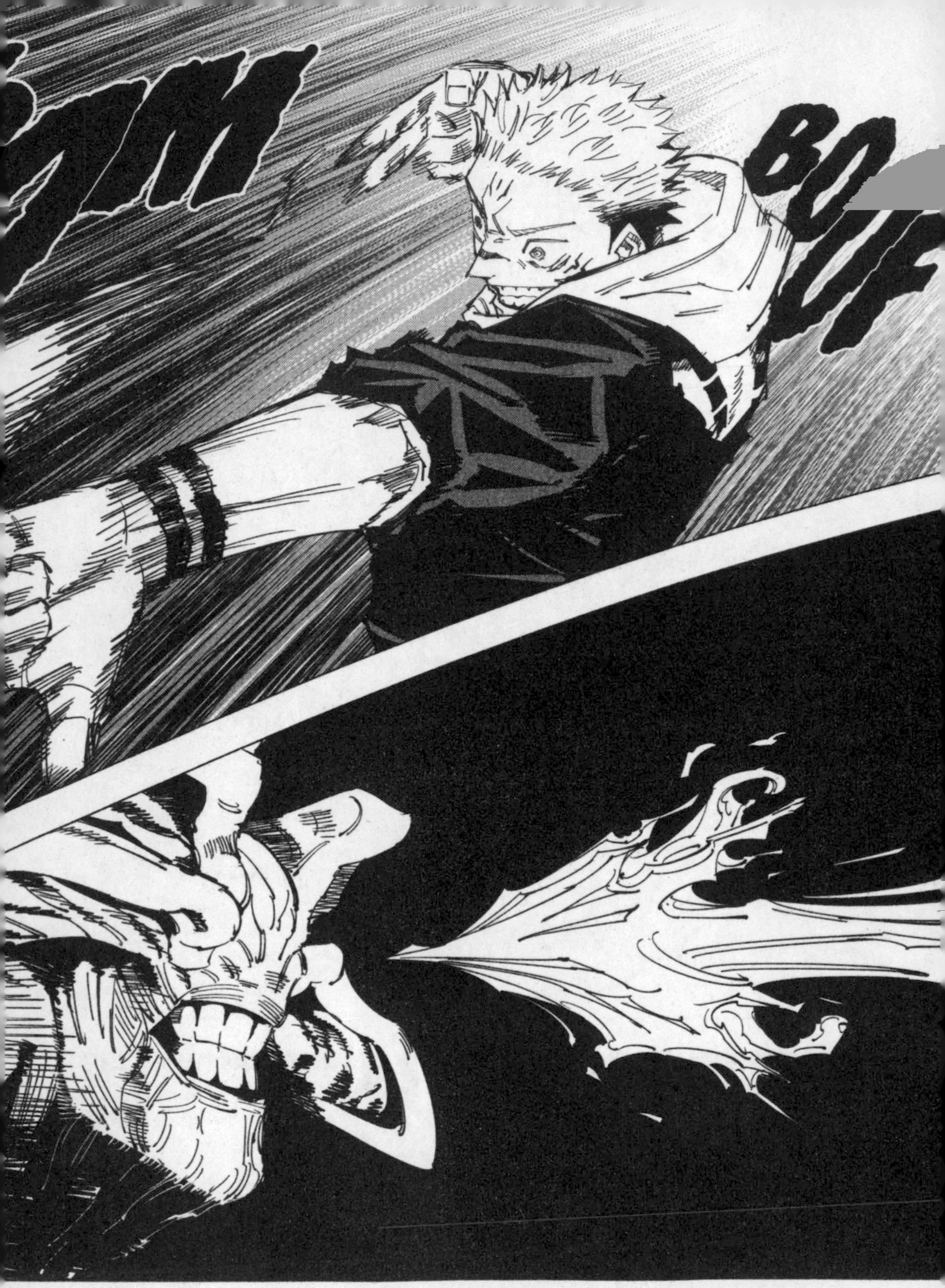
BOUF

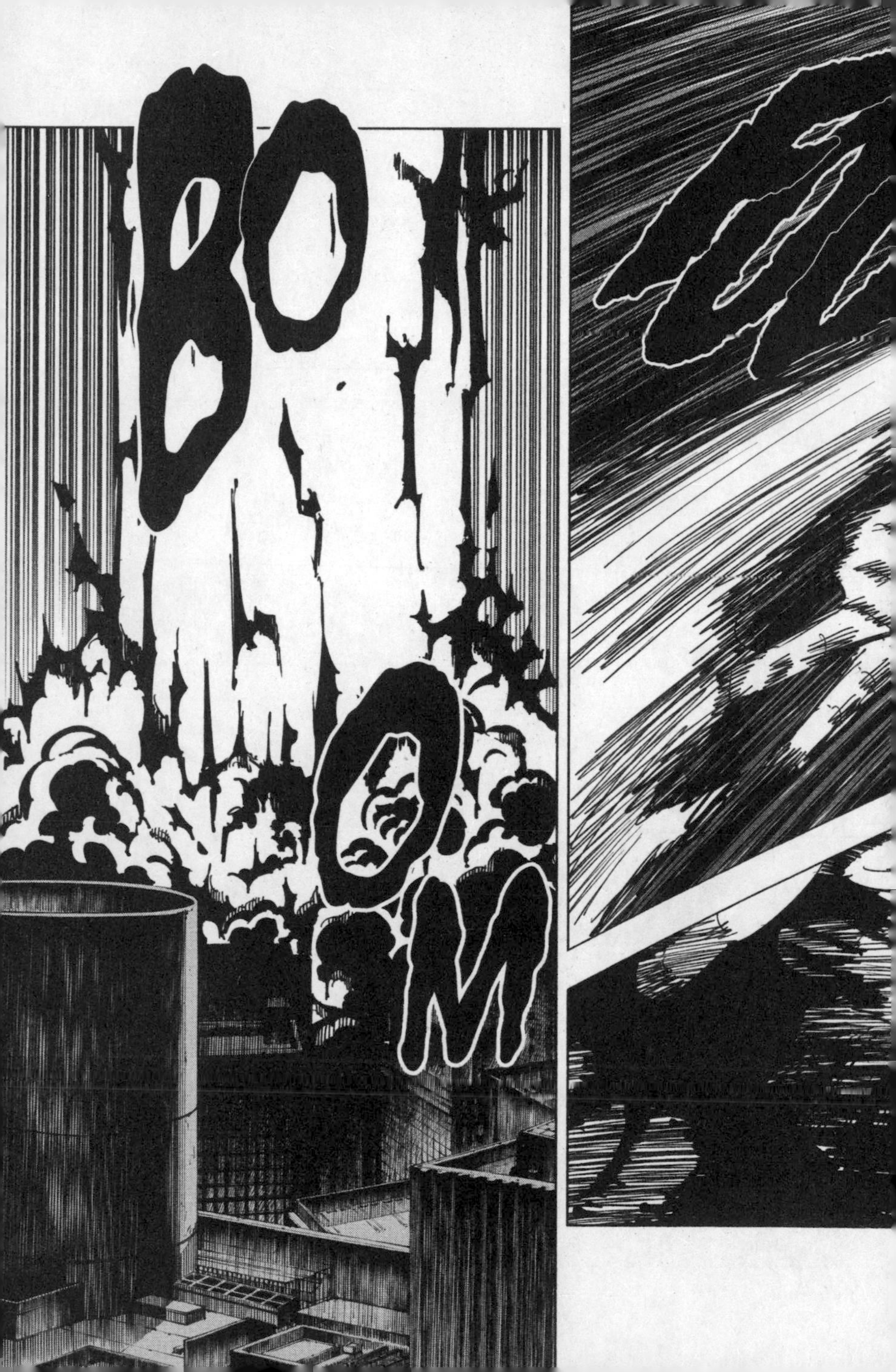
BOOM

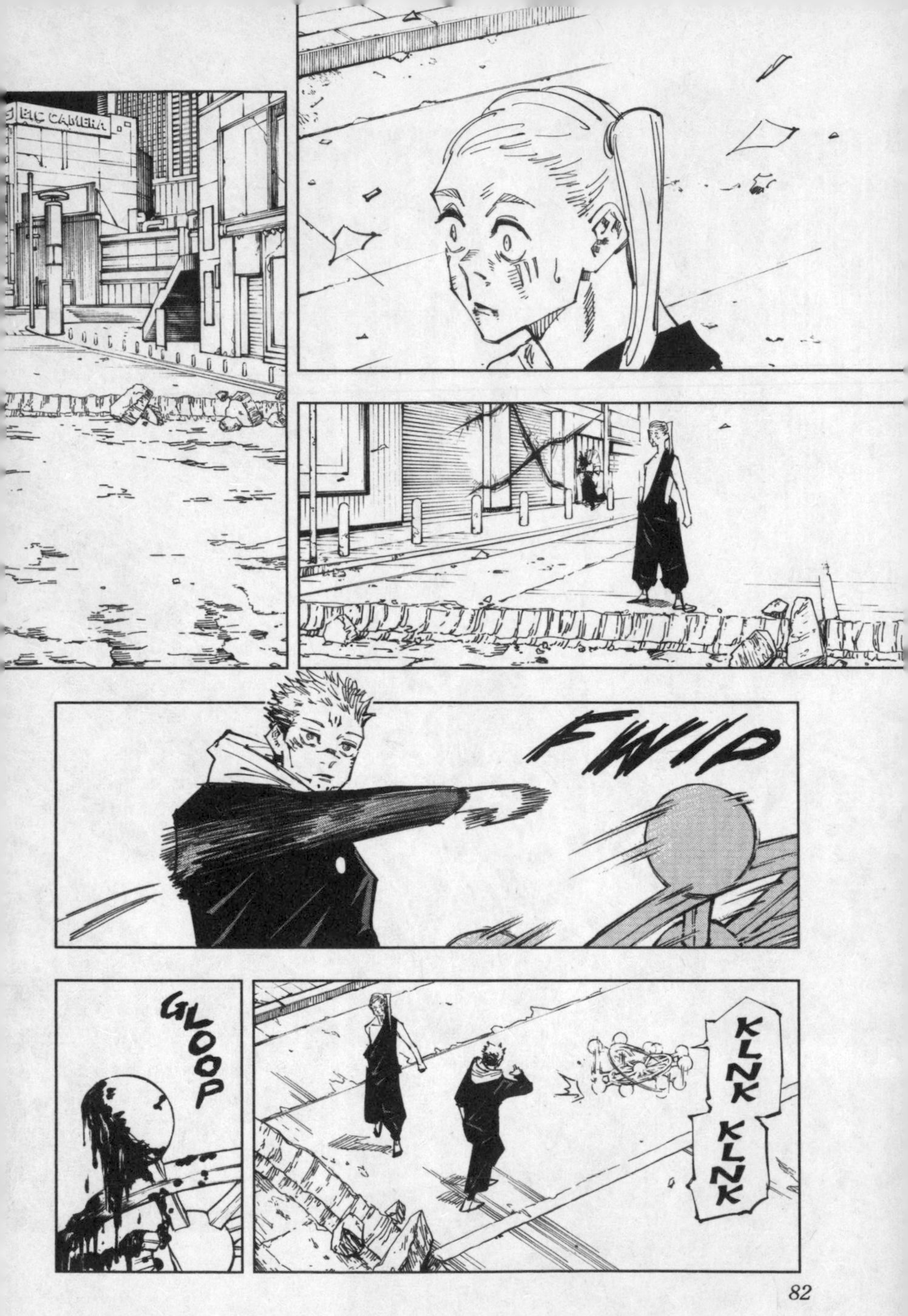
BIC CAMERA
FWIP
KLNK KLNK
GLOOP

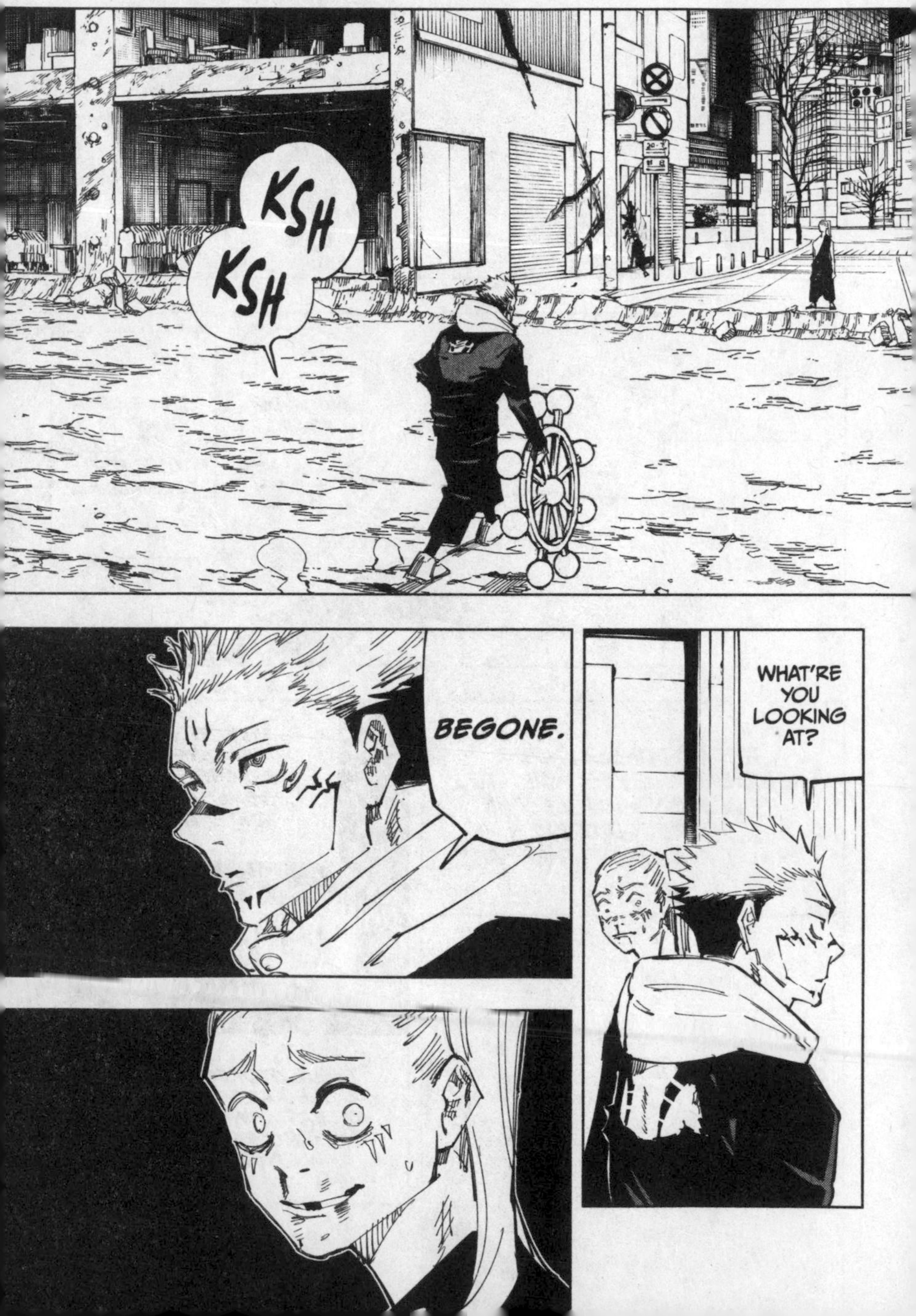
KSH KSH
WHAT'RE YOU LOOKING AT?
BEGONE.

I'M OUTTA HERE!

I'LL BE ON MY WAY!

I...

MY LUCK NEVER RUNS OUT!

I SURVIVED AGAIN!

CURSE USER HARUTA SHIGEMO'S CURSED TECHNIQUE...

...STORES MIRACLES.

THE MARKINGS UNDER SHIGEMO'S EYES INDICATE HOW MANY MIRACLES HE HAS STORED, BUT EVEN HE IS NOT AWARE OF THIS FACT.

ONCE AGAIN, I LIVE ...

LITTLE EVERYDAY MIRACLES ARE ERASED FROM SHIGEMO'S MEMORY AND STORED.

FOR EXAMPLE...

4:44 44

HEY! ALL THE SAME NUMBER!

THESE STORED MIRACLES ARE THEN RELEASED WHEN SHIGEMO'S LIFE IS IN DANGER.

84

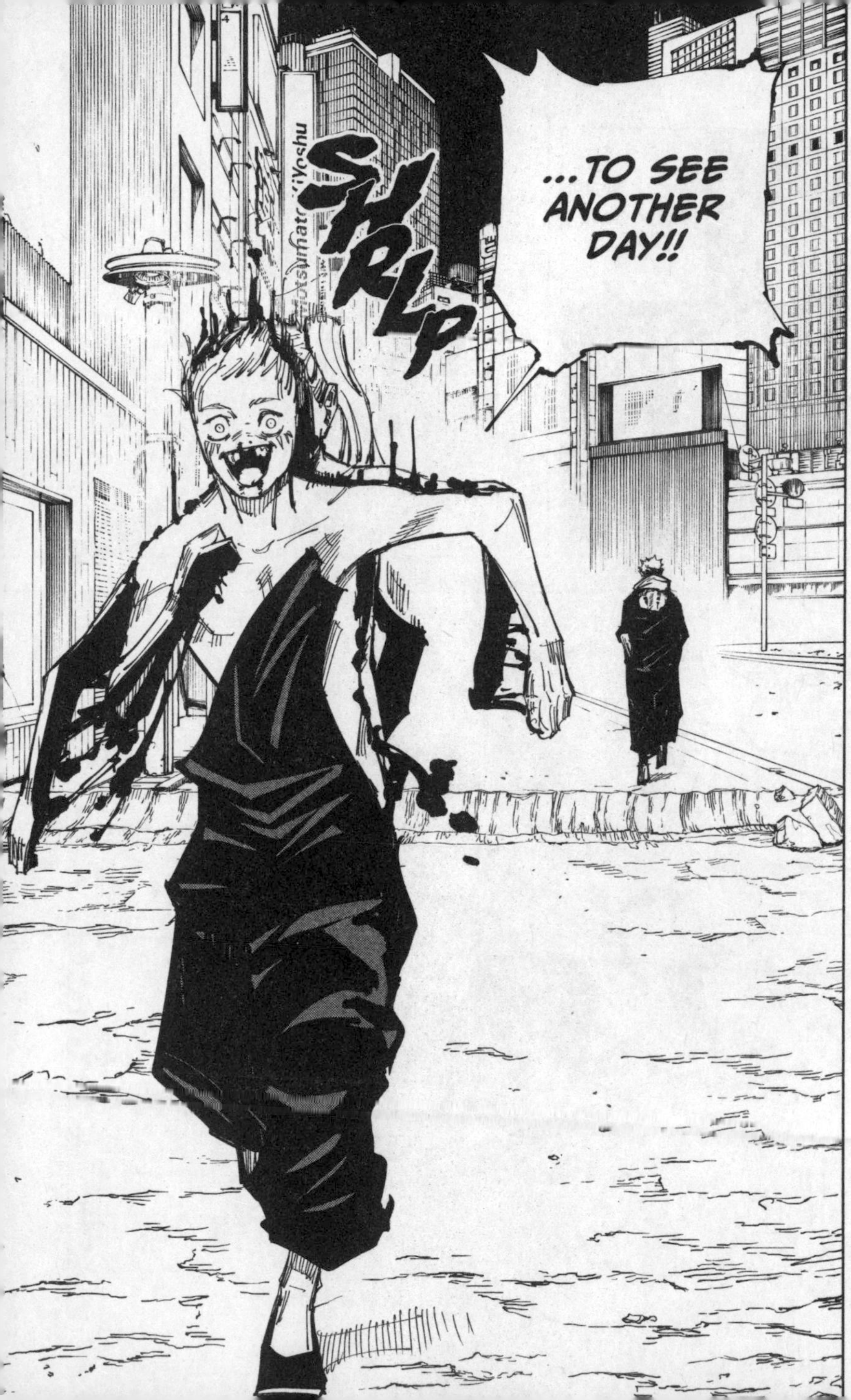
...TO SEE ANOTHER DAY!!
SHRLP

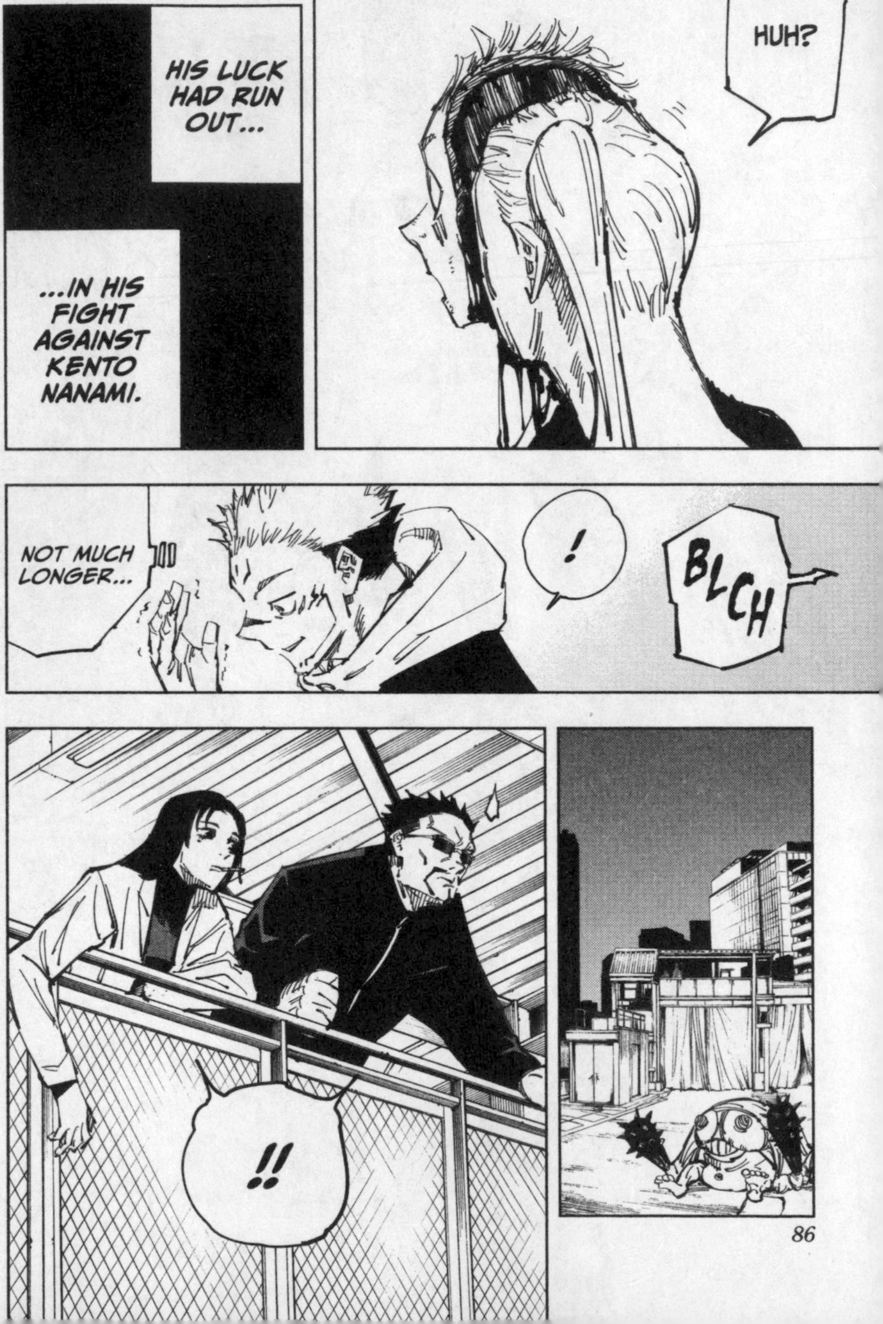
HUH?
HIS LUCK HAD RUN OUT...
...IN HIS FIGHT AGAINST KENTO NANAMI.
BLCH
!
NOT MUCH LONGER...
!!

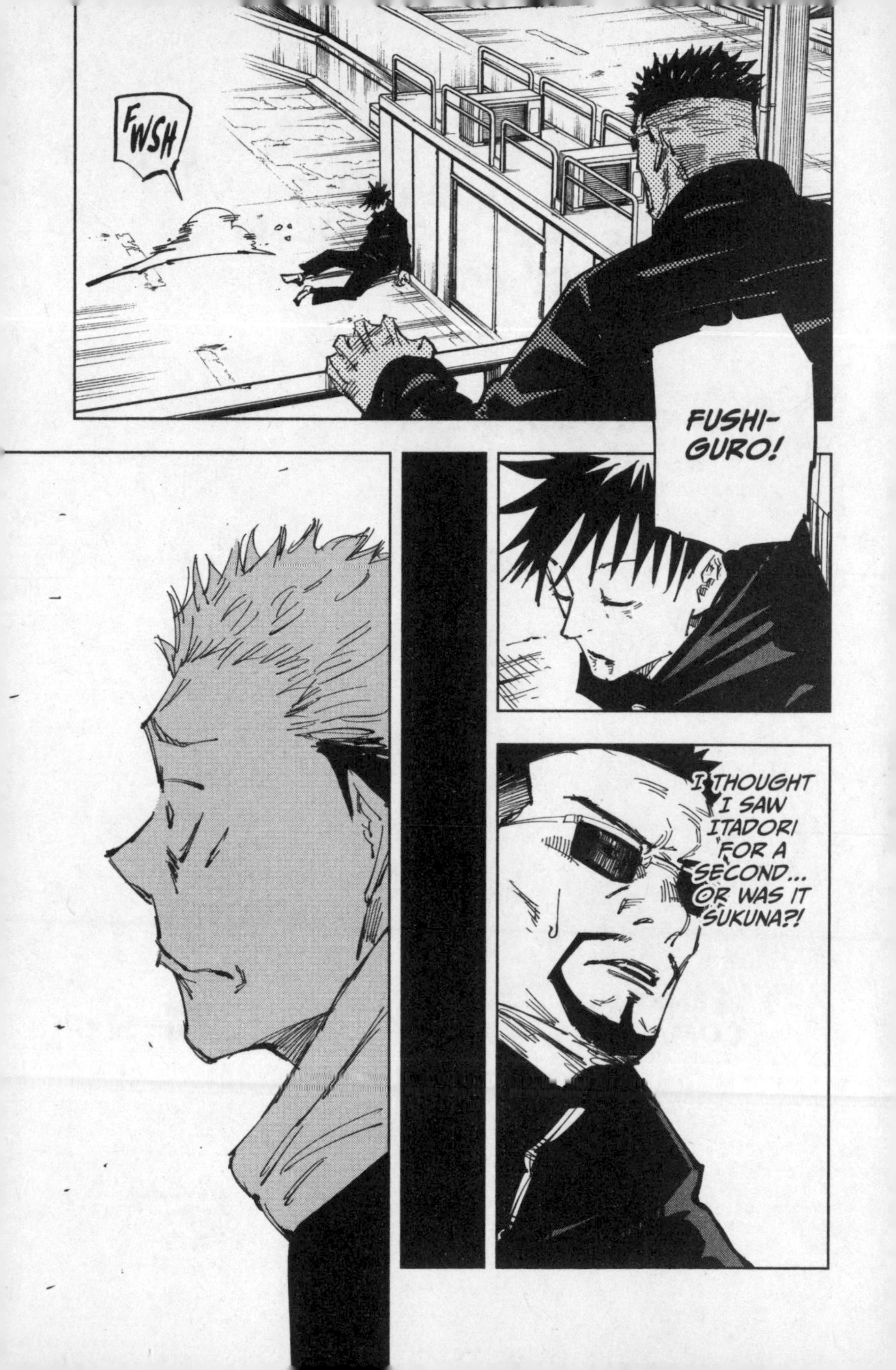
FWSH
FUSHI-GURO!
I THOUGHT I SAW ITADORI FOR A SECOND... OR WAS IT SUKUNA?!

THE 2020 VALENTINES RANKINGS THAT I SERIOUSLY ALMOST FORGOT

RANKINGS (VALENTINES RECEIVED)	CHARACTER	
17 (1)	OKKOTSU	SUKUNA
	PAPAGURO	HAIBARA
	PANDA	JUNPEI
	HANAMI	KAMO (NORITOSHI)

GENERAL COMMENT

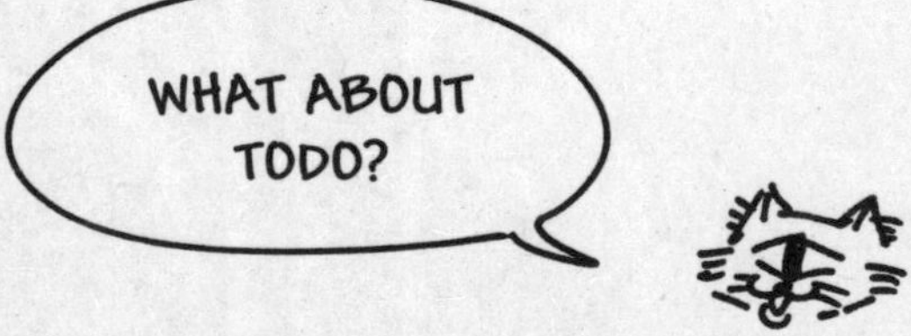
WHAT ABOUT TODO?

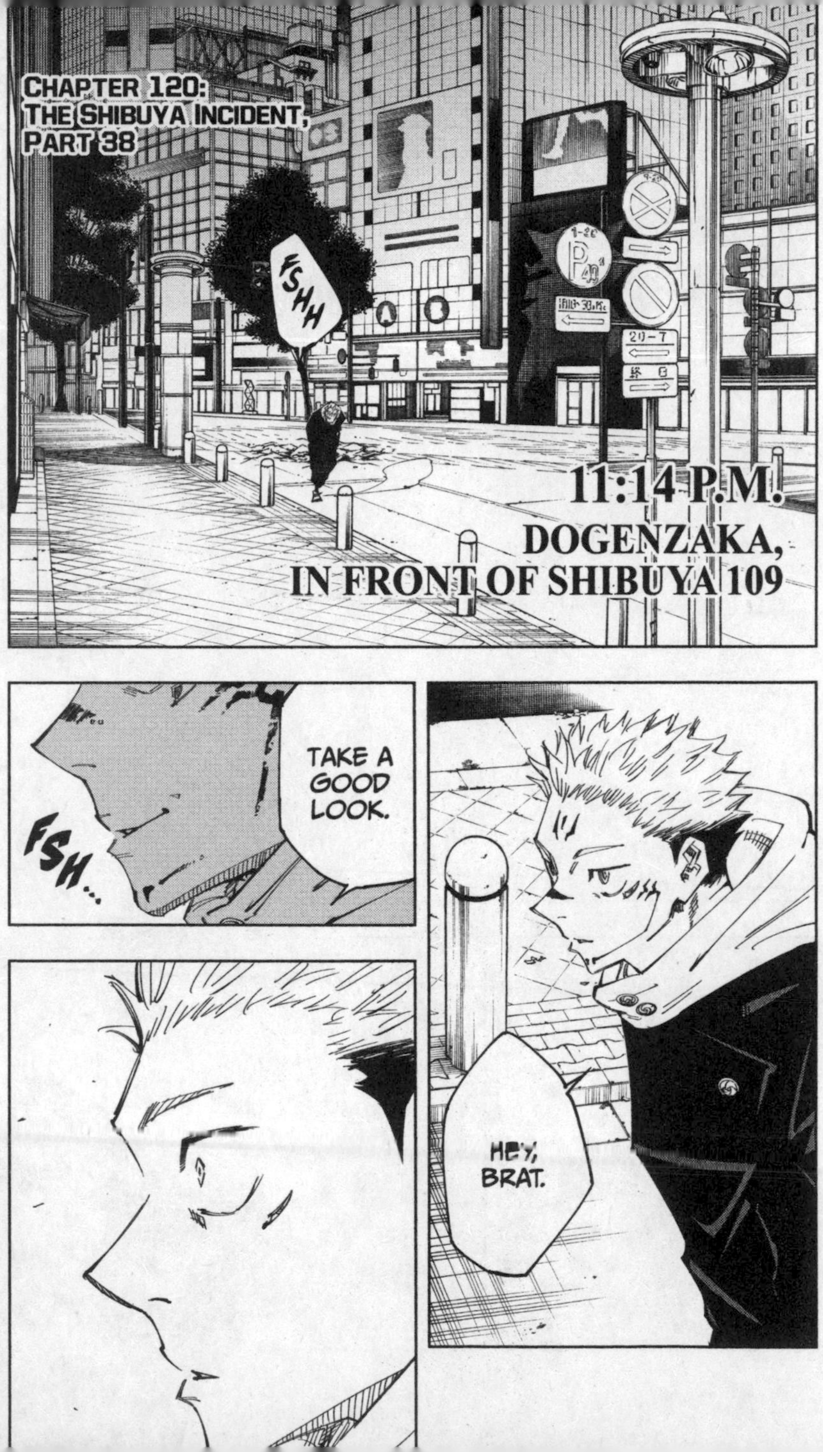
CHAPTER 120:
THE SHIBUYA INCIDENT,
PART 38
FSHH
11:14 P.M.
DOGENZAKA,
IN FRONT OF SHIBUYA 109
HEY, BRAT.
TAKE A GOOD LOOK.
FSH...

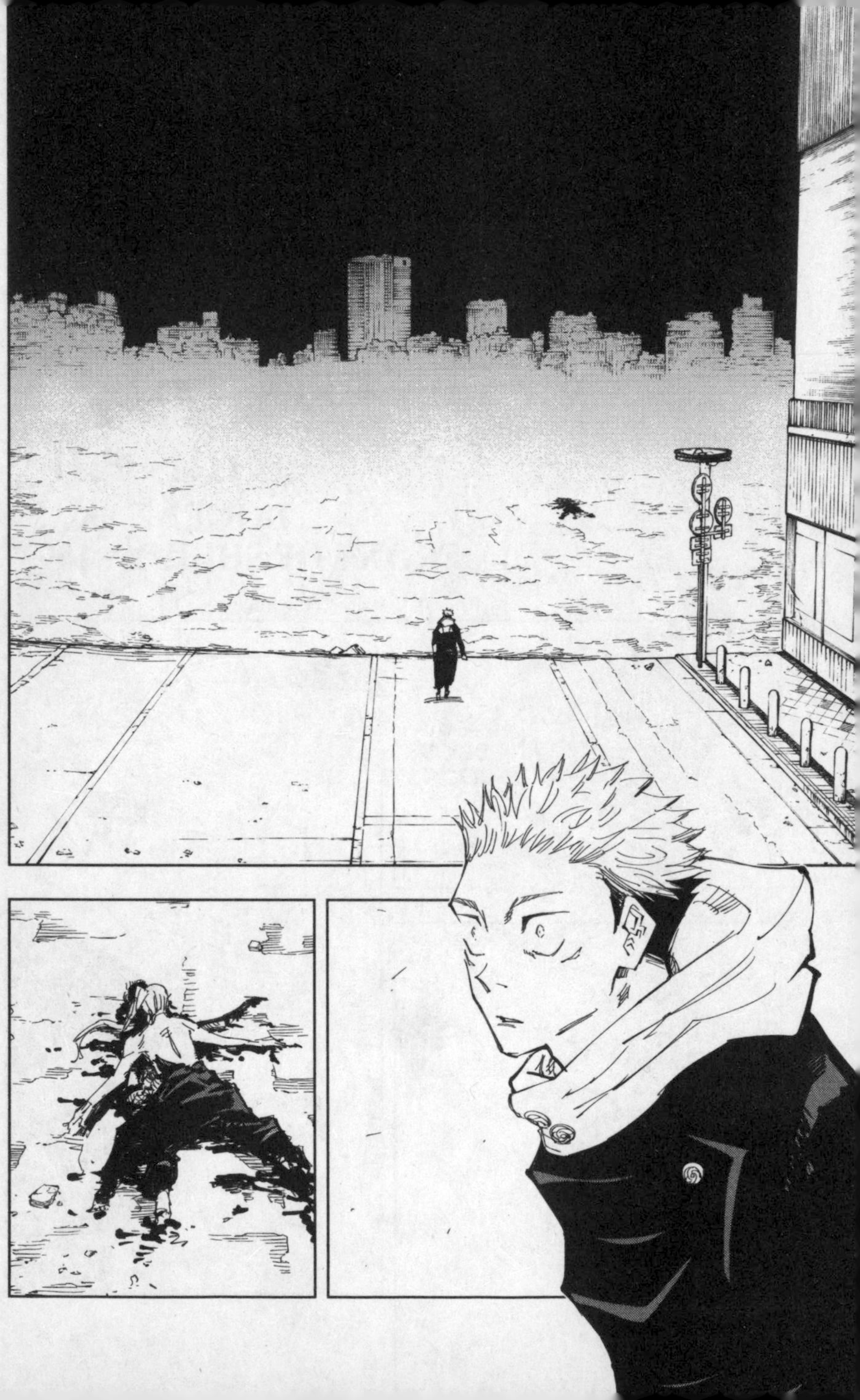

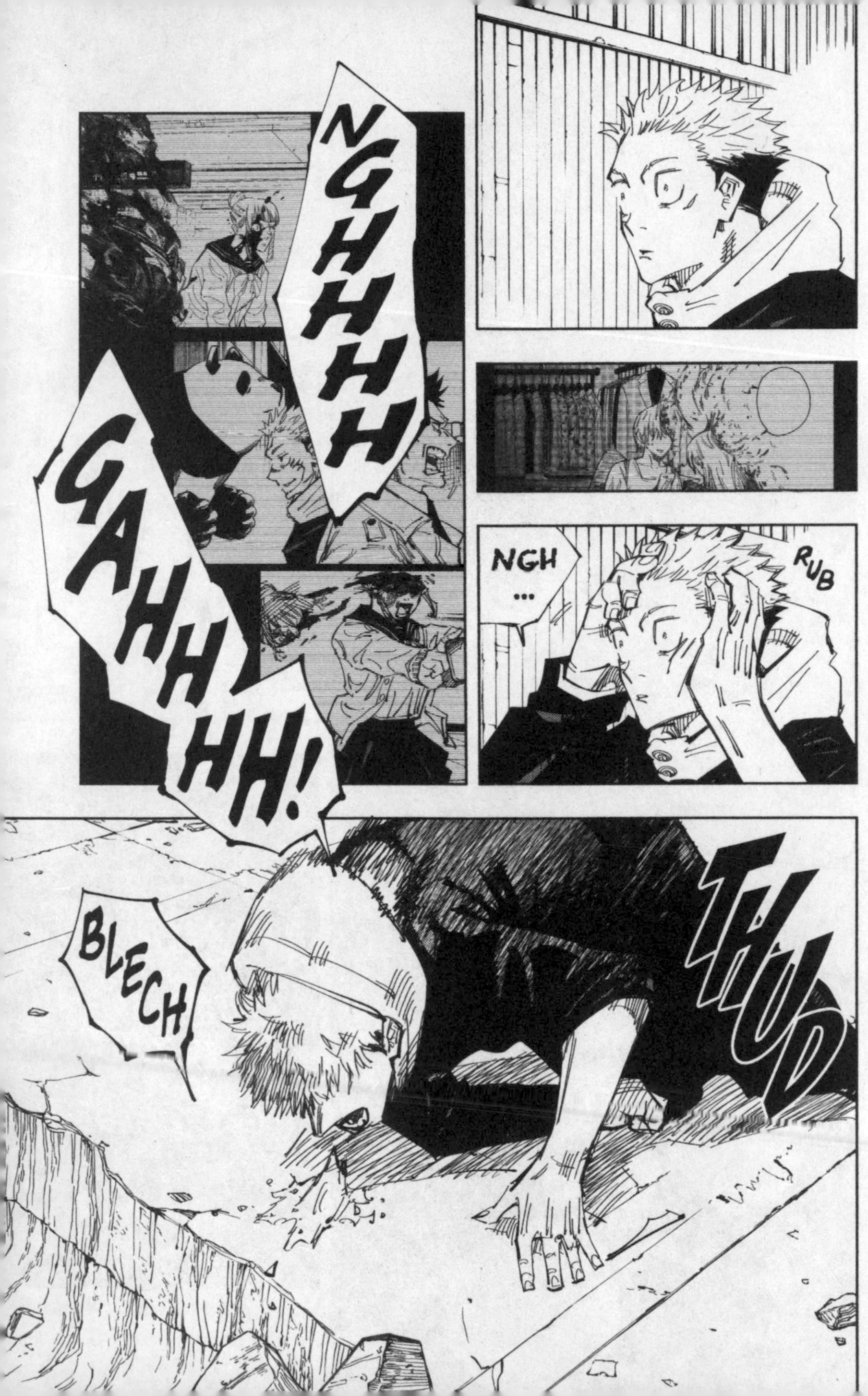
NGH ...
RUB
NGHHHHH
GAHHHHH!
THUD
BLECH

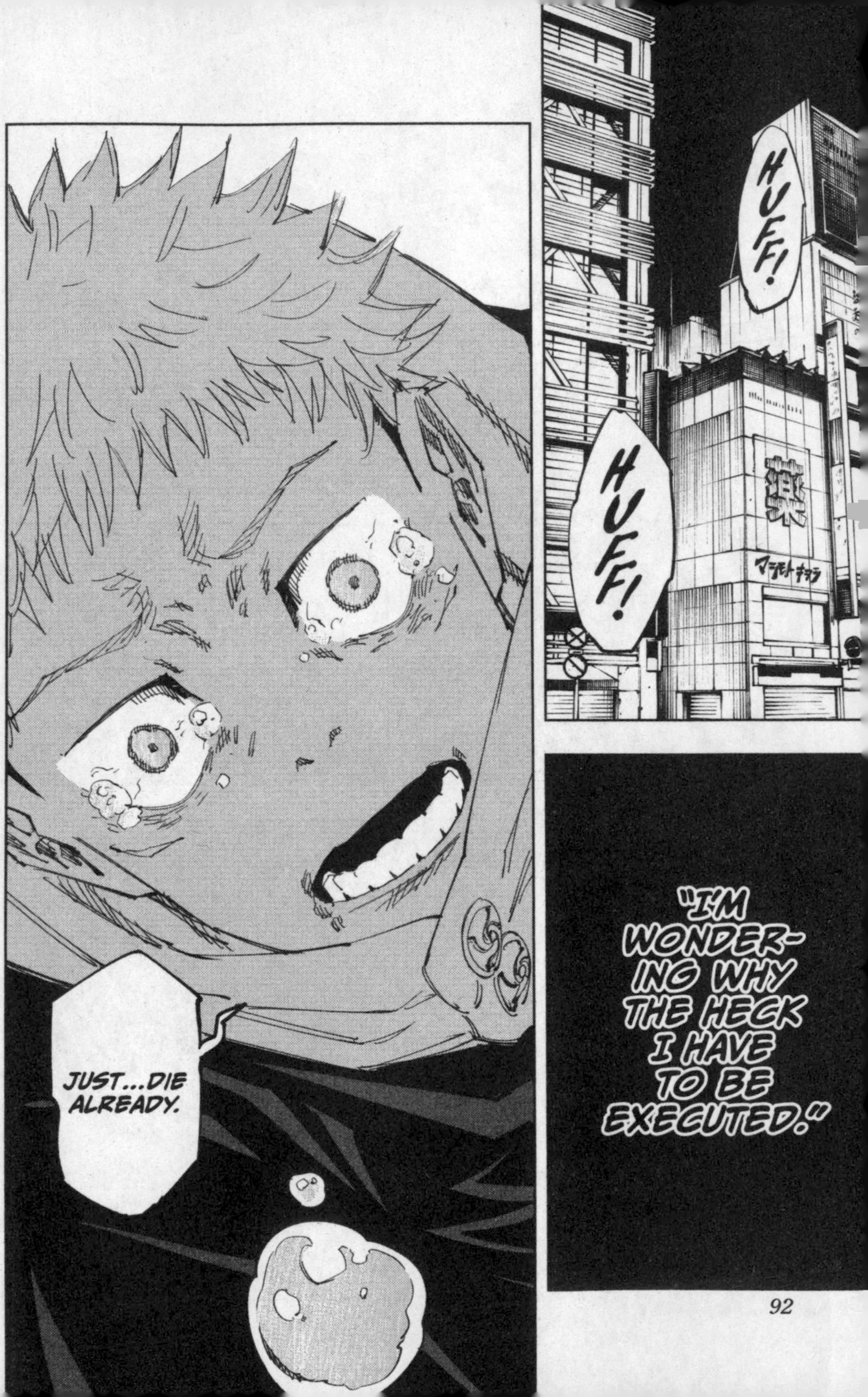
HUFF!
HUFF!
"I'M WONDERING WHY THE HECK I HAVE TO BE EXECUTED."
JUST...DIE ALREADY.

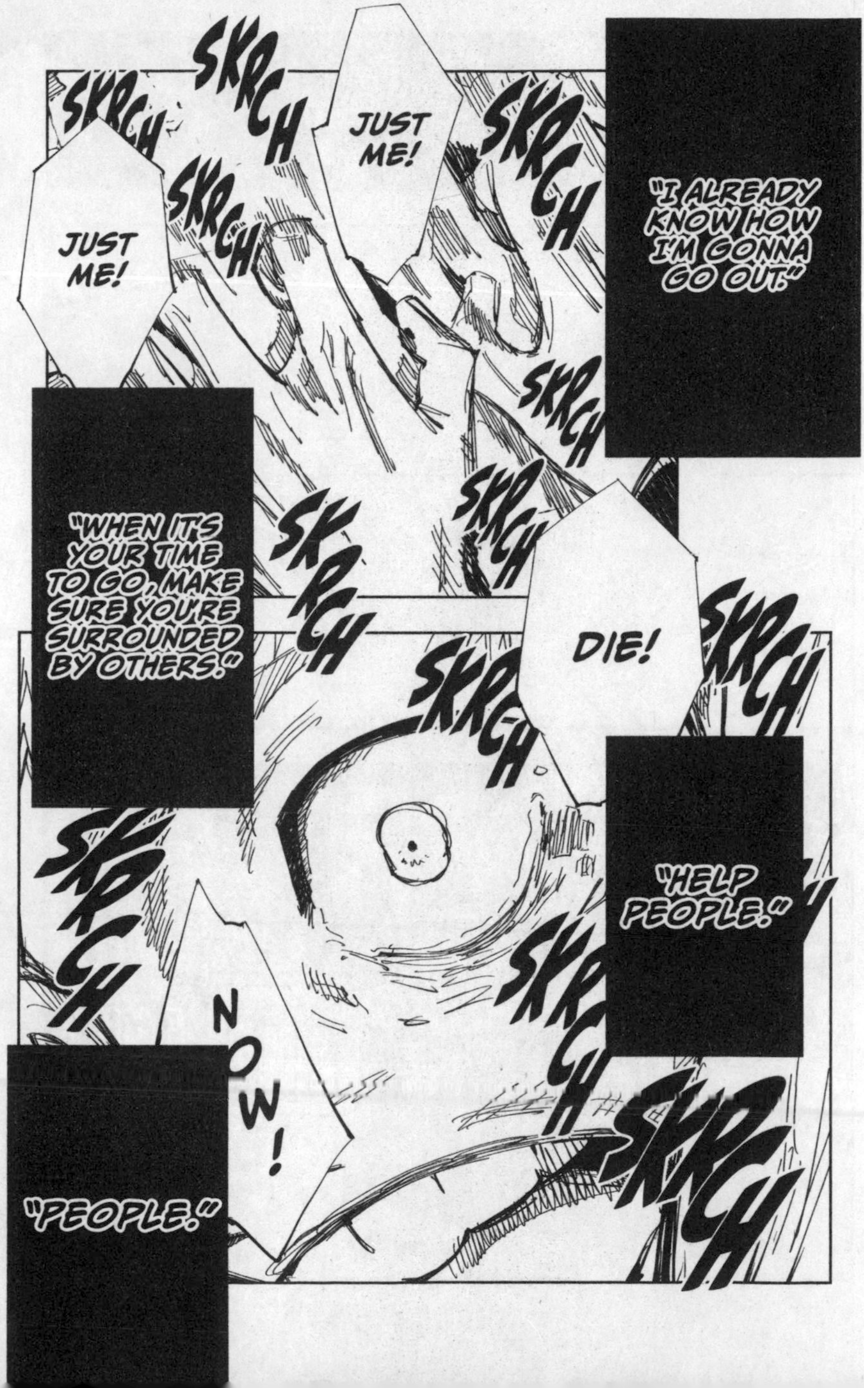
"I ALREADY KNOW HOW I'M GONNA GO OUT."
SKRCH
JUST ME!
SKRCH
SKRCH
JUST ME!
SKRCH
SKRCH
SKRCH
SKRCH
"WHEN IT'S YOUR TIME TO GO, MAKE SURE YOU'RE SURROUNDED BY OTHERS."
SKRCH
DIE!
SKRCH
SKRCH
"HELP PEOPLE."
SKRCH
SKRCH
SKRCH
NOW!
"PEOPLE."

BECAUSE OF YOU...

I NEED TO MOVE.

...I'M NOTHING BUT A MURDERER.

I NEED TO FIGHT.

WITH HOW THINGS HAVE GONE...

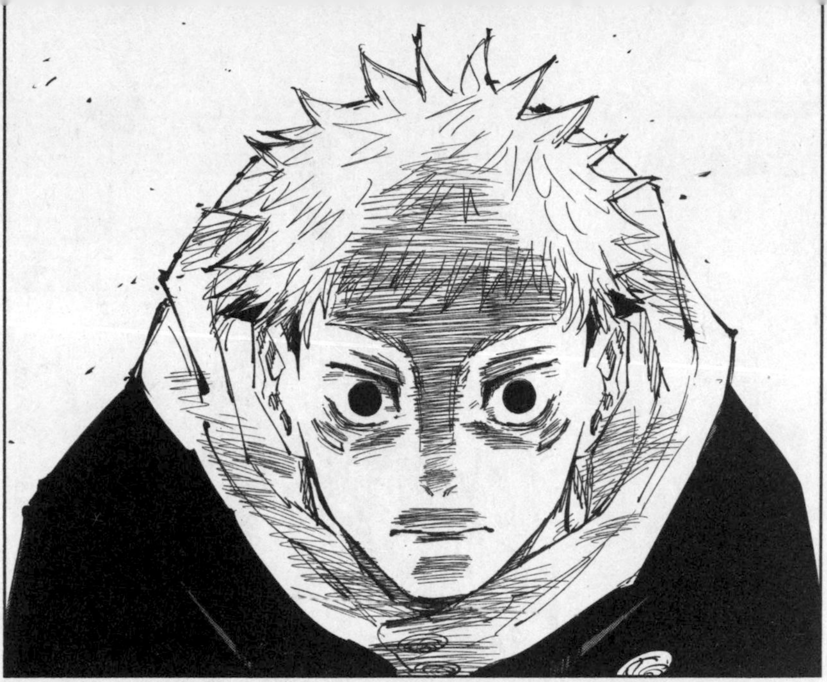

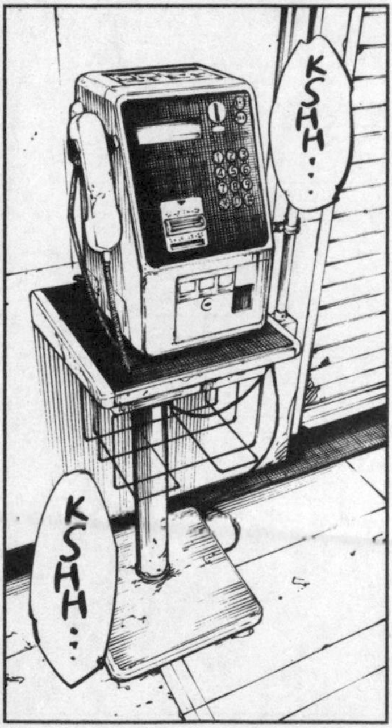
KSHH...
KSHH...

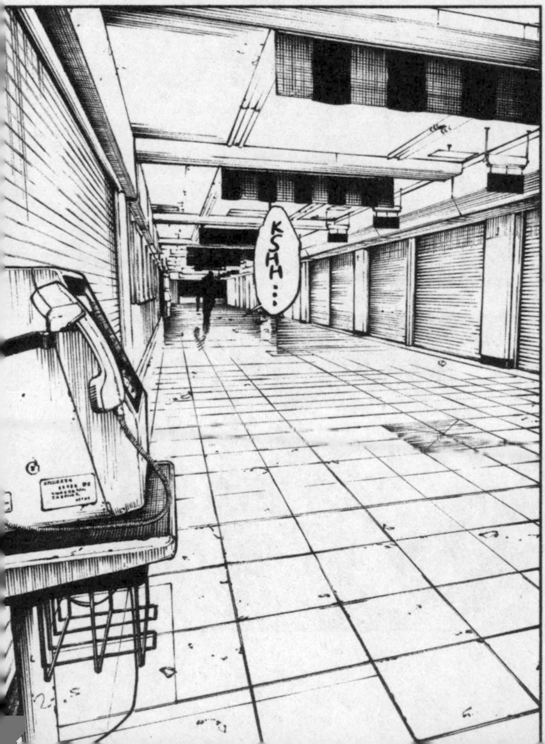
KSHH...

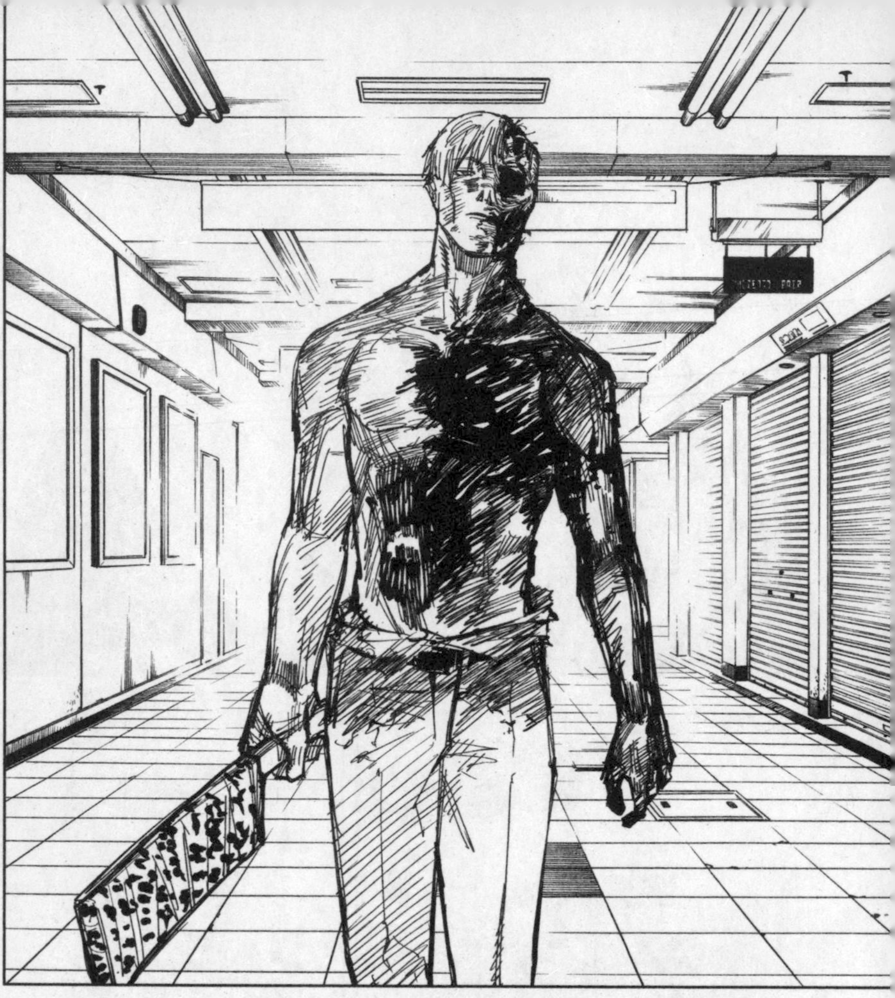

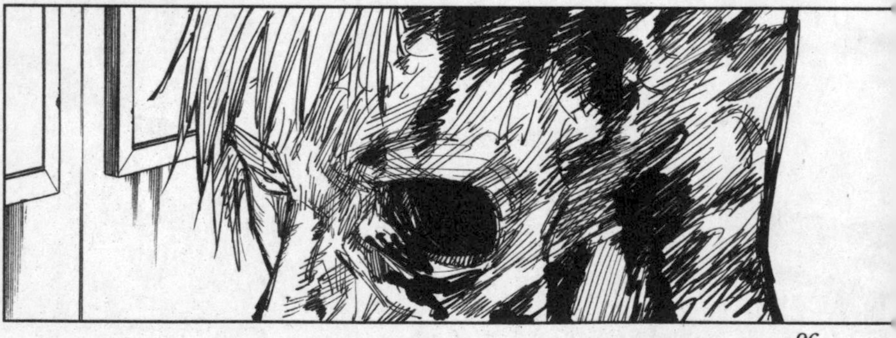

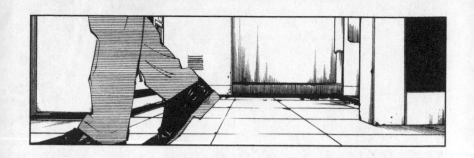

PHOTO ID

←出口 A7

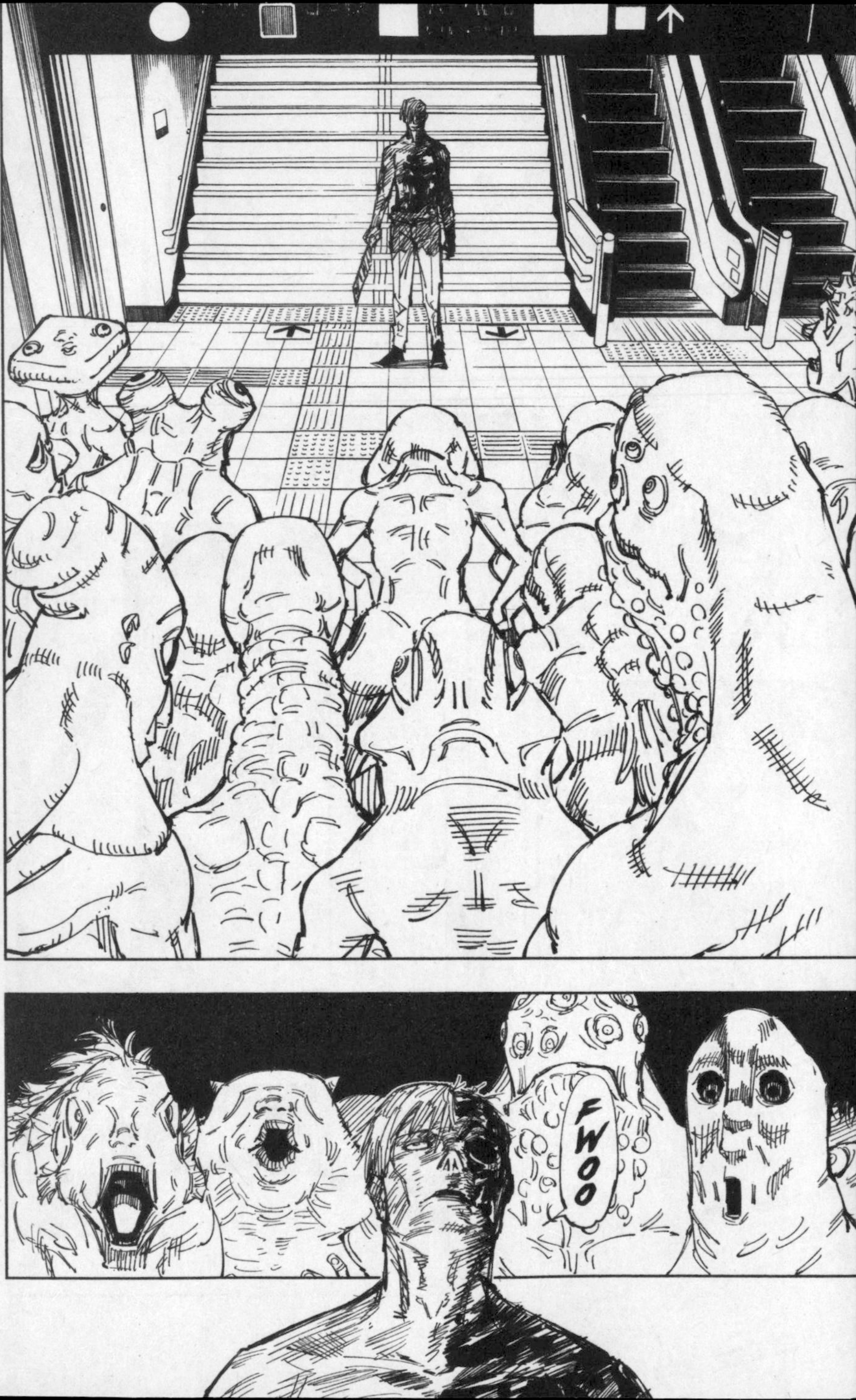
FWOO

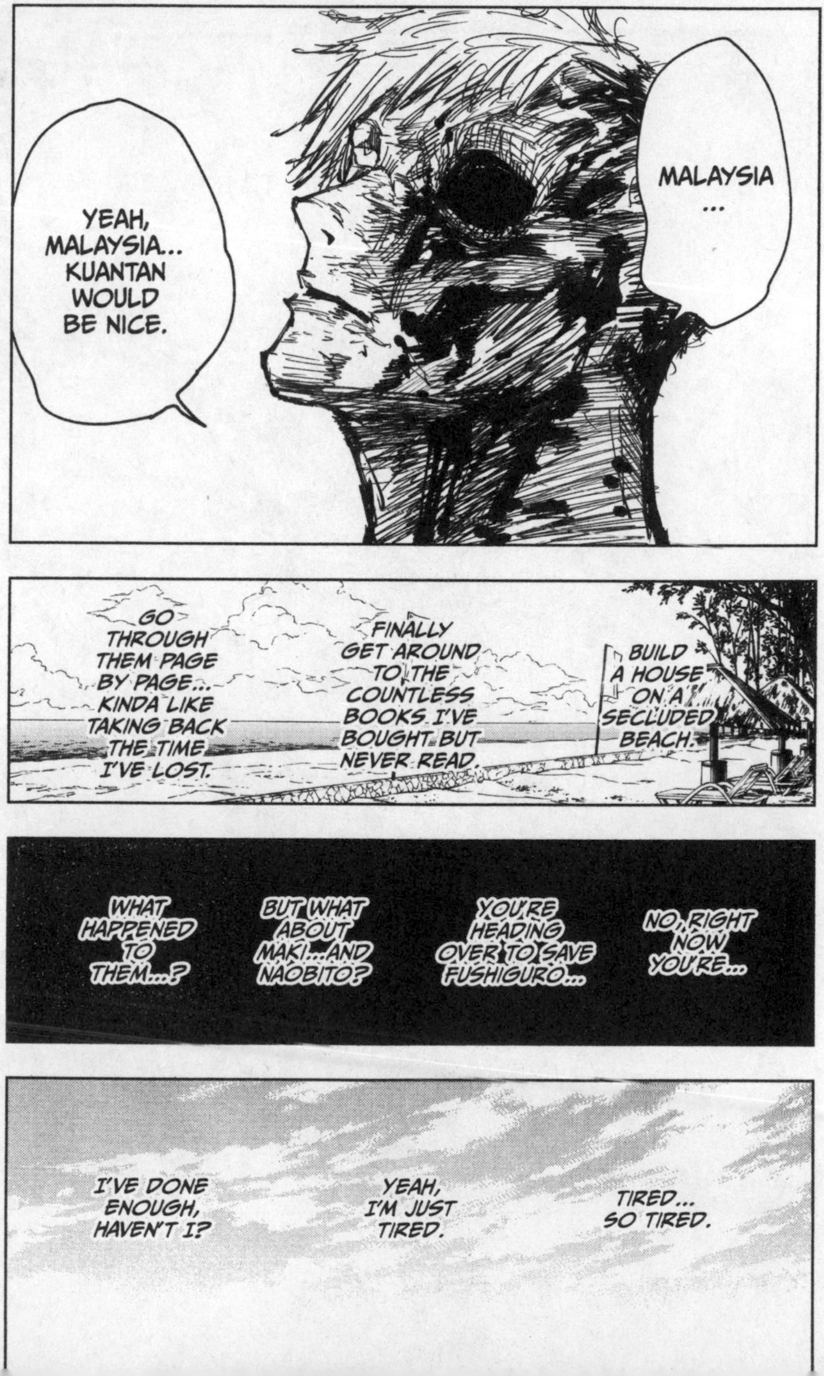
MALAYSIA ...
YEAH, MALAYSIA... KUANTAN WOULD BE NICE.
BUILD A HOUSE ON A SECLUDED BEACH.
FINALLY GET AROUND TO THE COUNTLESS BOOKS I'VE BOUGHT BUT NEVER READ.
GO THROUGH THEM PAGE BY PAGE... KINDA LIKE TAKING BACK THE TIME I'VE LOST.
NO, RIGHT NOW YOU'RE...
YOU'RE HEADING OVER TO SAVE FUSHIGURO...
BUT WHAT ABOUT MAKI... AND NAOBITO?
WHAT HAPPENED TO THEM...?
TIRED... SO TIRED.
YEAH, I'M JUST TIRED.
I'VE DONE ENOUGH, HAVEN'T I?

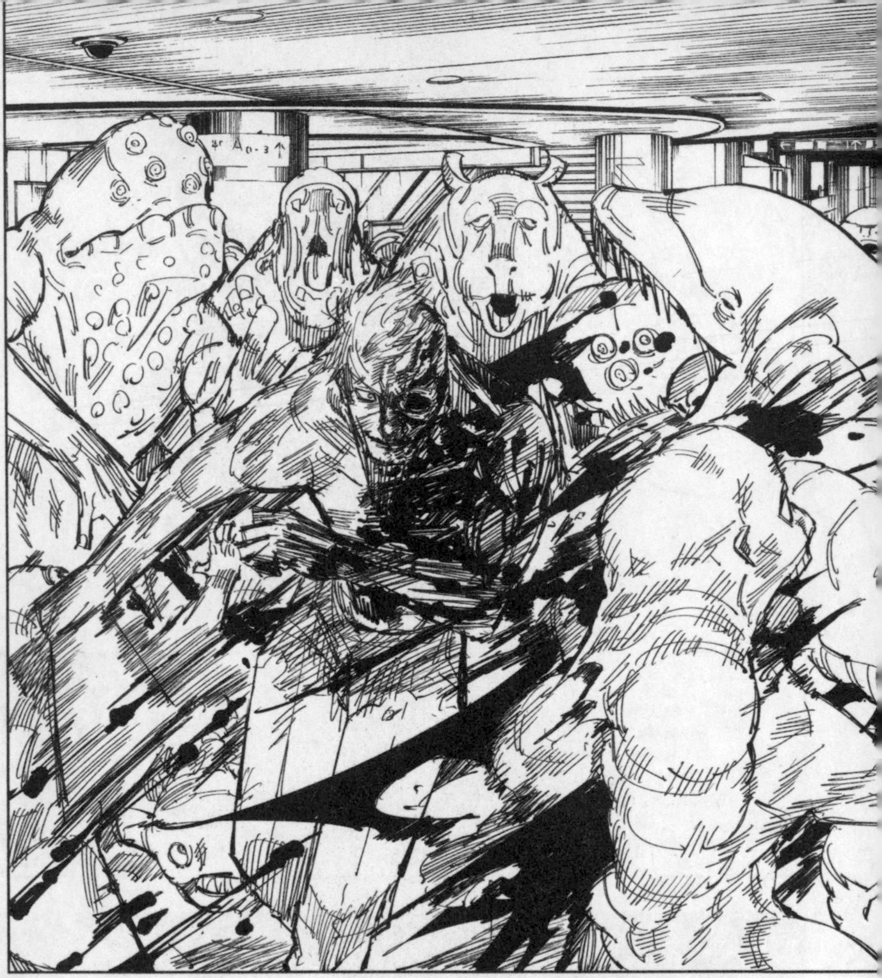
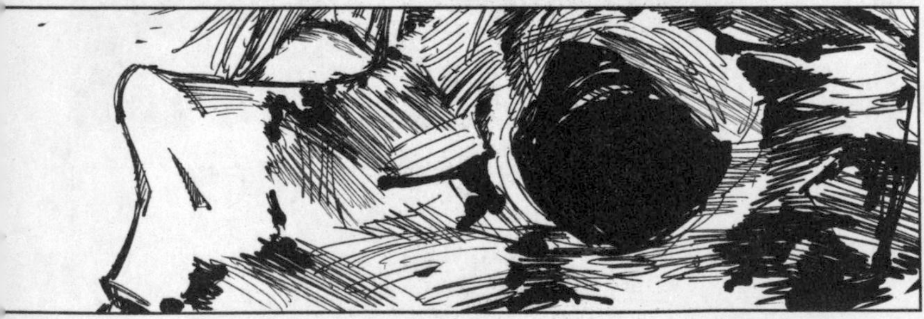

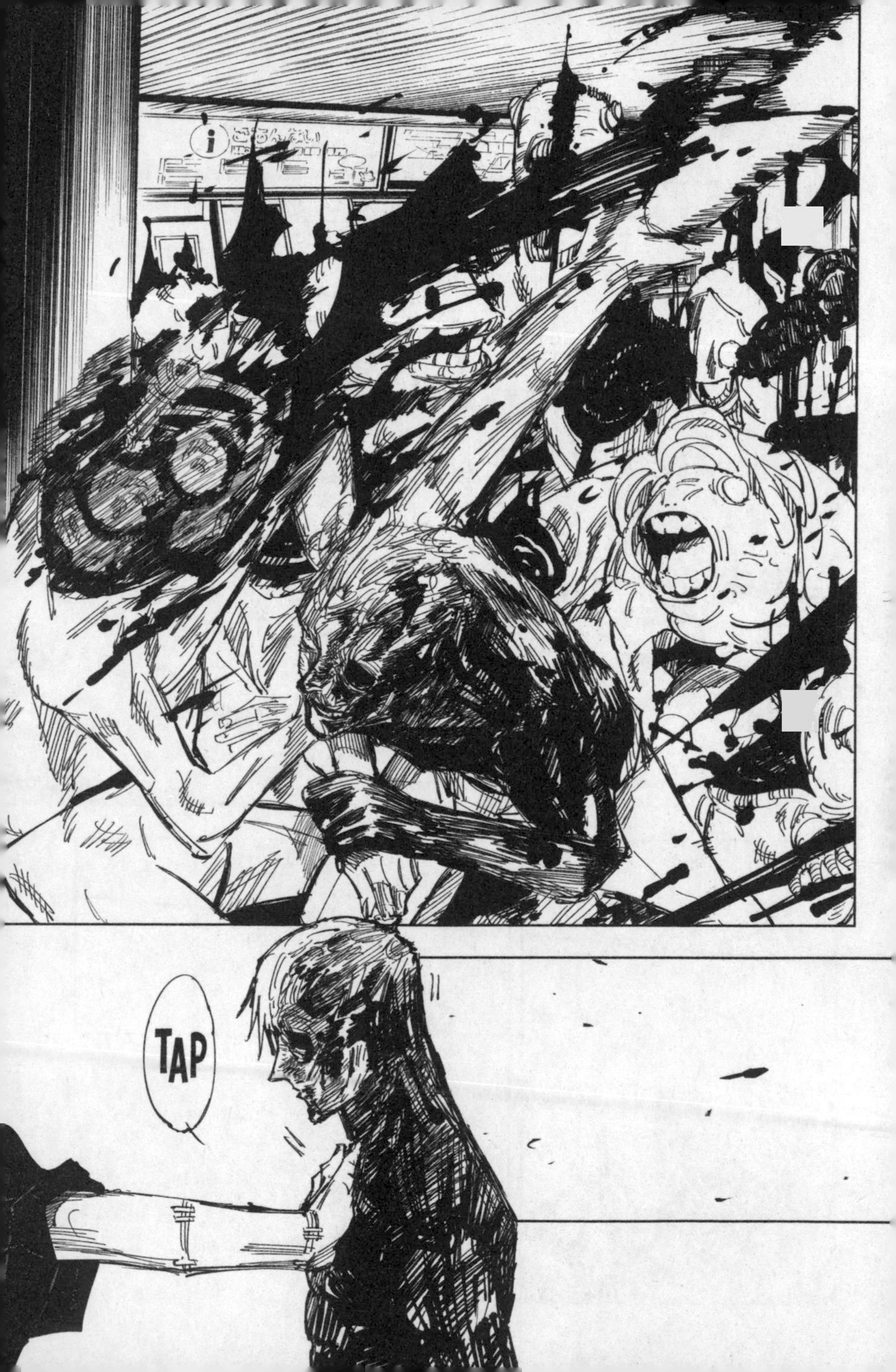
TAP

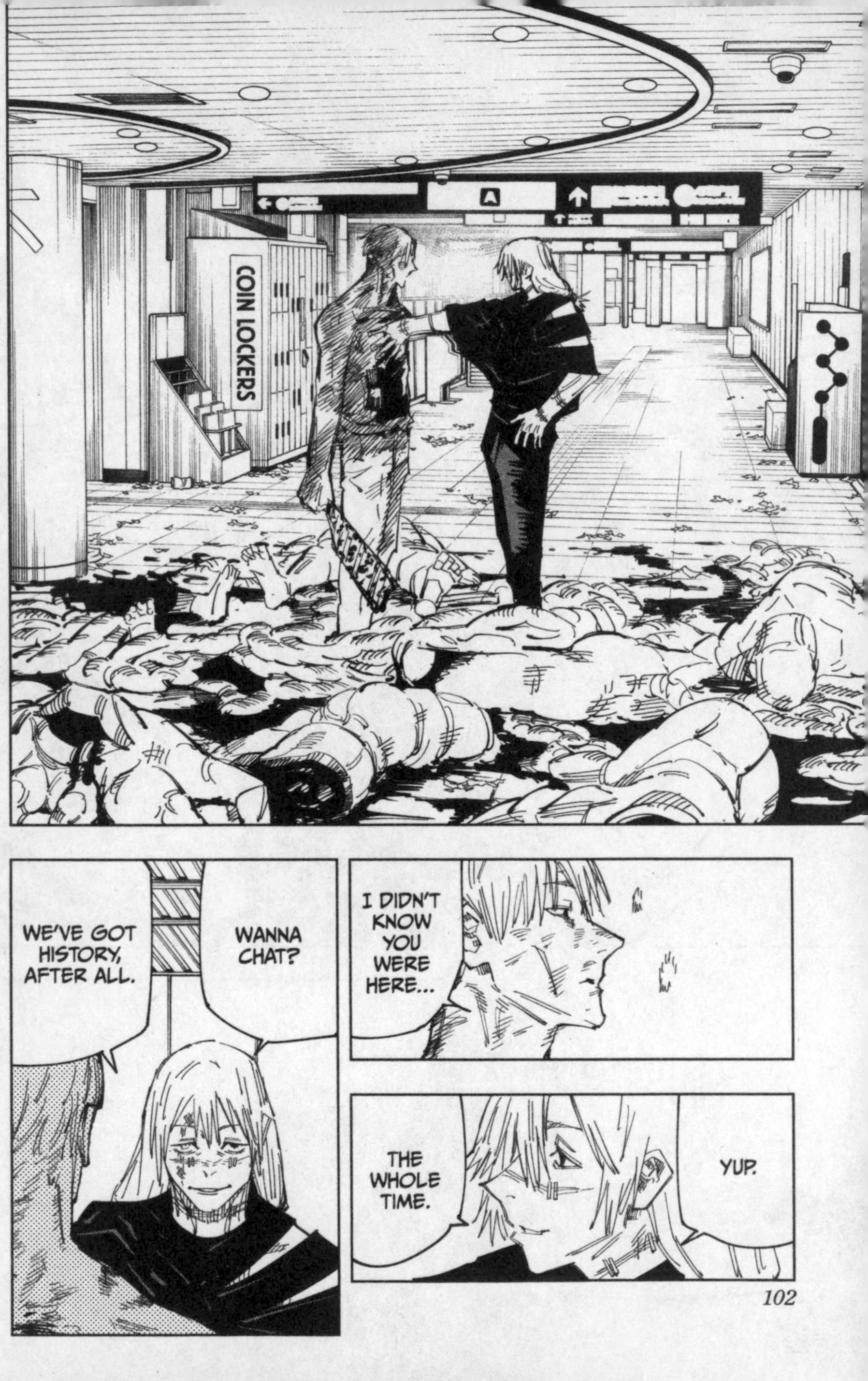
COIN LOCKERS
I DIDN'T KNOW YOU WERE HERE...
THE WHOLE TIME.
YUP.
WANNA CHAT?
WE'VE GOT HISTORY, AFTER ALL.

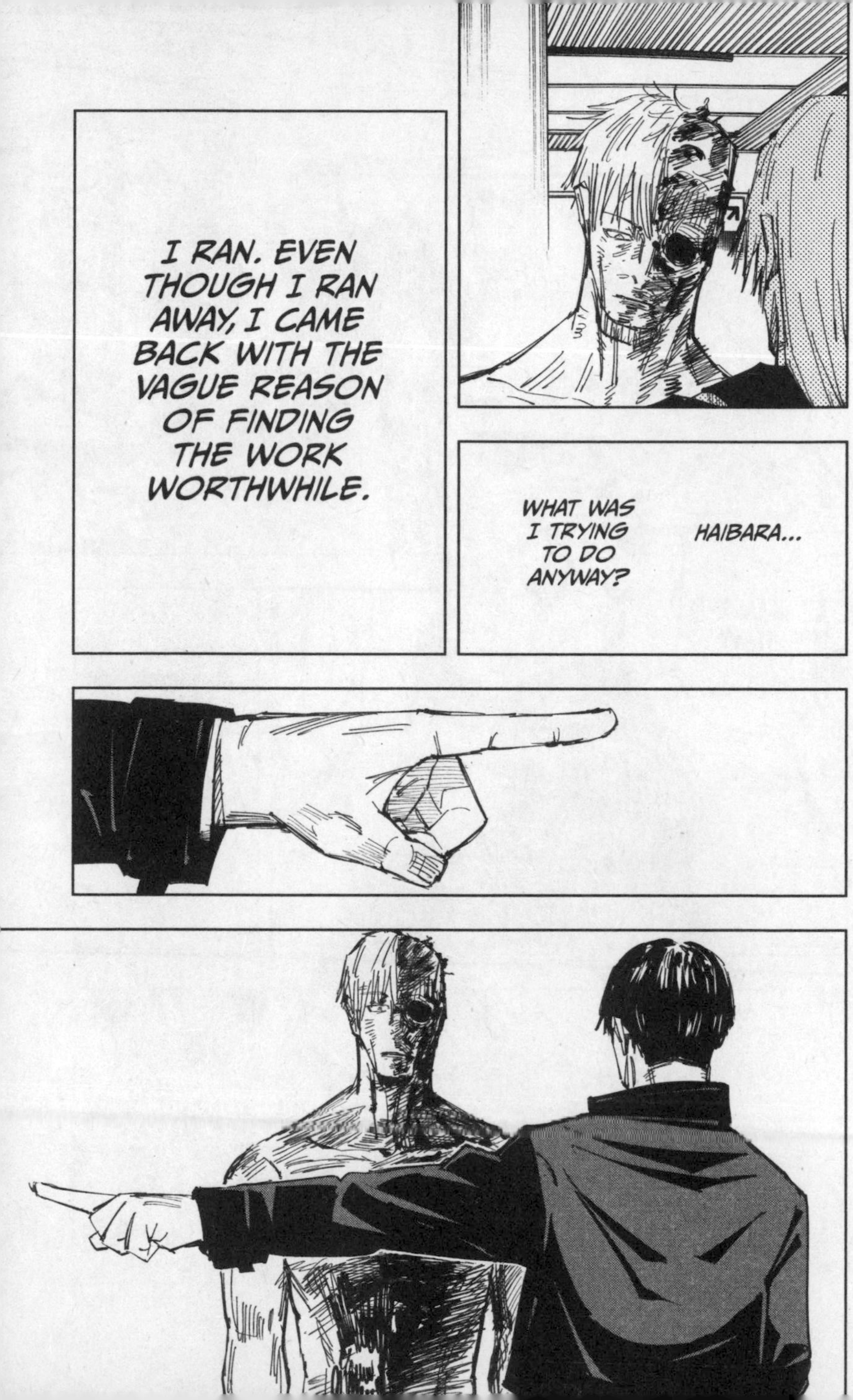
HAIBARA...
WHAT WAS I TRYING TO DO ANYWAY?
I RAN. EVEN THOUGH I RAN AWAY, I CAME BACK WITH THE VAGUE REASON OF FINDING THE WORK WORTHWHILE.

NANA-MIN!

ITADORI.

IT'LL JUST END UP BECOMING A CURSE FOR HIM.

NO, HAIBARA. THAT'S NOT RIGHT. I CAN'T SAY THAT TO HIM.

ITADORI...

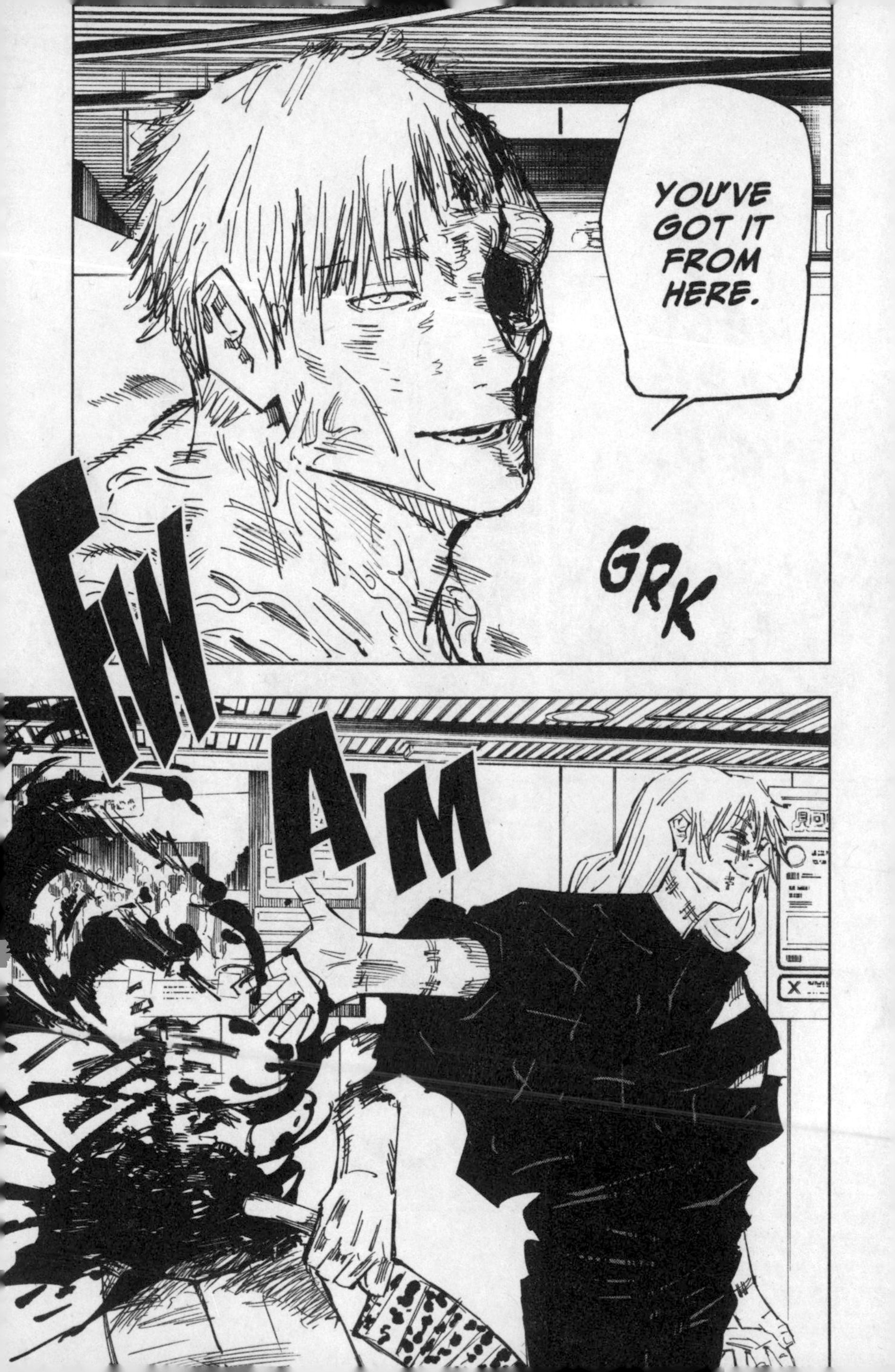
YOU'VE GOT IT FROM HERE.
GRK
FWAM

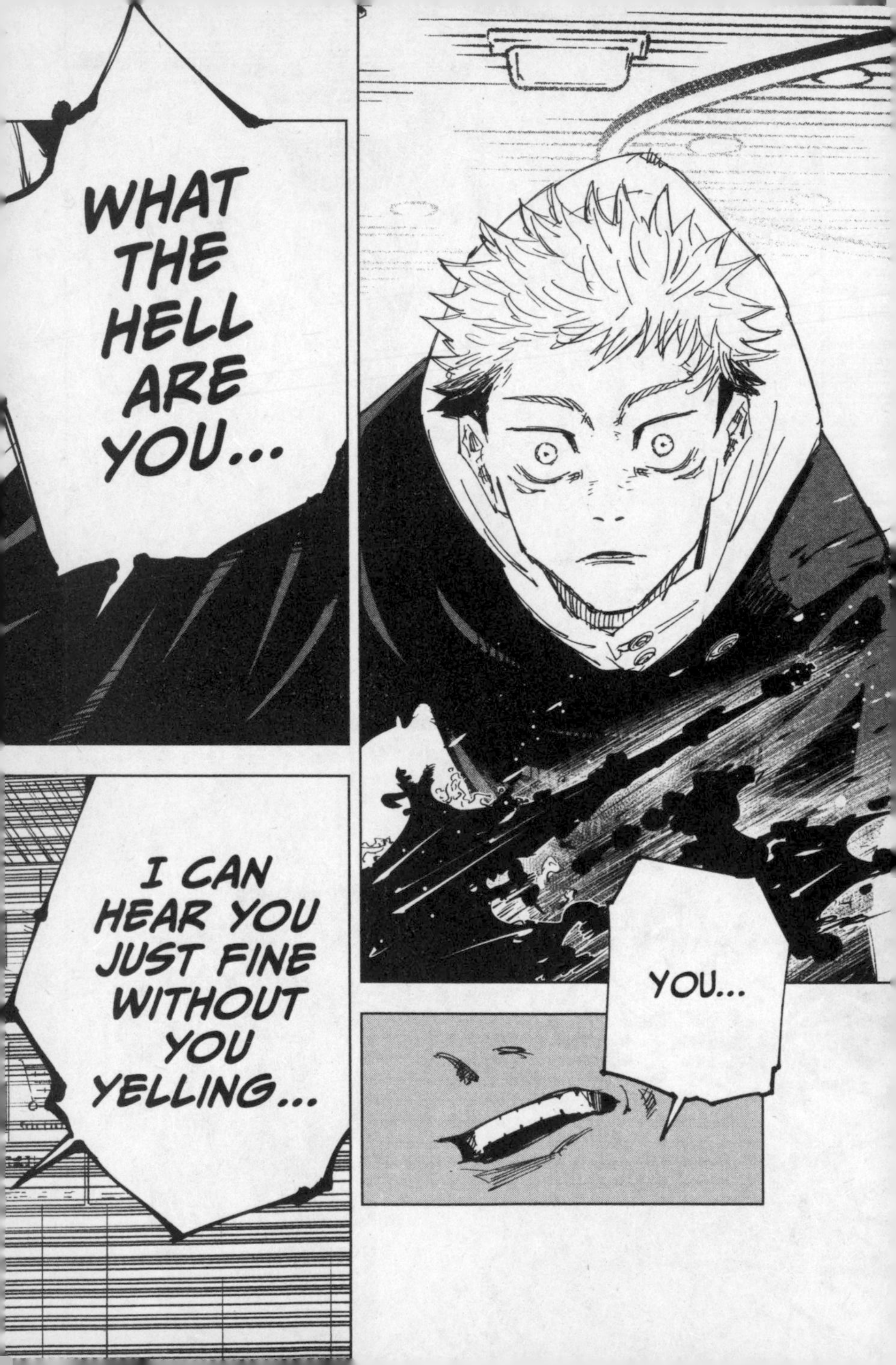
YOU...
WHAT THE HELL ARE YOU...
I CAN HEAR YOU JUST FINE WITHOUT YOU YELLING...

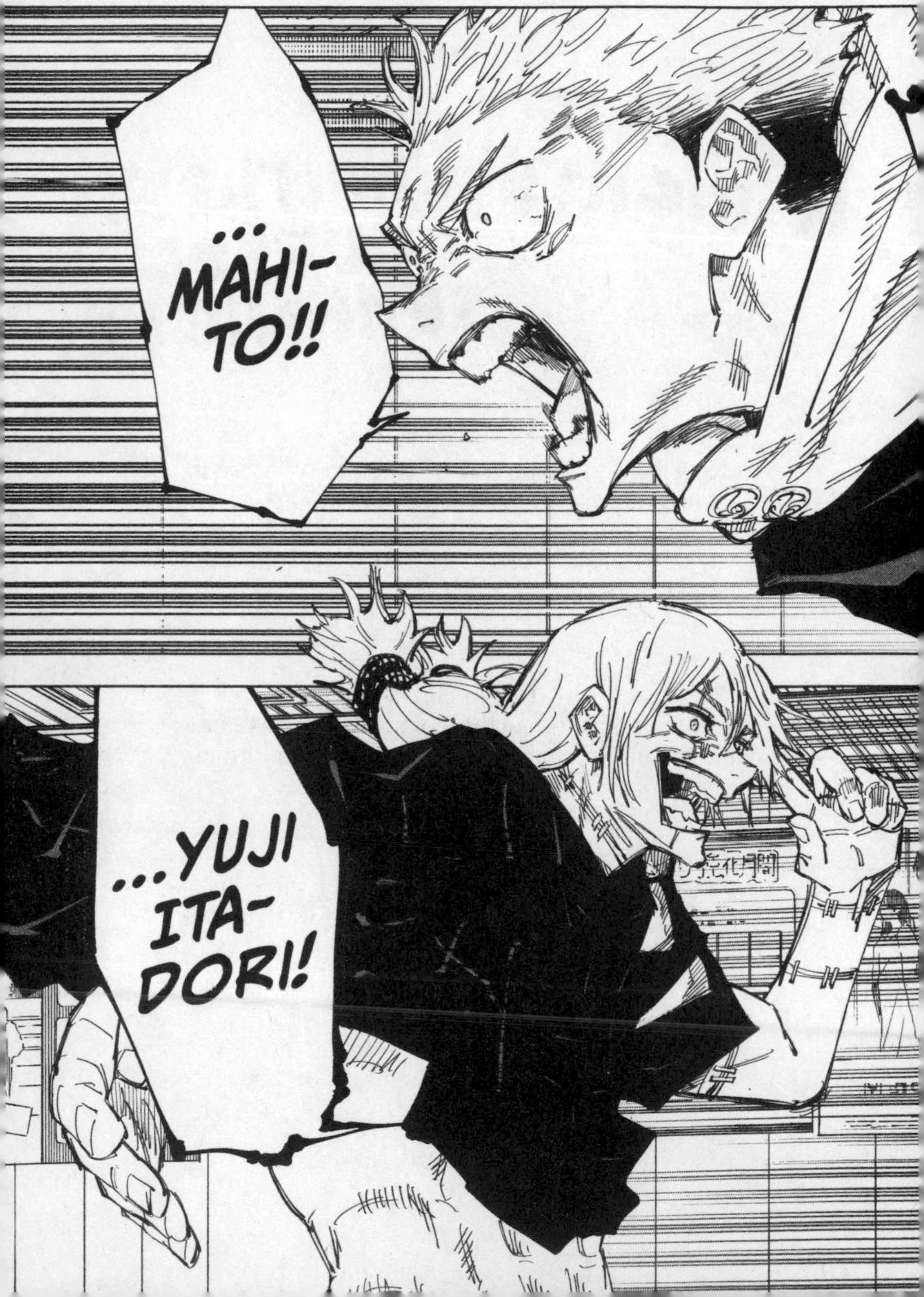
...MAHI-TO!!
...YUJI ITA-DORI!

GETTING IT RIGHT!! LIMITLESS CURSED TECHNIQUE

• Now that the anime has begun, more people in Japan and overseas will check out *Jujutsu Kaisen*. Because of that, I can't keep bluffing my way through stuff. Yes, I'm talking about Gojo's cursed technique.

• So I asked my editor to find someone knowledgeable about mathematics for their input, and the inquiry in the *Jump* editorial staff turned up T-san, who has a master's degree in engineering (information geometry)!!

• I hope to share what I've learned in this volume and the next.

• I should've done this from the start!!

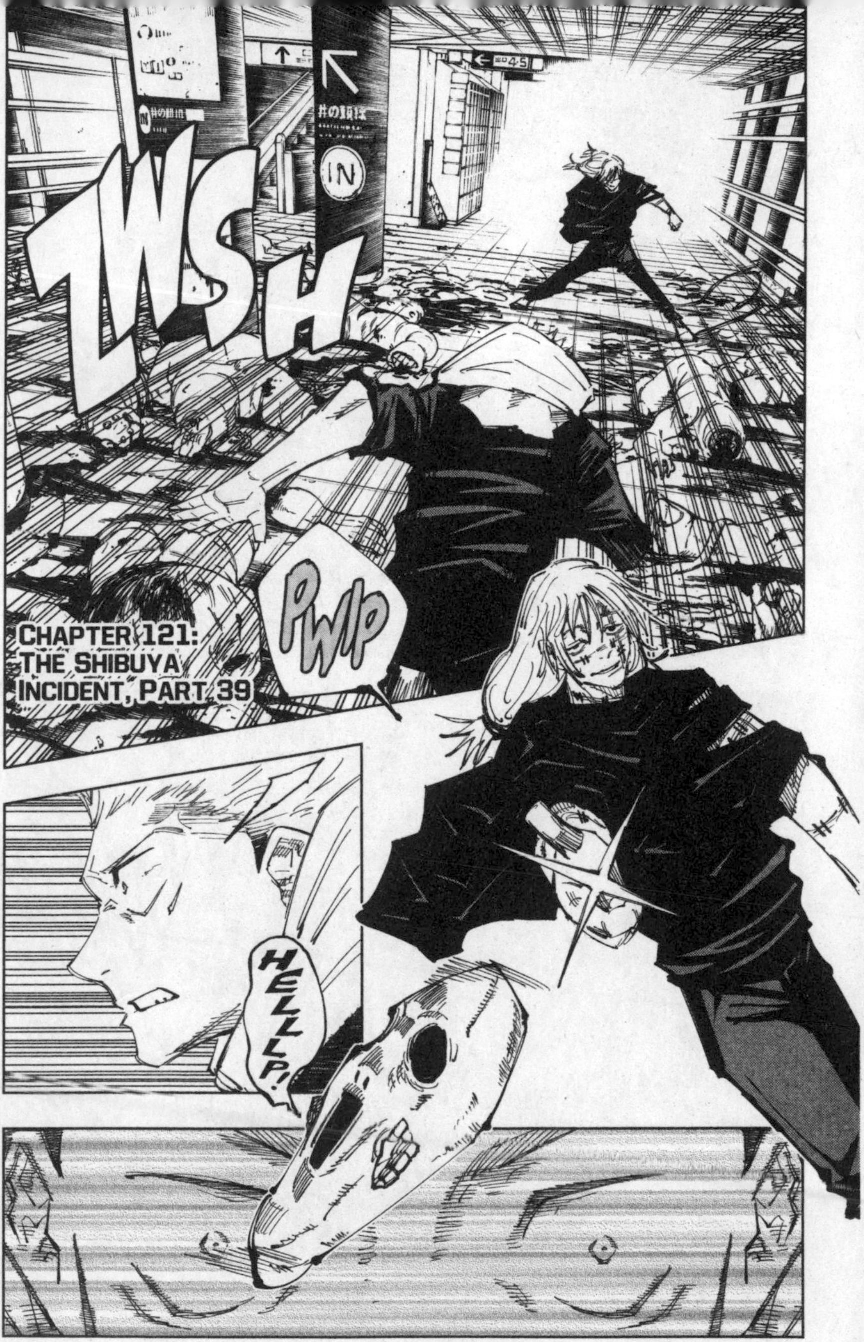
ZWSH
PWIP
Chapter 121:
The Shibuya
Incident, Part 39
HELLLP!

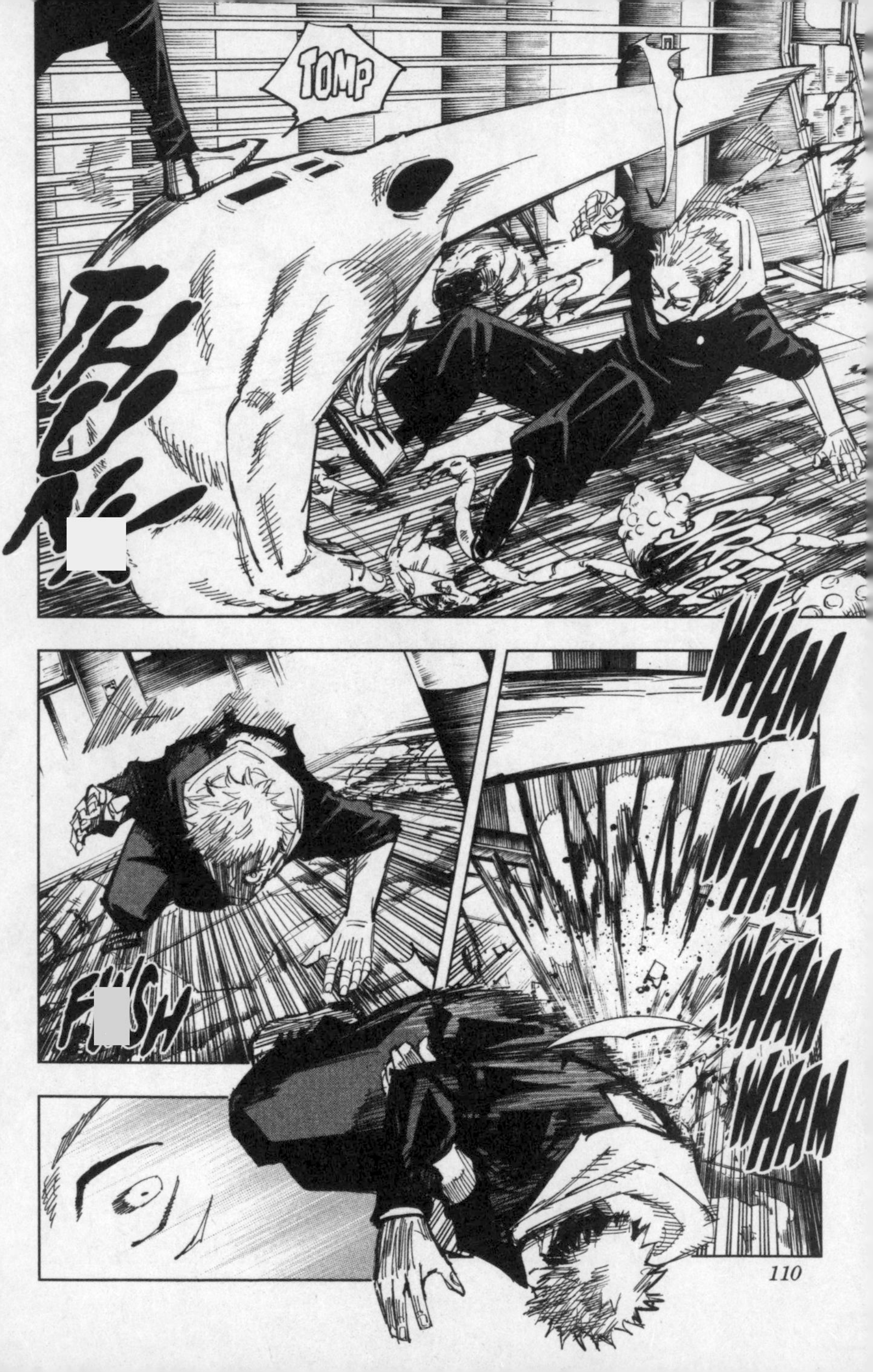
TOMP
WHAM
WHAM
WHAM
WHAM
WHAM

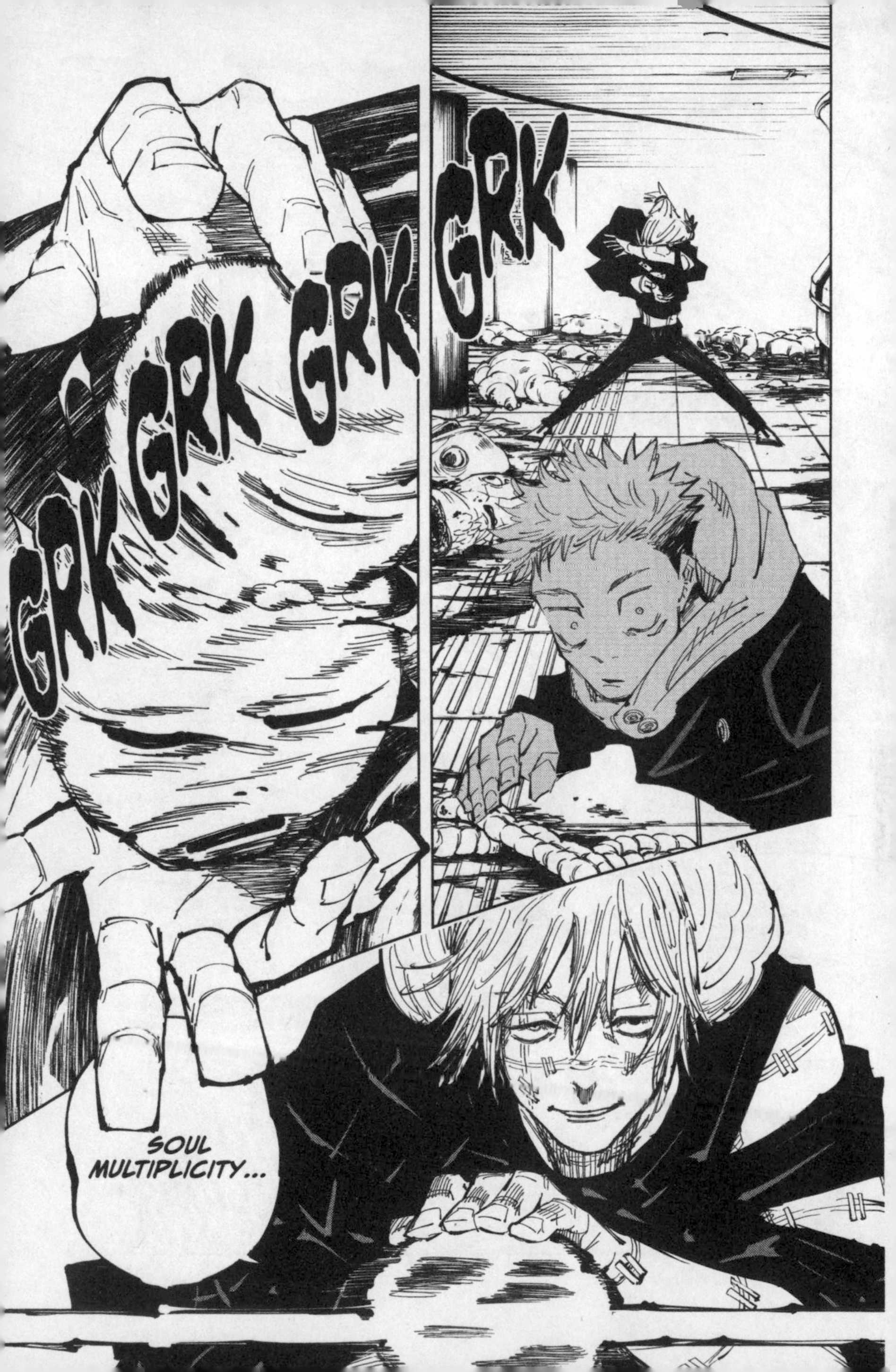
GRK GRK
GRK GRK GRK GRK
SOUL MULTIPLICITY...

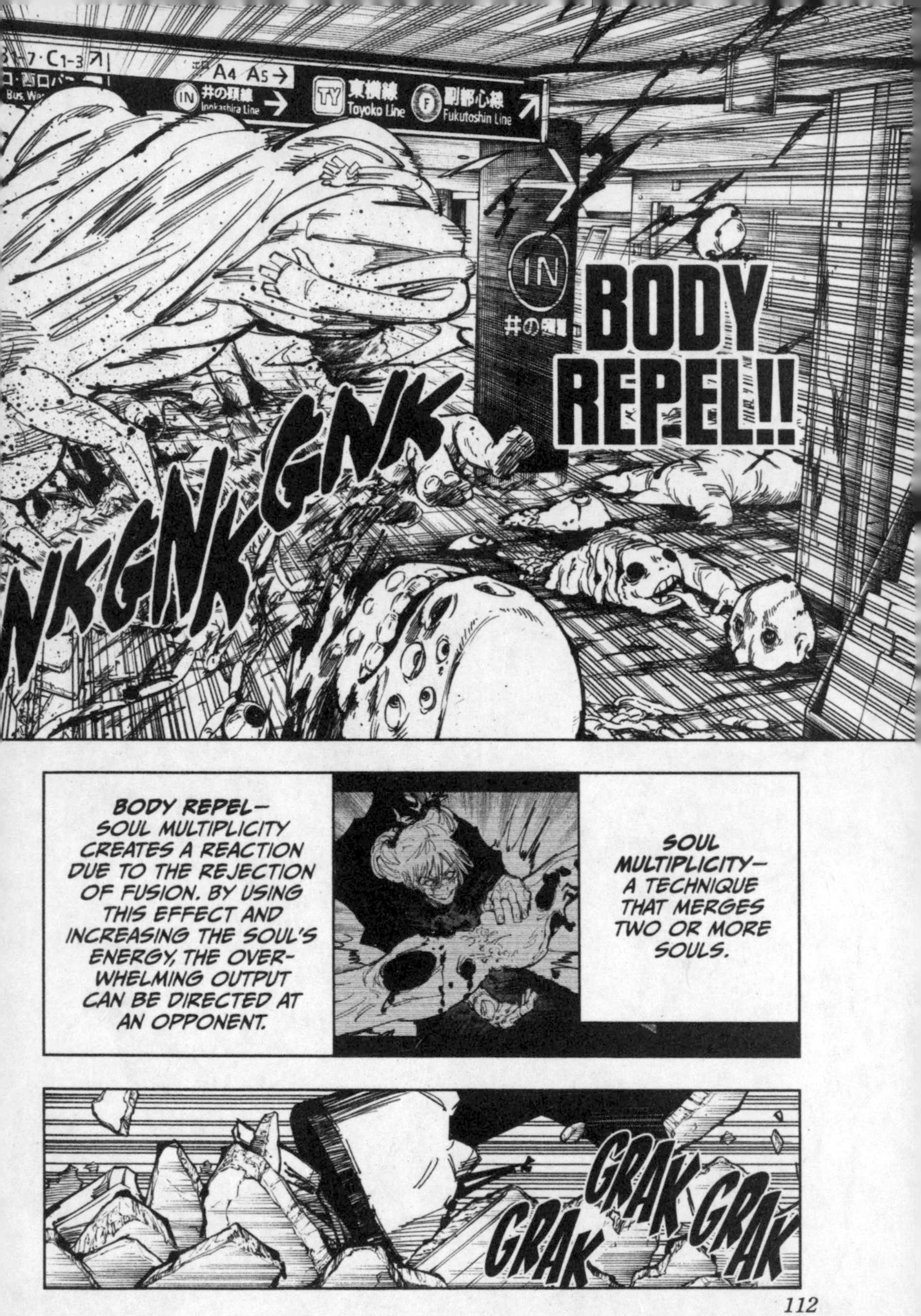
A4 A5
井の頭線
Inokashira Line
東横線
Toyoko Line
副都心線
Fukutoshin Line
IN
BODY REPEL!!
NKGNKGNKGNK
SOUL MULTIPLICITY— A TECHNIQUE THAT MERGES TWO OR MORE SOULS.
BODY REPEL— SOUL MULTIPLICITY CREATES A REACTION DUE TO THE REJECTION OF FUSION. BY USING THIS EFFECT AND INCREASING THE SOUL'S ENERGY, THE OVERWHELMING OUTPUT CAN BE DIRECTED AT AN OPPONENT.
GRAK GRAK GRAK GRAK

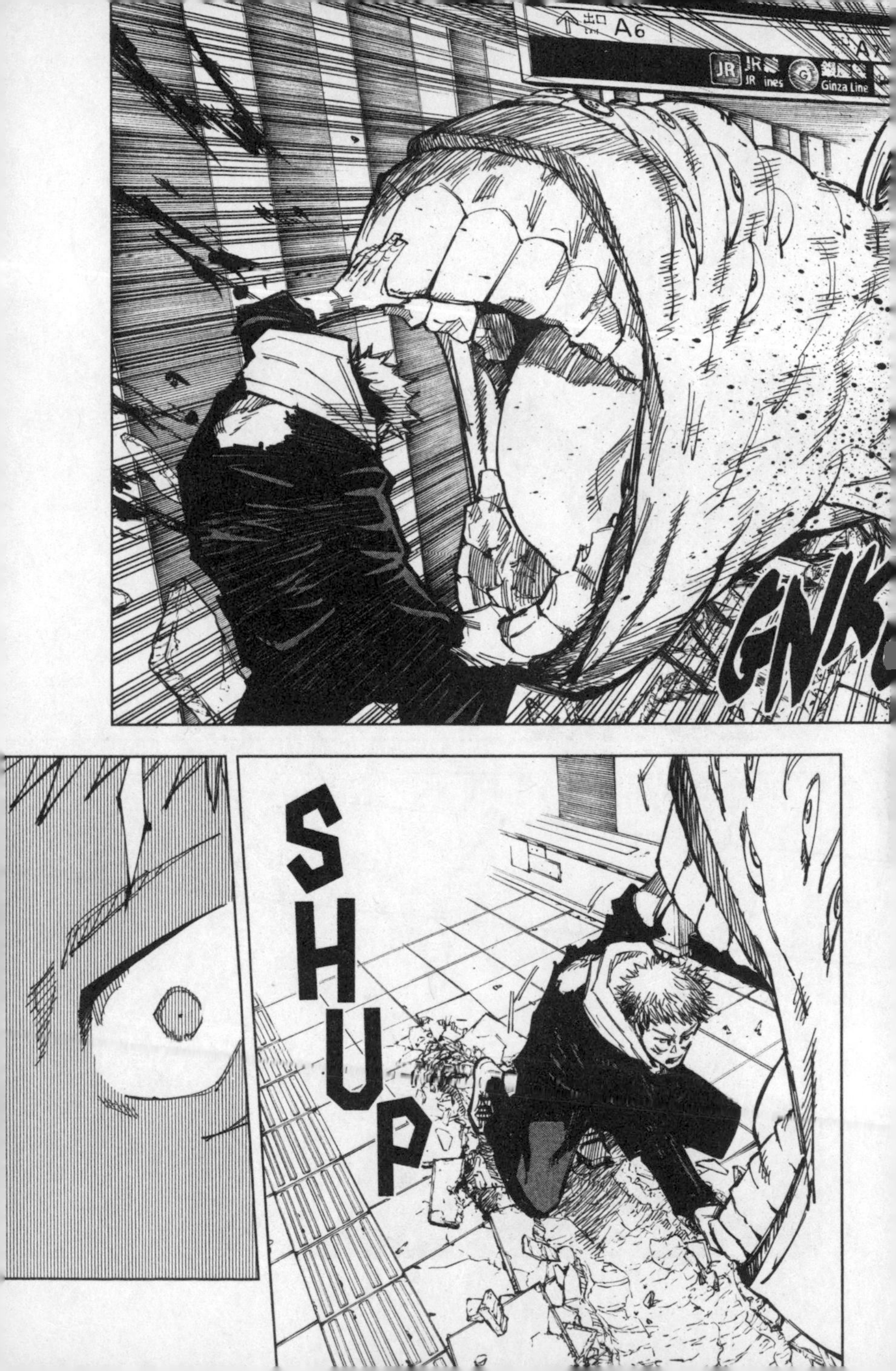
出口 A6
Ginza Line
GNK
SHUP

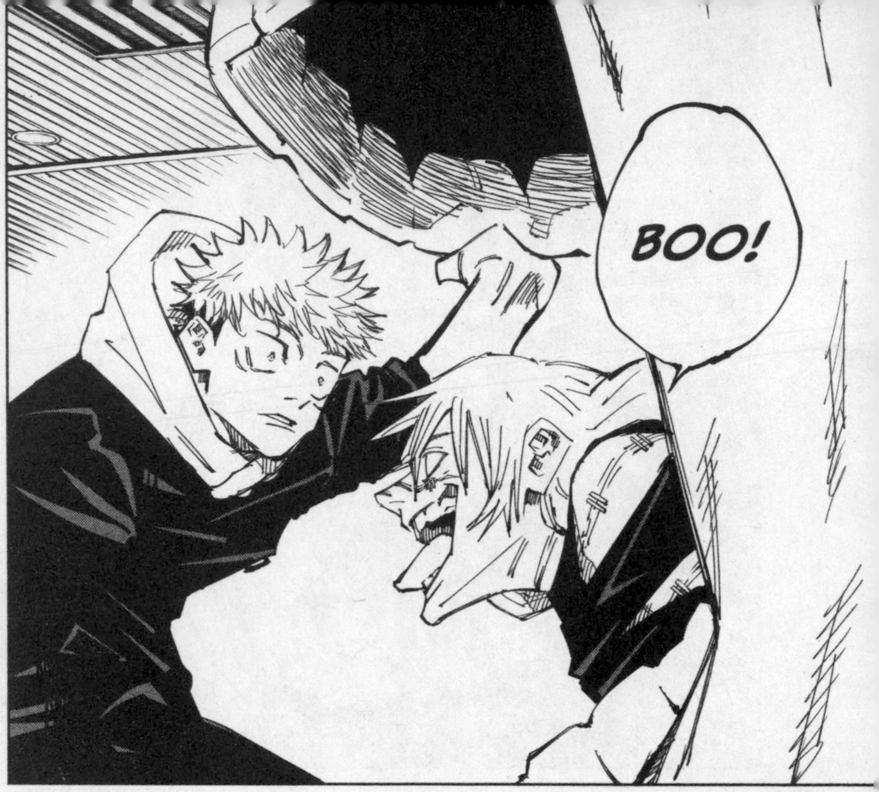
BOO!

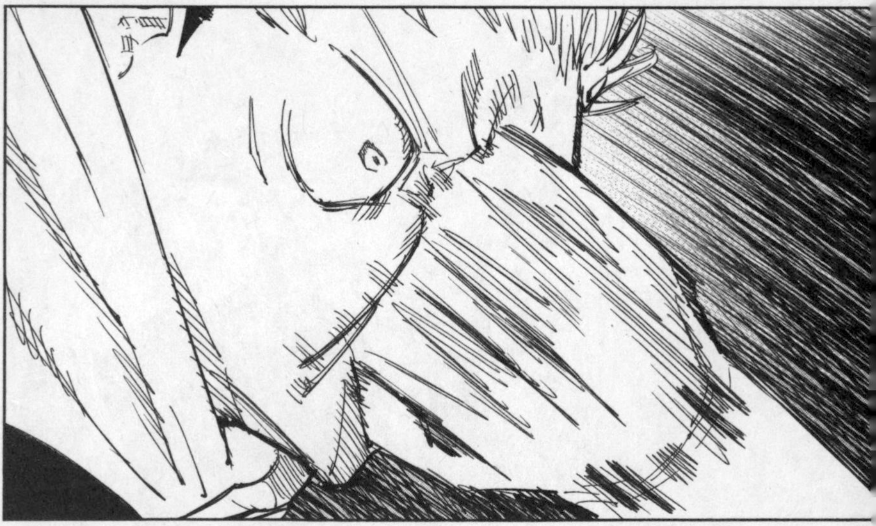

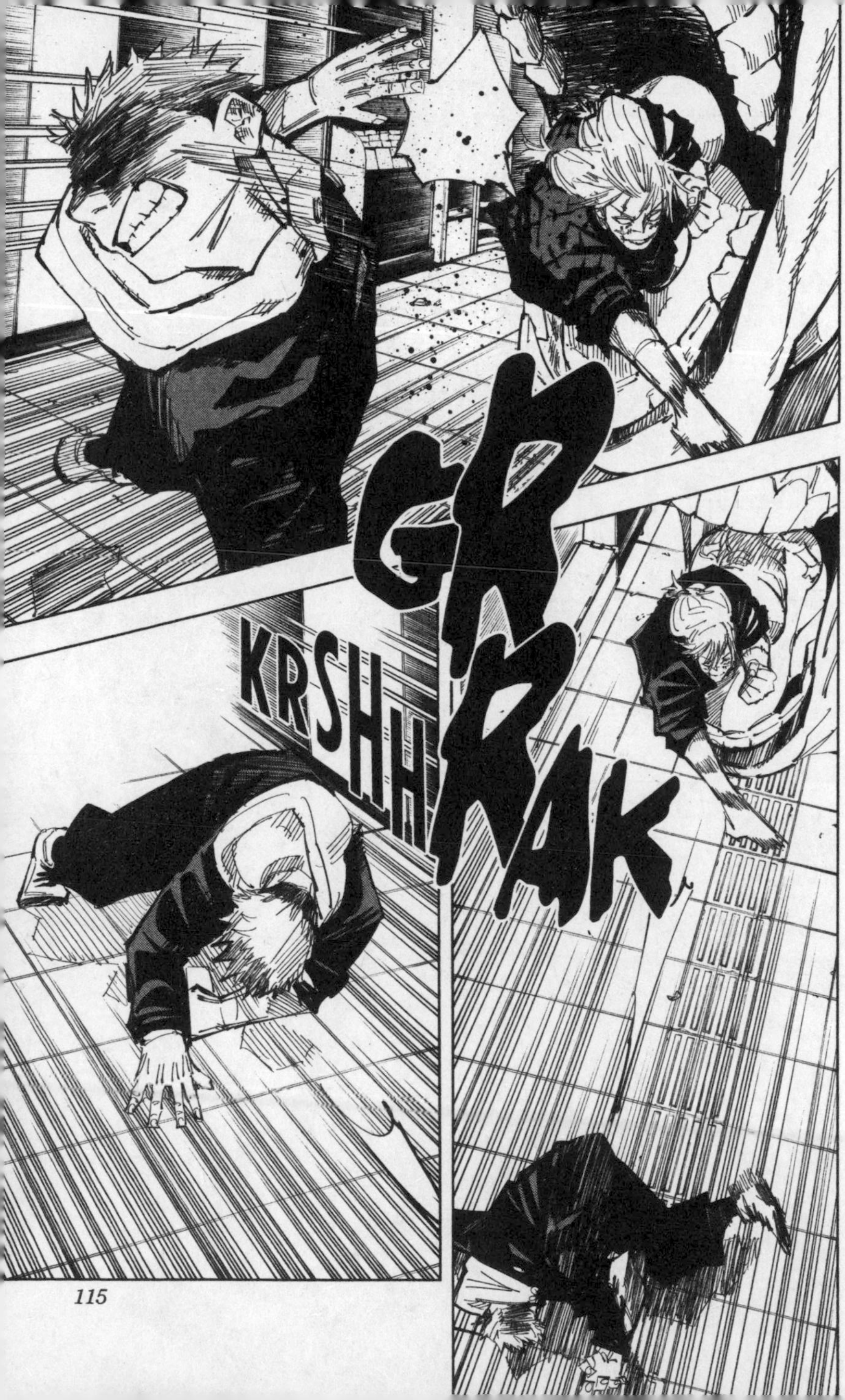
GRRAK
KRSHH

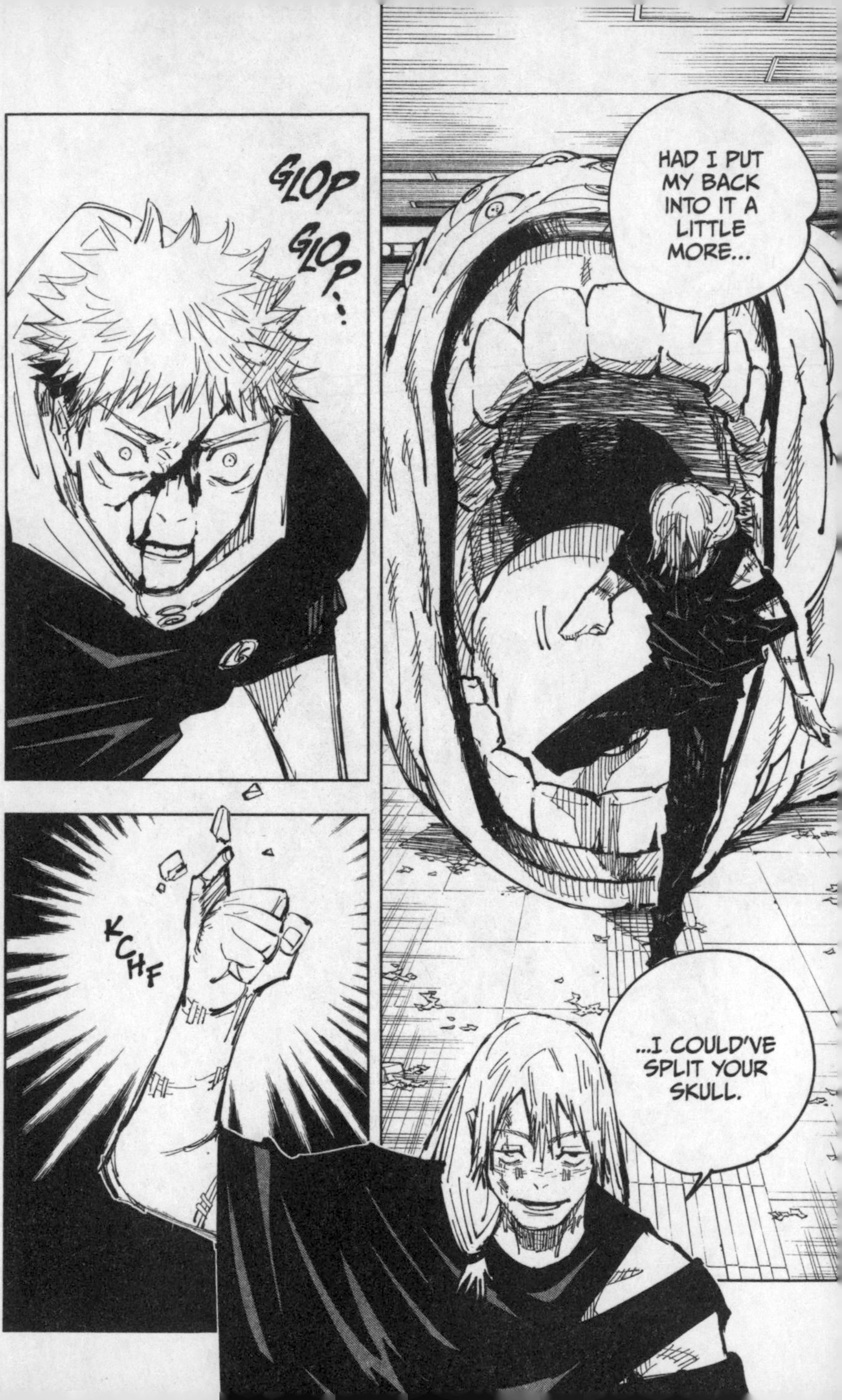
HAD I PUT MY BACK INTO IT A LITTLE MORE...
...I COULD'VE SPLIT YOUR SKULL.
GLOP
GLOP...
KCHF

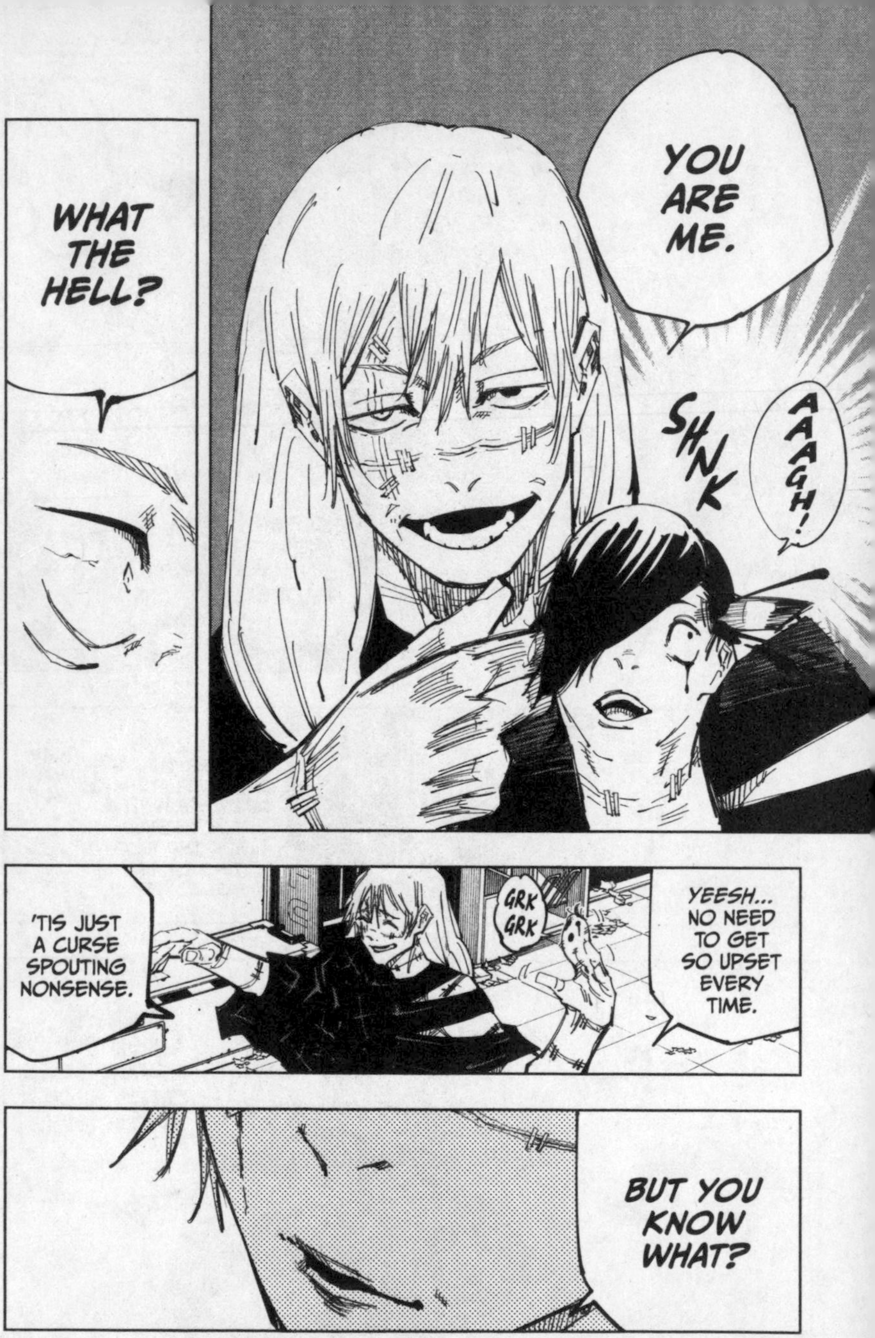
YOU ARE ME.
SHNK
AAAGH!
WHAT THE HELL?
YEESH... NO NEED TO GET SO UPSET EVERY TIME.
GRK GRK
'TIS JUST A CURSE SPOUTING NONSENSE.
BUT YOU KNOW WHAT?

ALL THAT BLAB-BERING...

UNTIL YOU ACCEPT THAT FACT...

YOU REALLY DON'T STOP TALKING.

I'LL MAKE SURE THOSE ARE YOUR DYING WORDS!

...THERE'S NO WAY YOU'LL EVER BEAT ME.

"YOU'VE GOT IT FROM HERE."

...A JUJUTSU SORCERER!

NANAMIN WOULDN'T LOSE HIS COOL.

NANA-MIN...

PROVE TO HIM THAT...

...I AM...

...YOU ARE...

GWOOOO

I'LL STICK WITH MANIPULATING LIMBS, WHICH SHOULDN'T BE A PROBLEM TO SACRIFICE JUST LIKE A MOMENT AGO.

"I NEED TO FOCUS ON CONCENTRATING MY BODY'S FORM TO MAINTAIN TOUGHNESS"...

IDLE TRANSFIGURATION DOESN'T WORK ON ITADORI.

INCREASING MY SIZE BY MANIPULATING MY SOUL WOULD JUST MAKE ME A BIGGER TARGET. THAT MIGHT AS WELL BE SUICIDE.

KRA KK

122

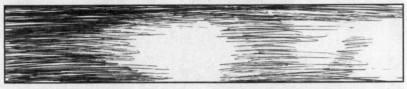

WHILE MAHITO'S FIST PIERCES THROUGH AIR...

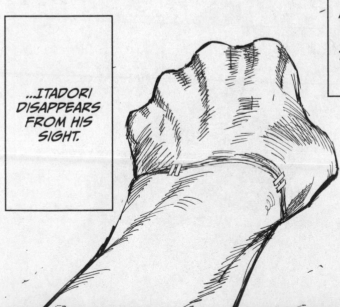

...ITADORI DISAPPEARS FROM HIS SIGHT.

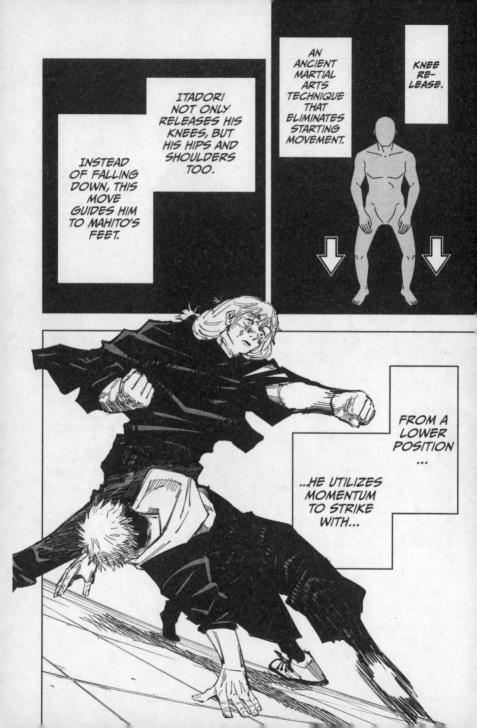

AN ANCIENT MARTIAL ARTS TECHNIQUE THAT ELIMINATES STARTING MOVEMENT.

KNEE RE-LEASE.

ITADORI NOT ONLY RELEASES HIS KNEES, BUT HIS HIPS AND SHOULDERS TOO.

INSTEAD OF FALLING DOWN, THIS MOVE GUIDES HIM TO MAHITO'S FEET.

FROM A LOWER POSITION...

...HE UTILIZES MOMENTUM TO STRIKE WITH...

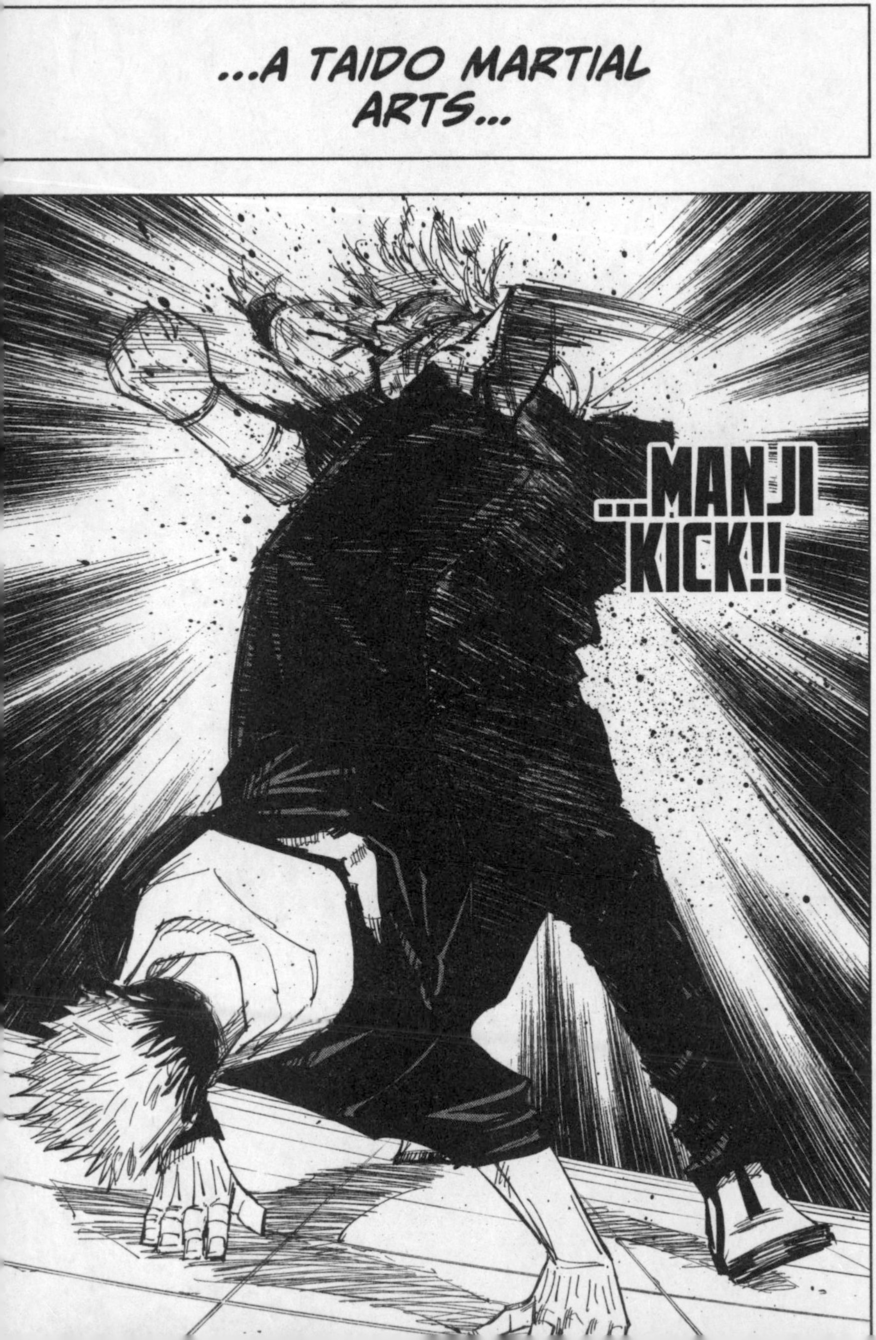
...A TAIDO MARTIAL ARTS...
...MANJI KICK!!

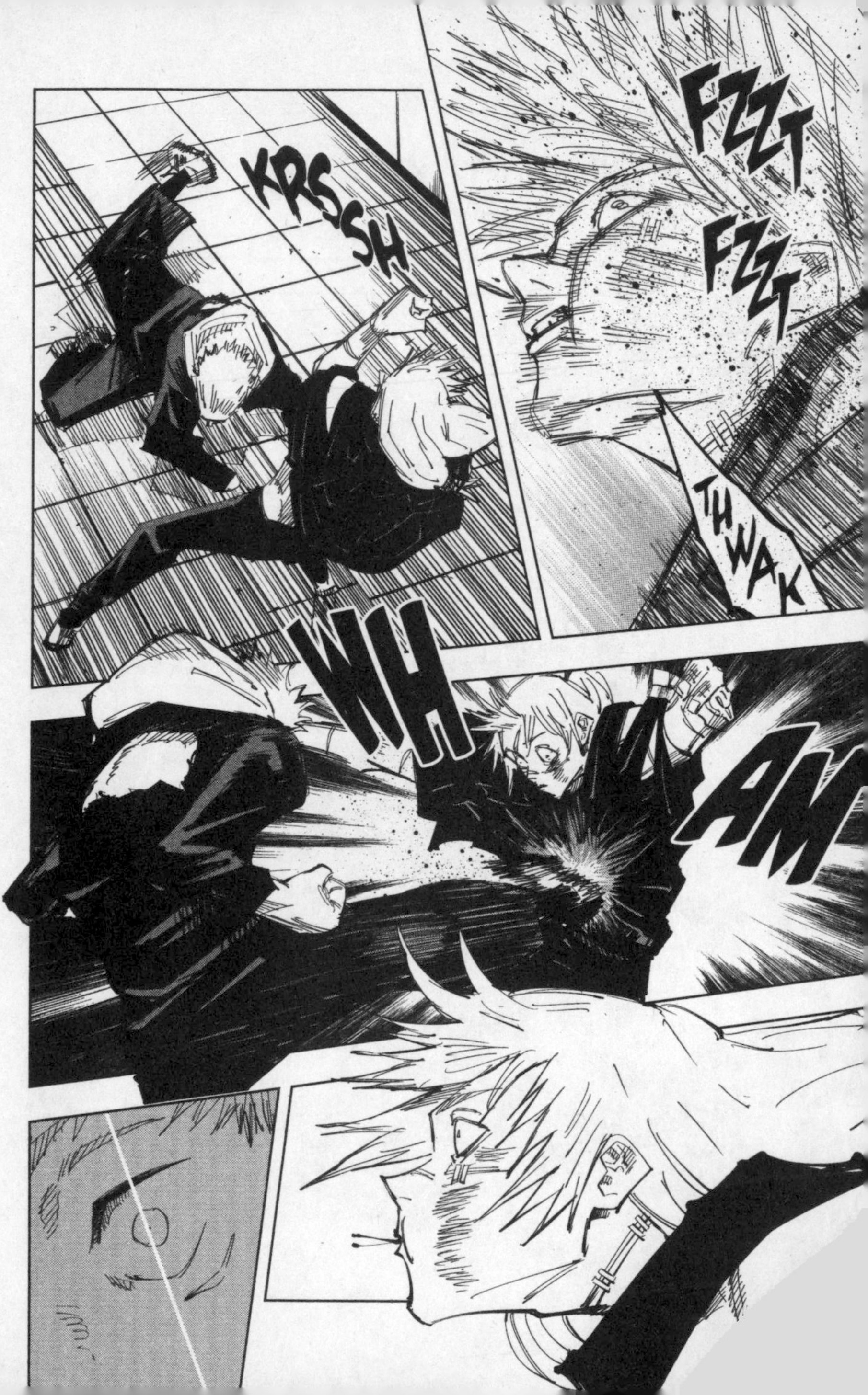
FZZT
FZZT
THWAK
KRSSSH
WH
AM

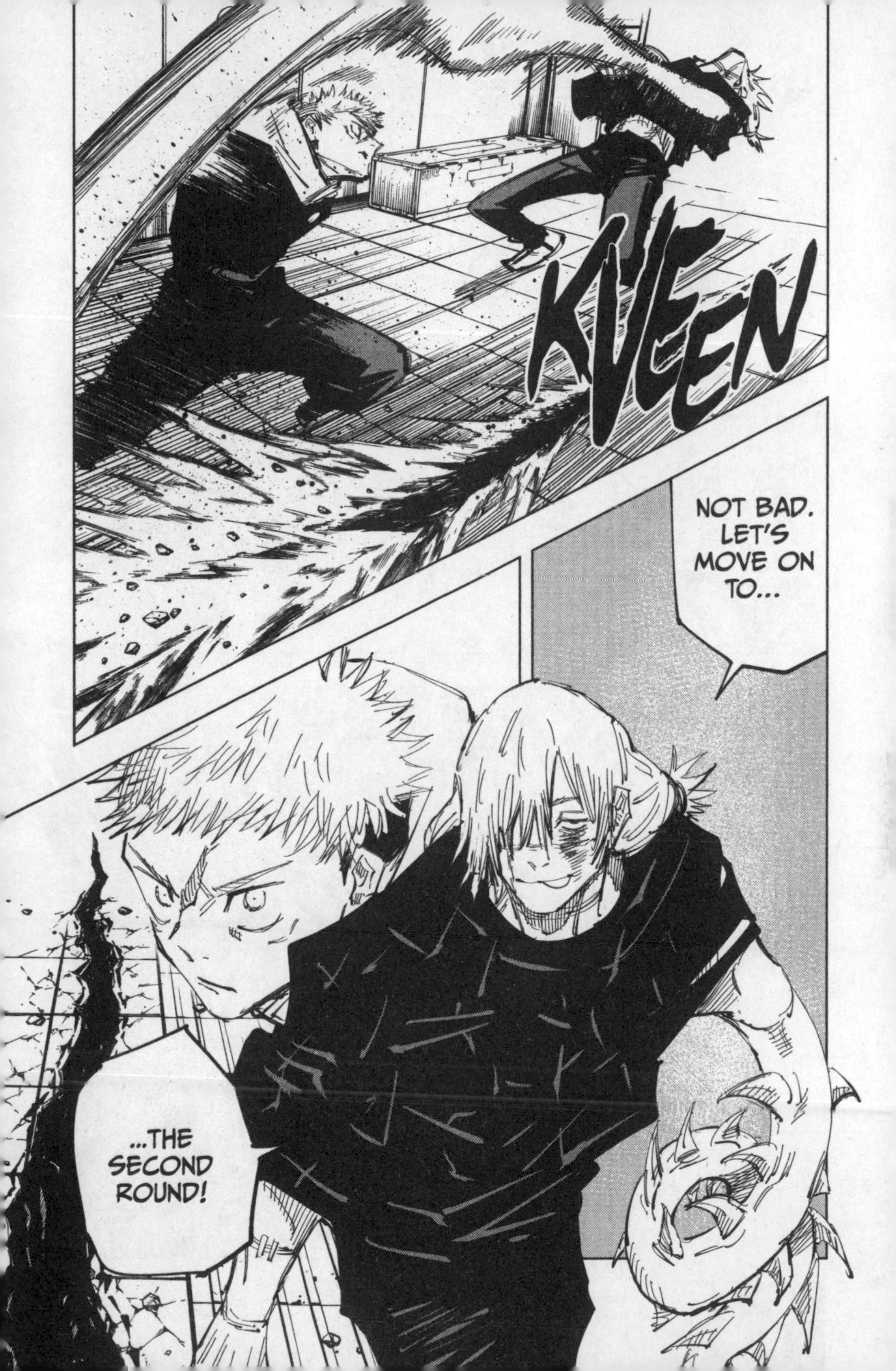
KVEEN
NOT BAD. LET'S MOVE ON TO...
...THE SECOND ROUND!

GETTING IT RIGHT!!
LIMITLESS CURSED TECHNIQUE ~INTRODUCTION~

T-SAN →

EDITOR

AKUTAMI

T-SAN CAME TO MY WORK-PLACE.

HM... I SEE...

...EXPLAINED IT LIKE THIS (IN THE GN BONUS CONTENT).

I READ THIS BOOK AND THEN...

TO BE CONTINUED IN VOLUME 15...

JUJUTSU

IT'S ALL WRONG!!

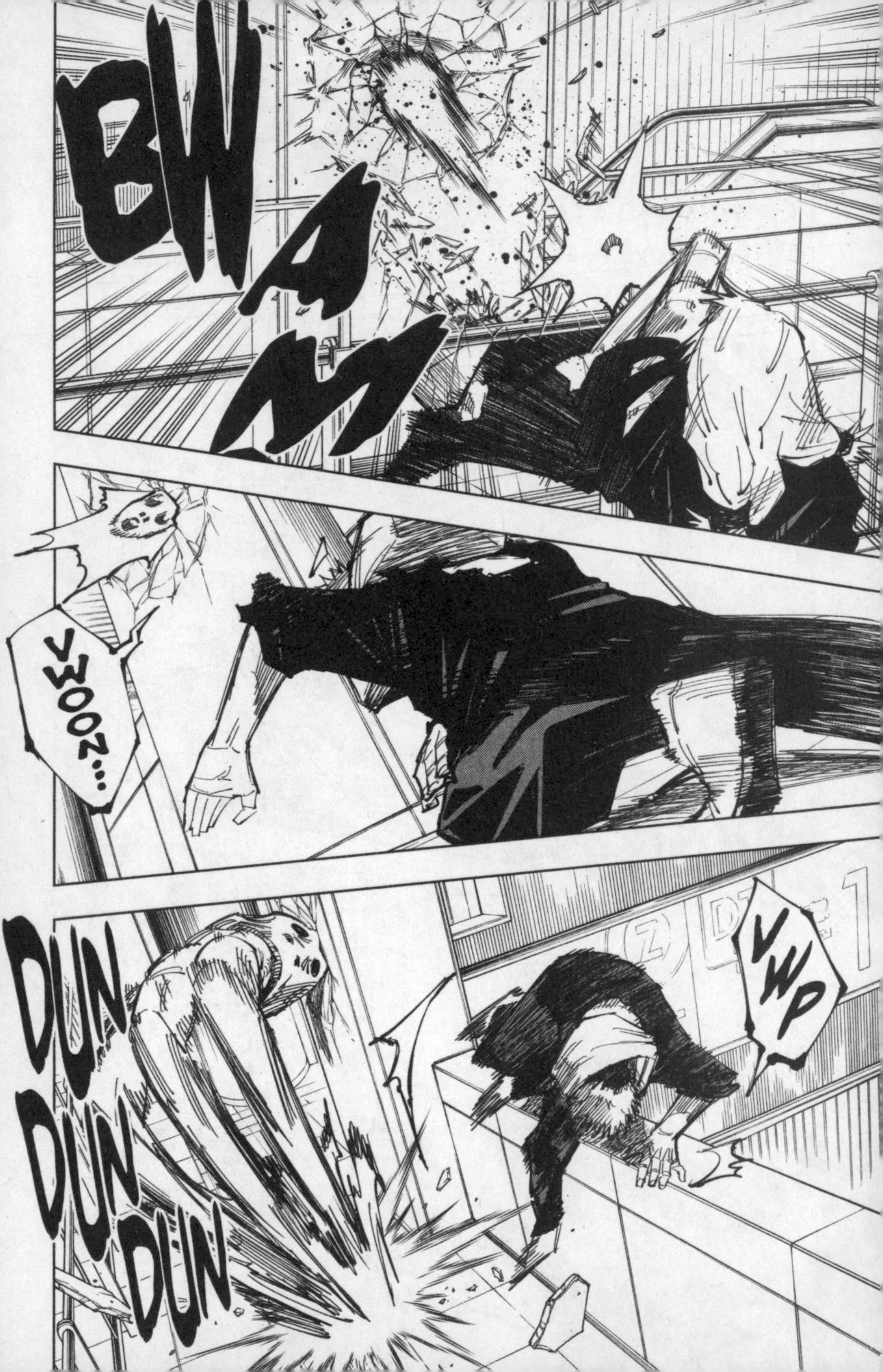
BWAM
VWOON...
VWP
DUN DUN DUN DUN

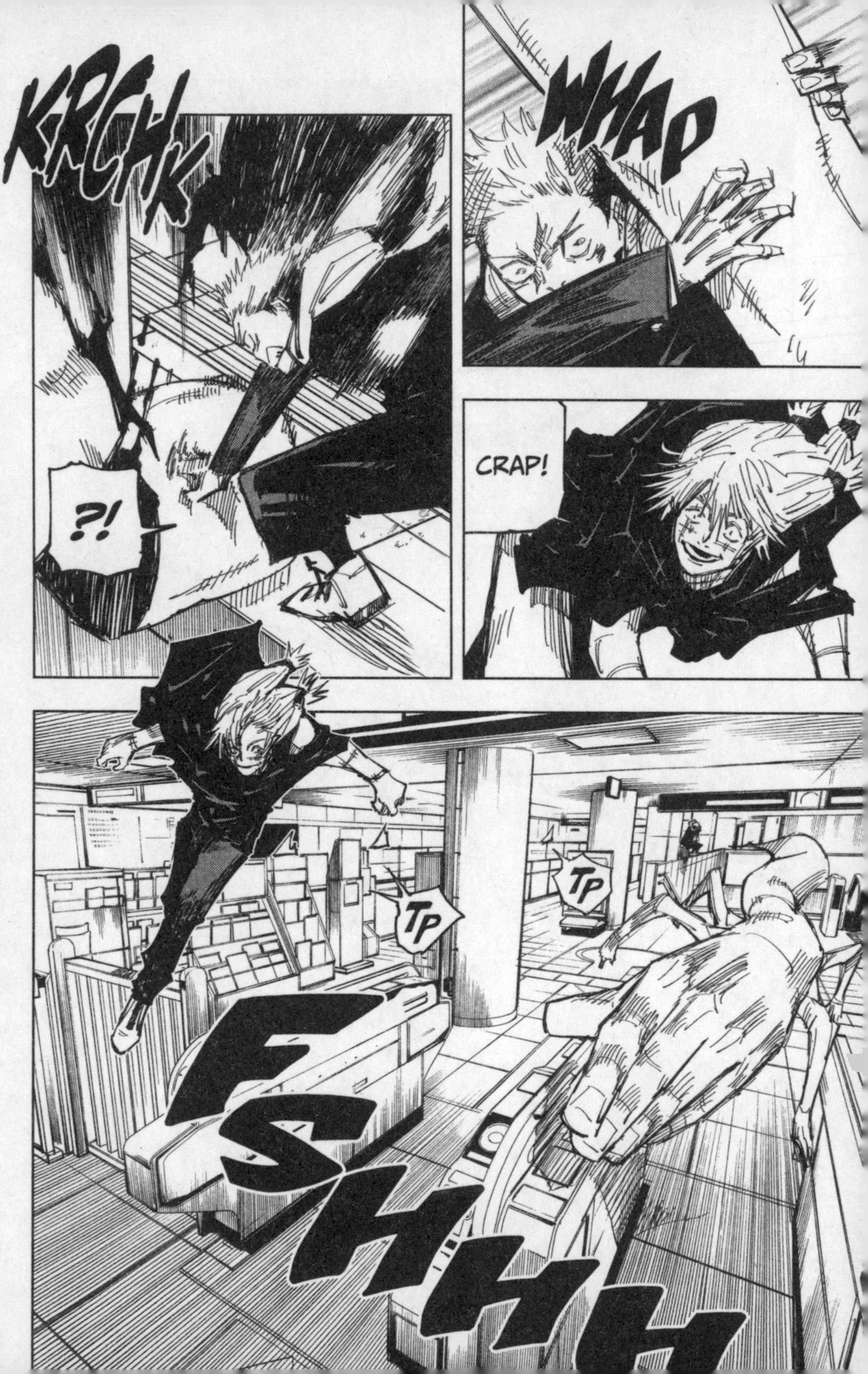
WHAP
CRAP!
KRCHK
?!
TP
TP
FSHHH

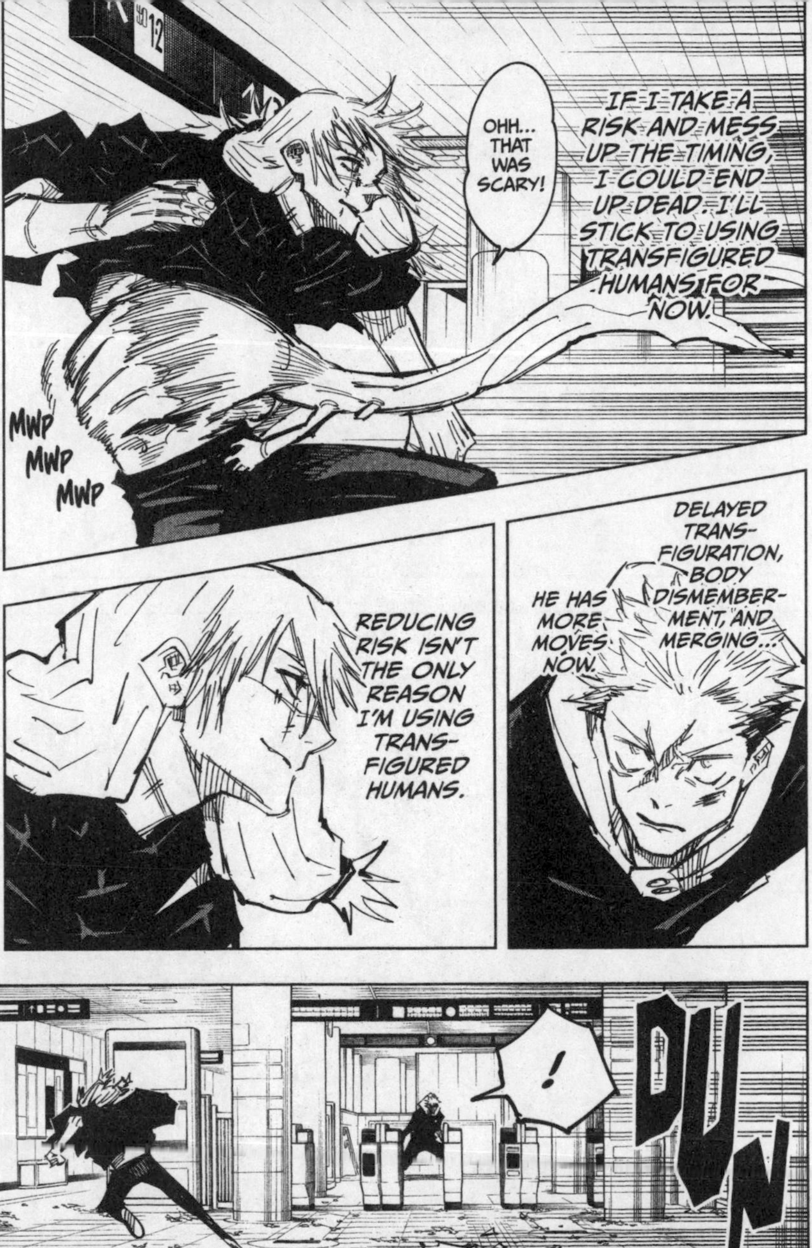
IF I TAKE A RISK AND MESS UP THE TIMING, I COULD END UP DEAD. I'LL STICK TO USING TRANSFIGURED HUMANS FOR NOW.
OHH... THAT WAS SCARY!
MWP MWP MWP
DELAYED TRANS-FIGURATION, BODY DISMEMBER-MENT, AND MERGING...
HE HAS MORE MOVES NOW.
REDUCING RISK ISN'T THE ONLY REASON I'M USING TRANS-FIGURED HUMANS.
DUN
!

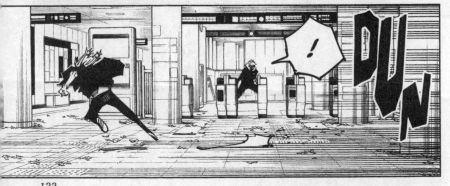

IT'S DANGEROUS OVER THERE WITH ALL THOSE MONSTERS!

HEY, COME THIS WAY!

A STUDENT ?!

SORRY, BUT NOWHERE'S SAFE IN SHIBUYA.

TRY TO STAY SOMEW—

WHERE'S MAHITO...?

UPSTAIRS!

134

DOWN THE HATCH!

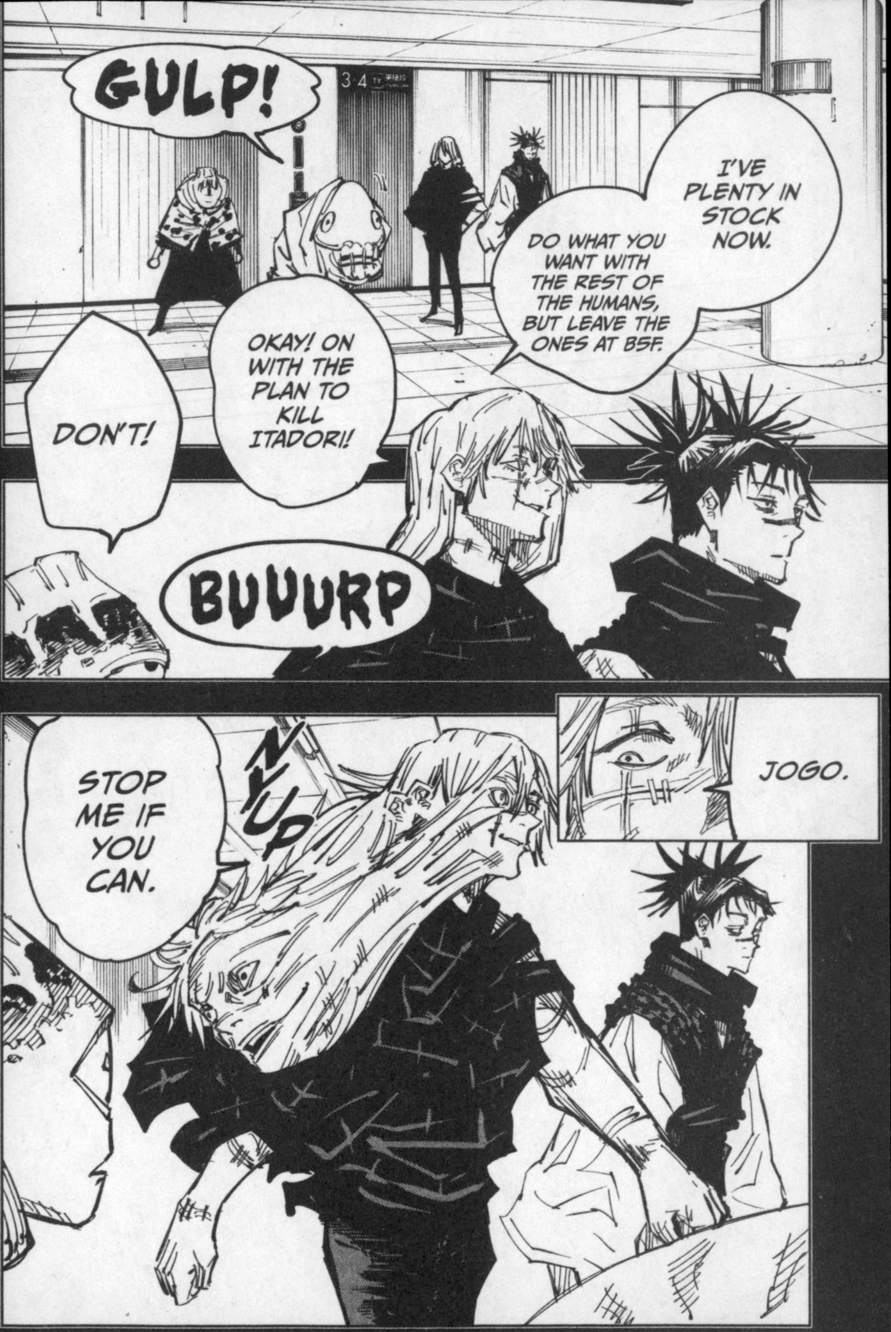
GULP!
I'VE PLENTY IN STOCK NOW.
DO WHAT YOU WANT WITH THE REST OF THE HUMANS, BUT LEAVE THE ONES AT B5F.
OKAY! ON WITH THE PLAN TO KILL ITADORI!
DON'T!
BUUURP
JOGO.
STOP ME IF YOU CAN.
NYUP

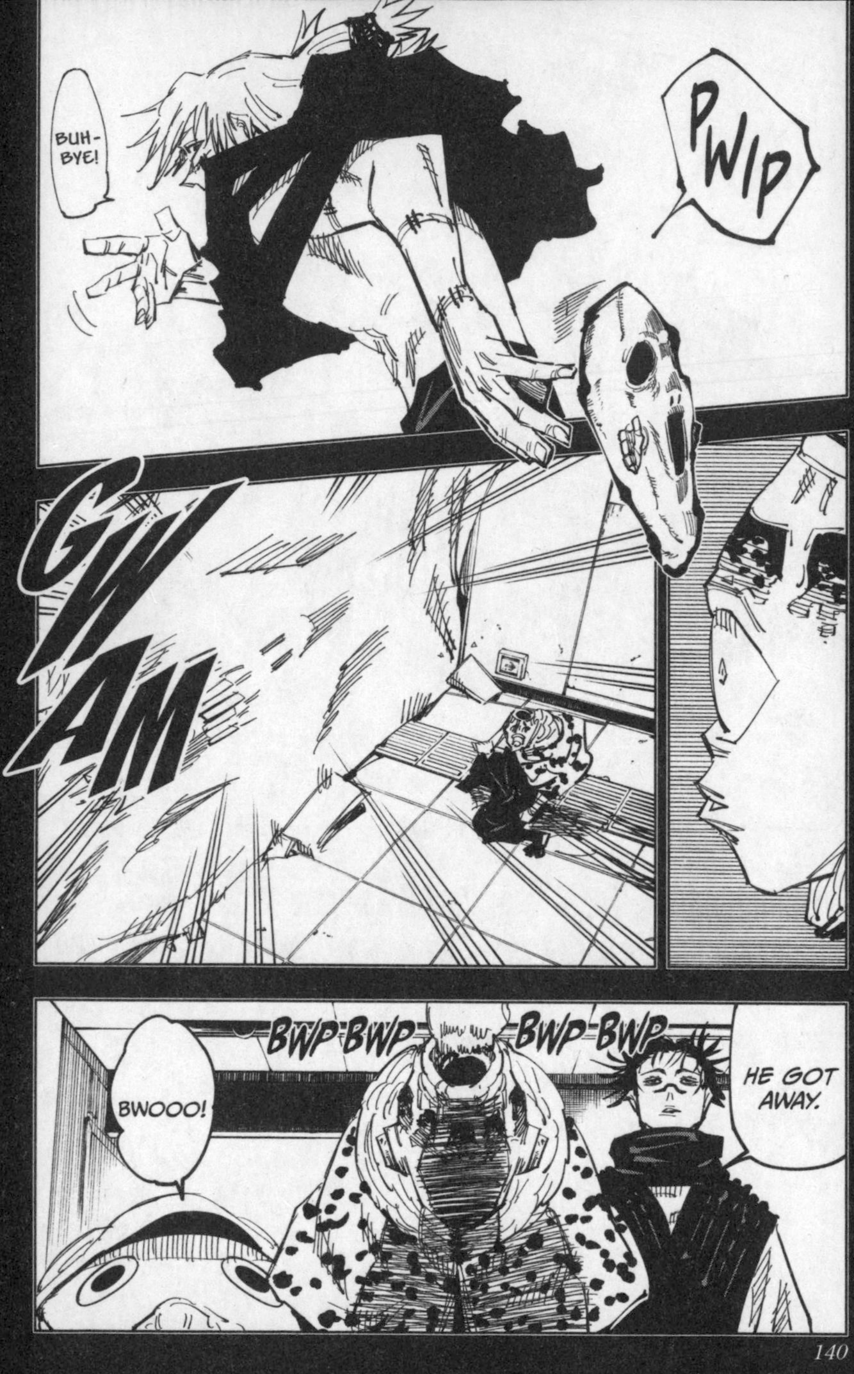
PWIP
BUH-BYE!
GWAM
HE GOT AWAY.
BWP BWP BWP BWP
BWOOO!

BWOOSH

MAHITOOO!

11:16 P.M.
DOGENZAKA KOJI

DID YOU SEE THAT?

WASN'T THAT CRAZY?

I WAS JUST THERE.

THE SPECIAL GRADE CURSED SPIRIT WHO'S BEEN CAUSING TROUBLE FOR OUR CLASS CLOWN?!

IT'S YOU, RIGHT?

PATCH-FACE...

!

142

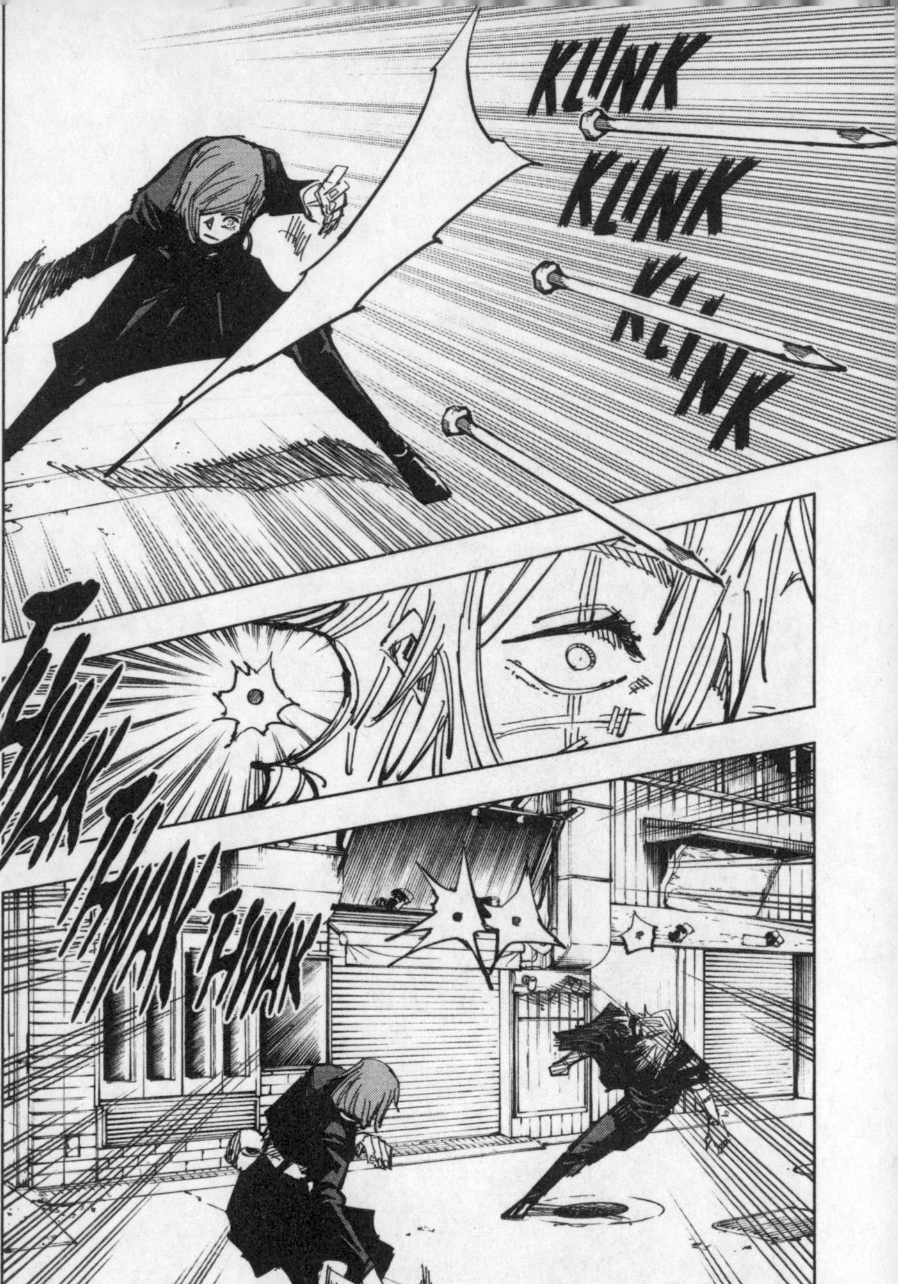
KLINK
KLINK
KLINK
THWAK
THWAK
THWAK

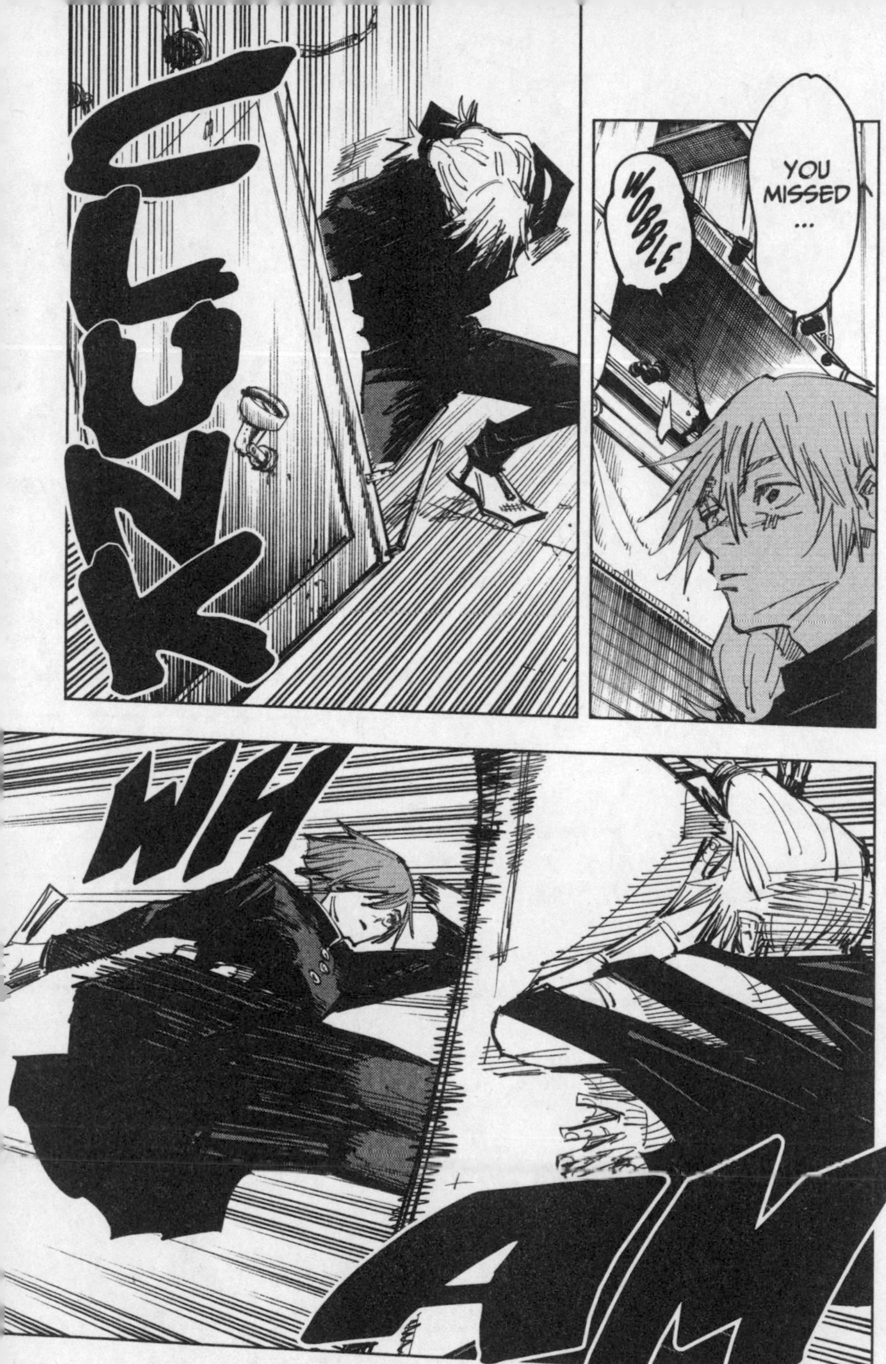
YOU MISSED ...
WOBBLE
STUCK
WHAM

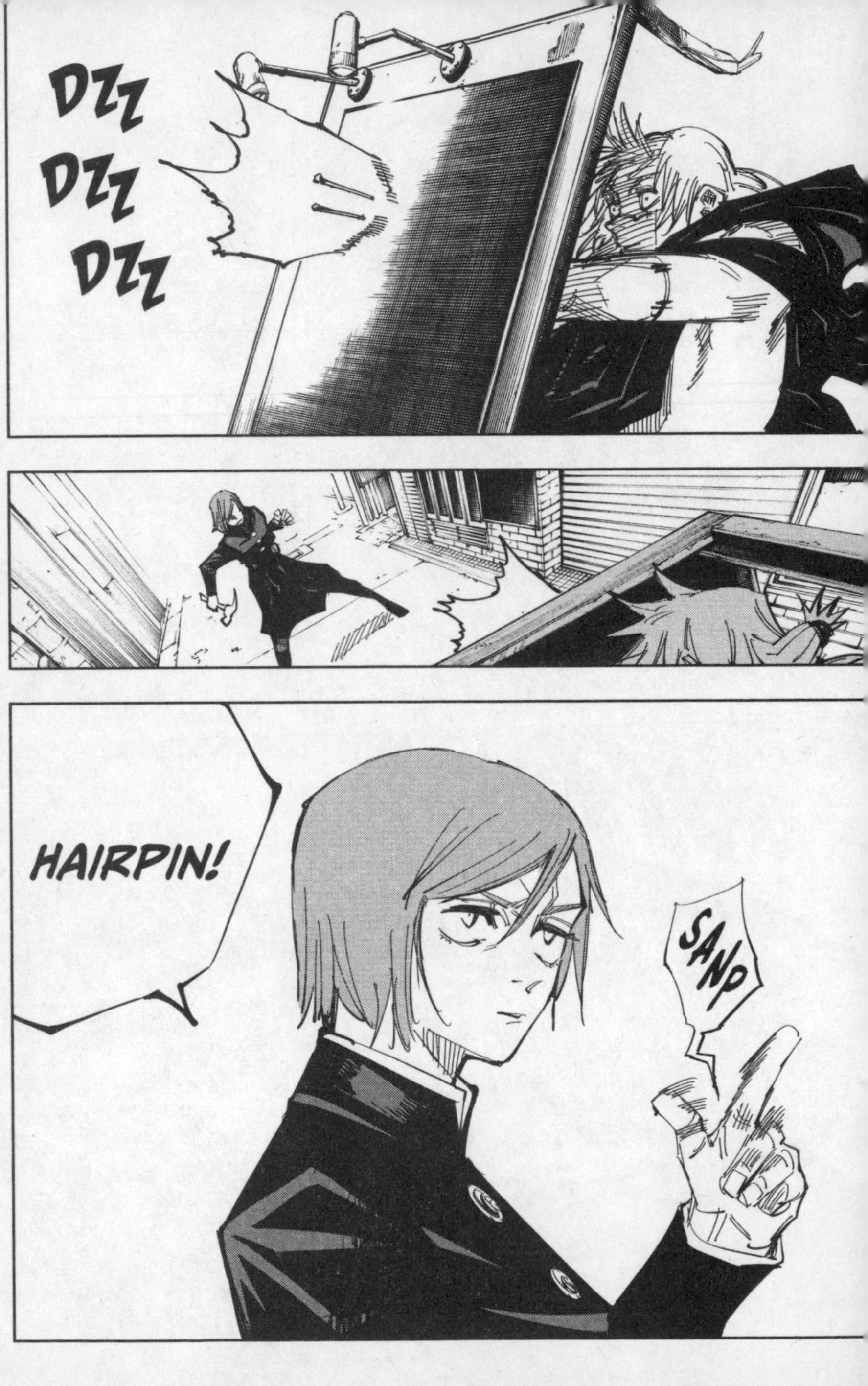
DZZ
DZZ
DZZ
HAIRPIN!
SNAP

WHAK WHAK

NOT BAD. BUT...

HA HA HA!

I'LL BRING HER DEAD BODY TO YUJI ITADORI!...

...AND DESTROY HIS SOUL!

...THAT WON'T WORK ON ME.

...I'D SAY SHE'S A FRIEND OF HIS.

JUDGING BY THE WAY SHE TALKS...

Extra Info

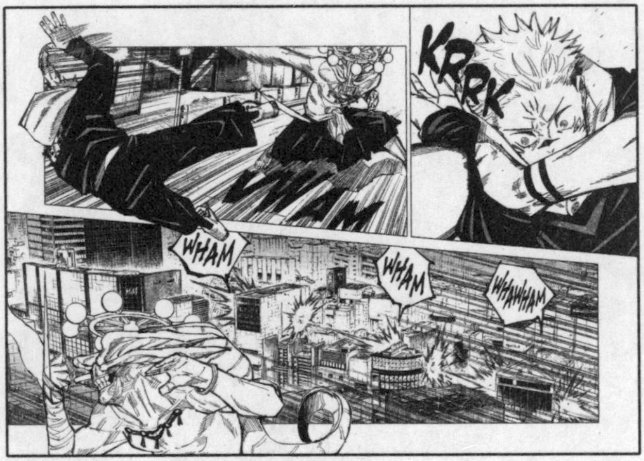

KRRK
VWAM
WHAM
WHAM
WHAWHAM

• Sukuna actually flew all the way outside the curtain in this scene.
• Since there was no particular effect on either Sukuna or Mahoraga and visually it had no particular bearing on the fight, I left it out.

DON'T DO IT, KUGISAKI!

NANAMI SAID SO TOO!

11:14 P.M.
SHOTO BUNKAMURA STREET
(OUTSIDE THE CURTAIN)

AND...WE DIDN'T TELL YOU SHOKO WAS HERE BECAUSE—

THE PARAMEDIC TEAM WAS PROBABLY LATE FOR THE SAME REASON.

BECAUSE YOU DIDN'T WANT ME DOING SOMETHING RECKLESS, RIGHT?

...WHILE THEY'RE STILL FIGHTING.

...I CAN'T JUST LEAVE...

EVEN SO...

149

CHAPTER 123: THE SHIBUYA INCIDENT, PART 41

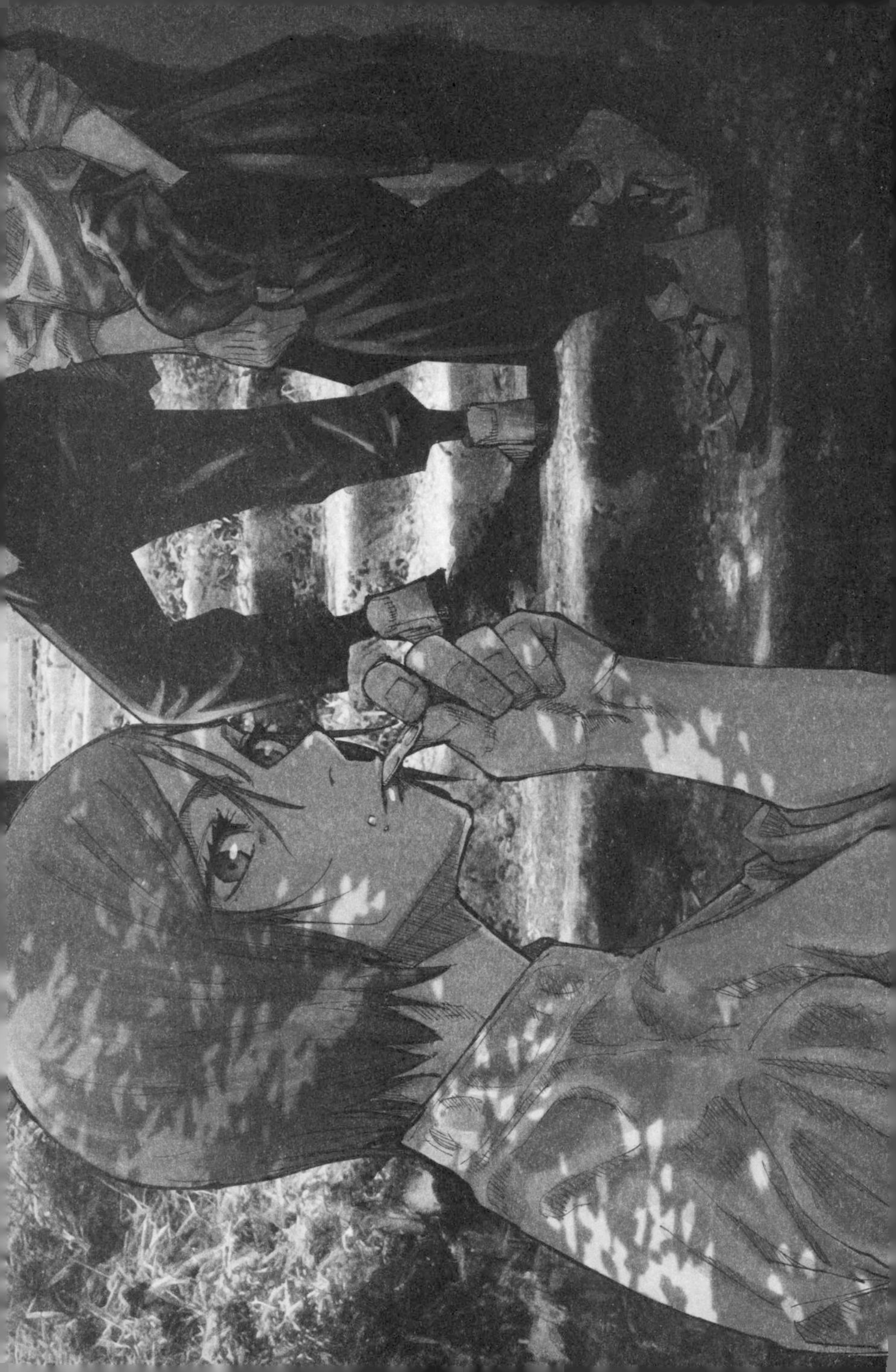

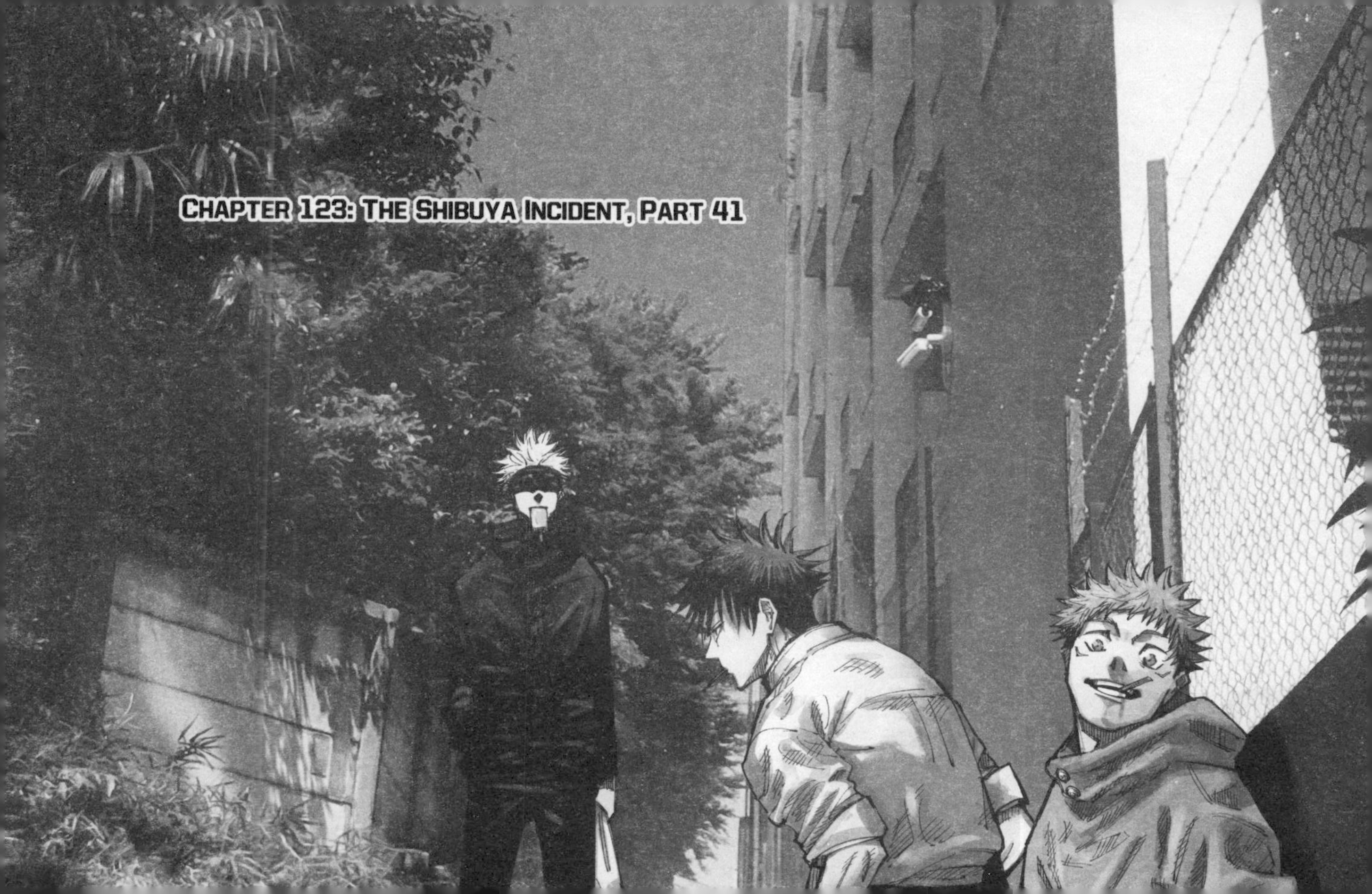
CHAPTER 123: THE SHIBUYA INCIDENT, PART 41

JUJUTSU KAISEN

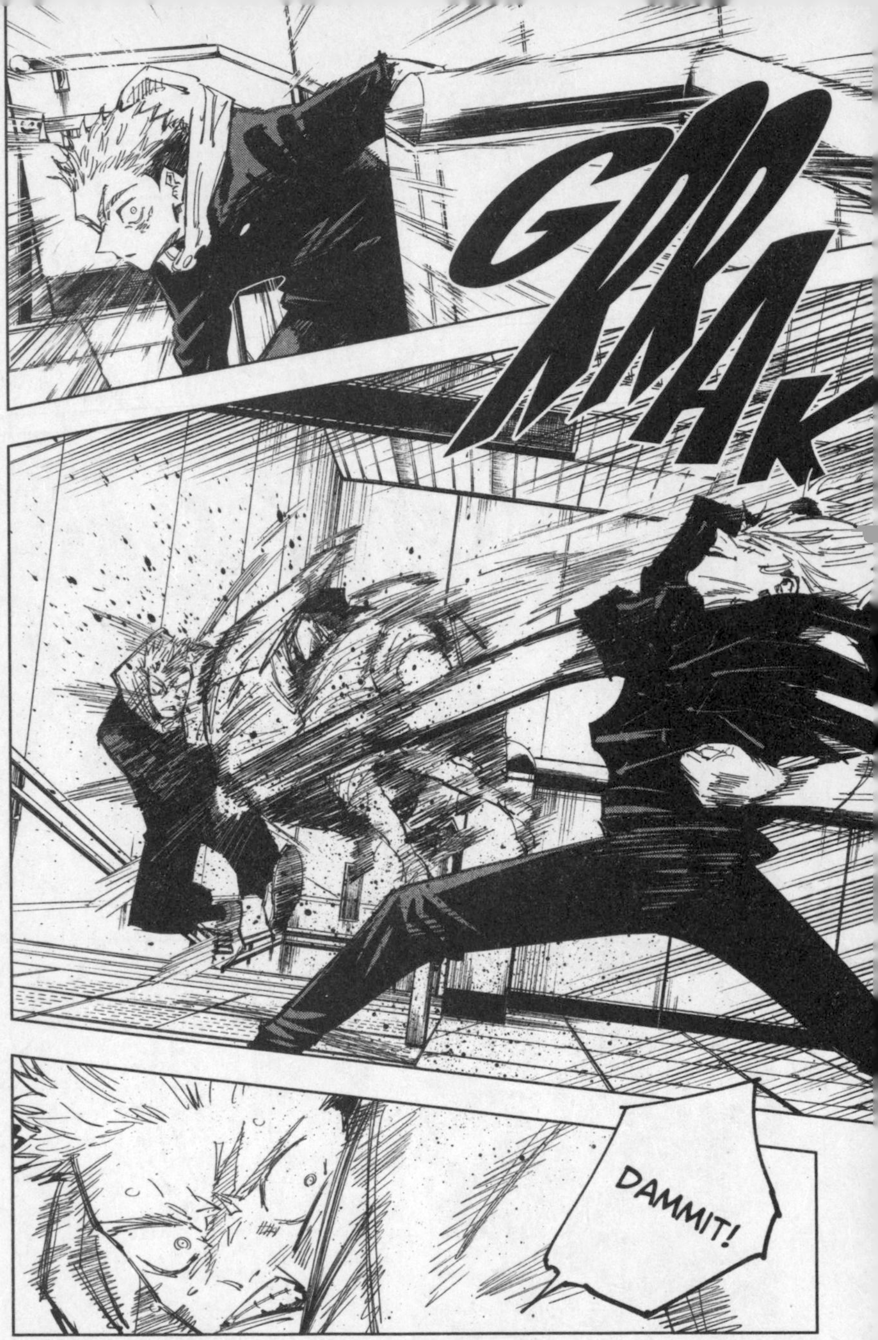
GWAK
DAMMIT!

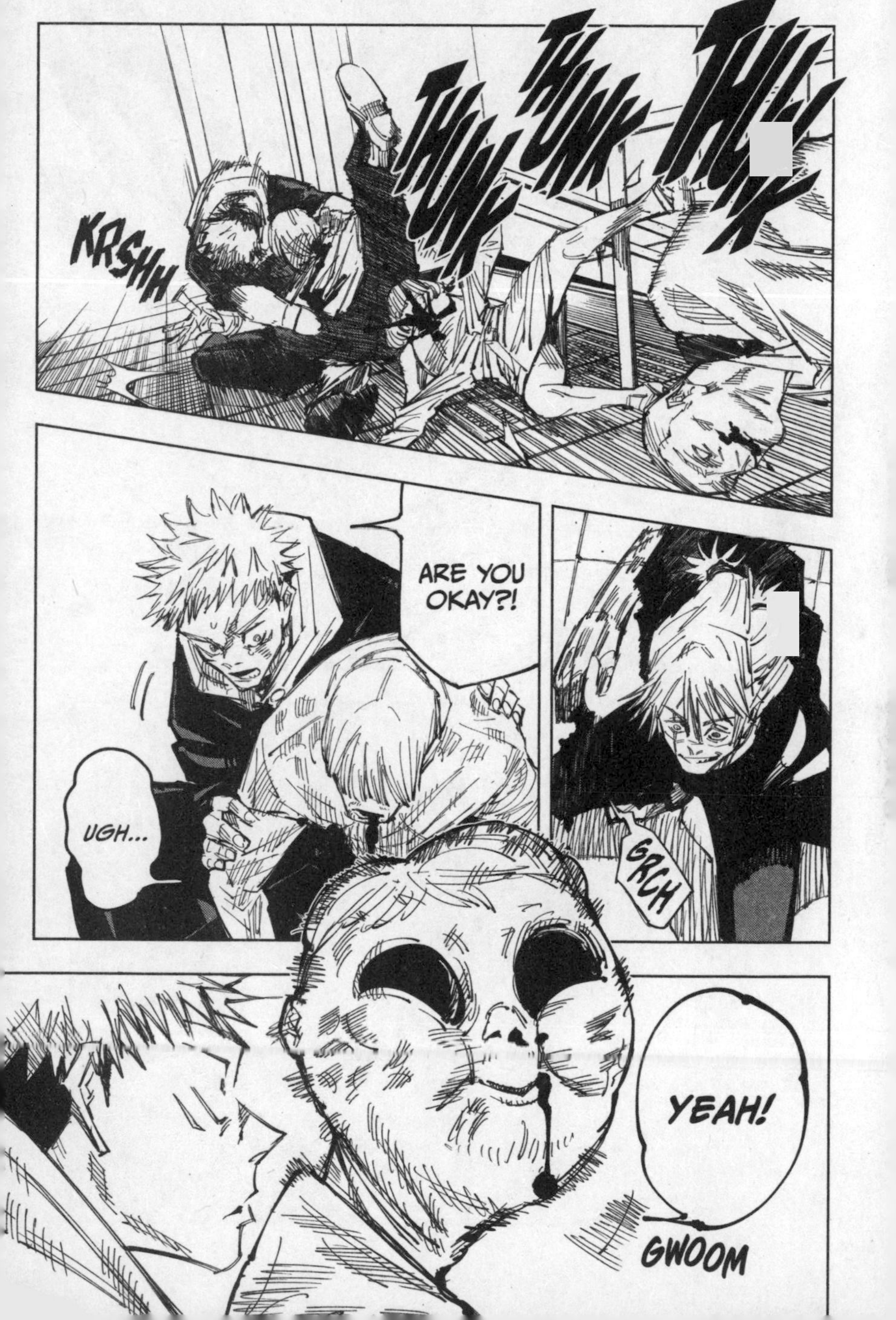
THUNK
THUNK
THUNK
KRSHH
GRCH
ARE YOU OKAY?!
UGH...
YEAH!
GWOOM

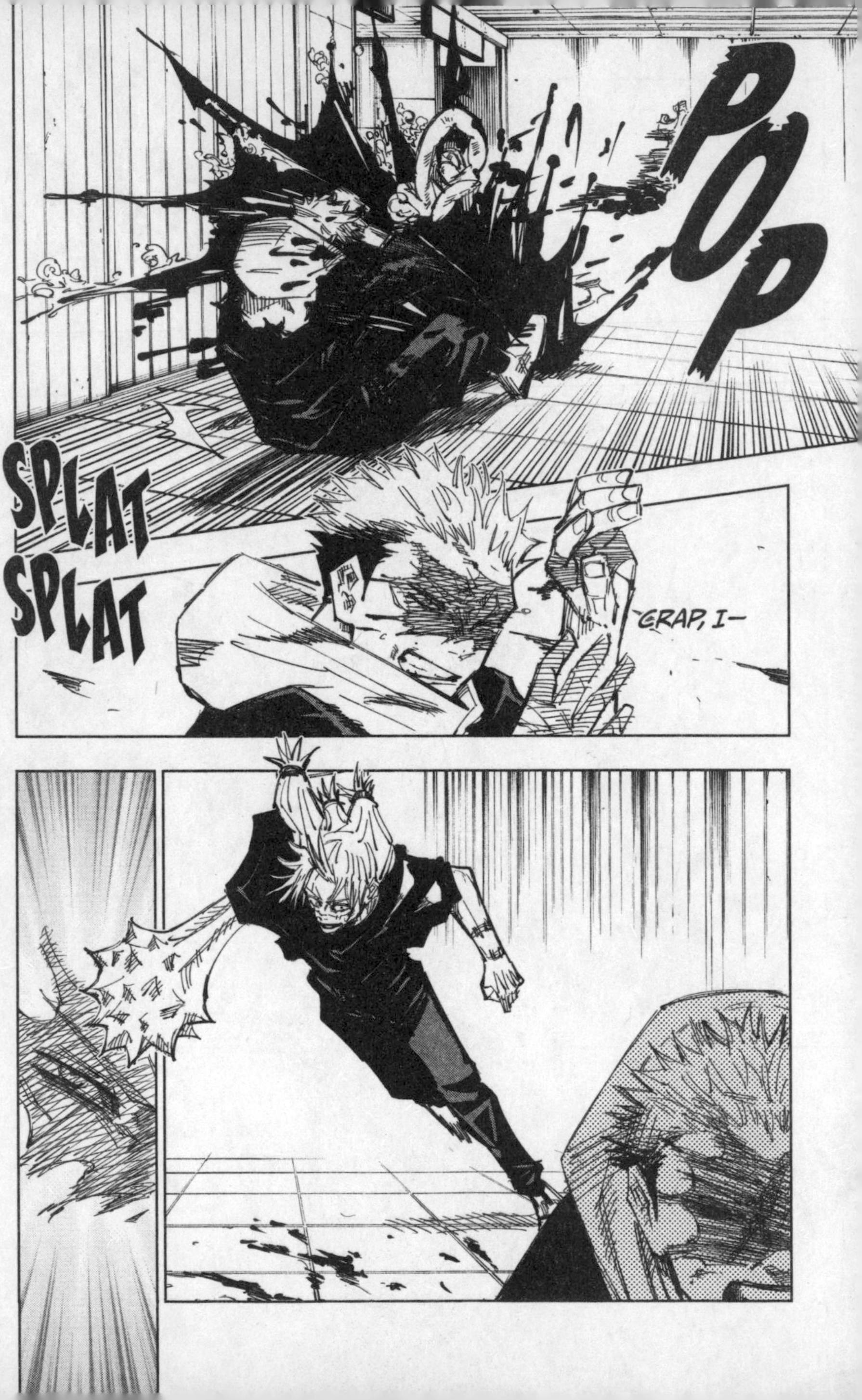
POP
SPLAT SPLAT
CRAP, I—

KLINK
KLINK

KLINK

KLINK

KLINK

VWUM

KRSH

I'M JUST A DOUBLE THOUGH.

SHE'S AVOIDING MY HANDS... THE 7:3 HAIRSTYLE SORCERER MUST HAVE WARNED HER.

HOW BORING.

I CAN CHANGE MY FORM LIKE THE ORIGINAL, BUT...

...I CAN'T MANIPULATE TRANSFIGURED HUMANS OR OTHER SOULS.

∧BUT THANKS FOR WEARING YOUR-SELF DOWN...

...FOR ME!

I'M NOT FIGHTING ITADORI. I CAN MANIPULATE MY FORM AS MUCH AS I WANT WITHOUT INCURRING RISKS.

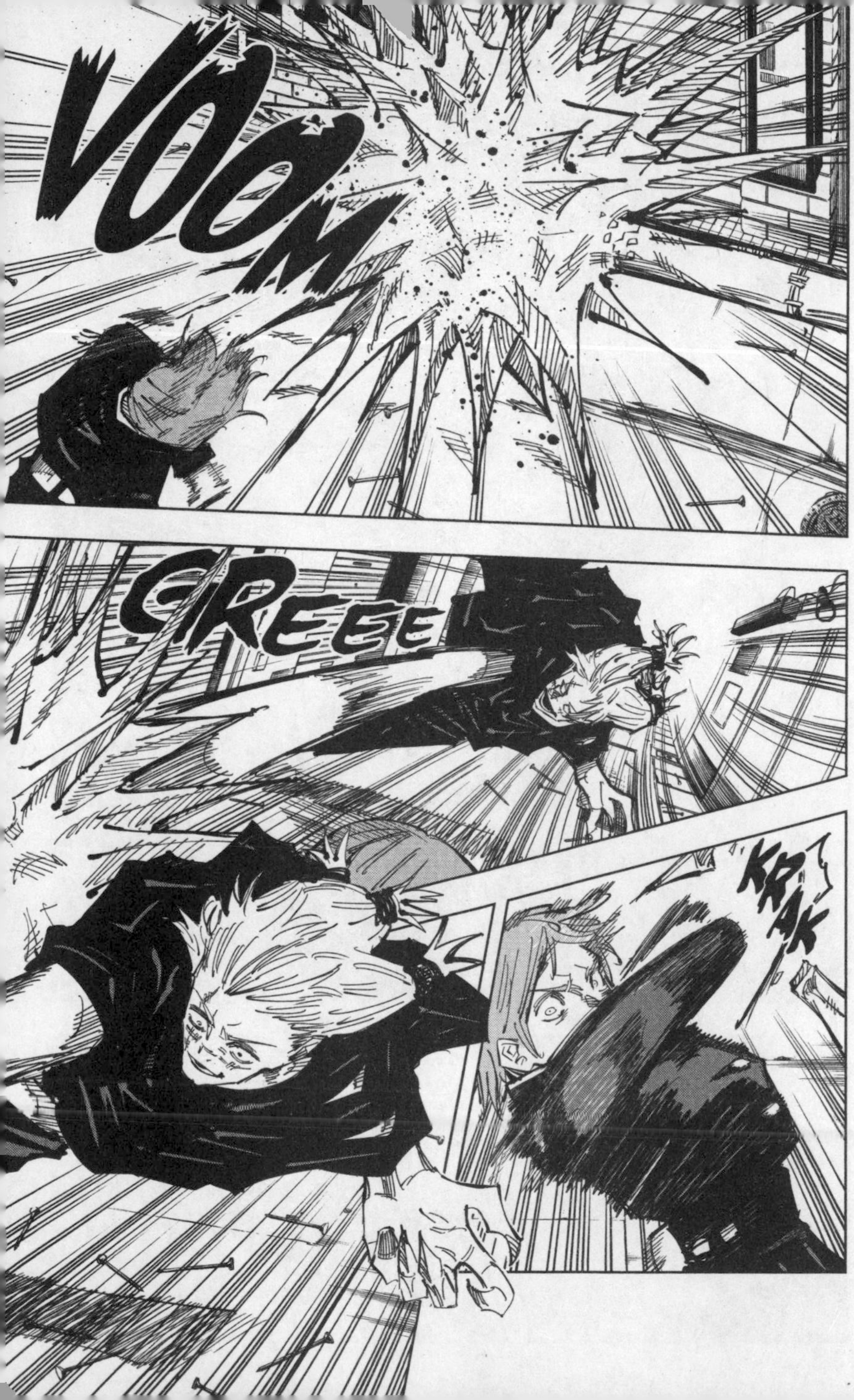
VOOM
CREEEE
KRAK

SOOO LAME!

... SOMETIMES YOU JUST GOTTA TRY!

I KNOW THAT, BUT...

SWP

KLINK

KLINK

2F

!

TP TP

VVP

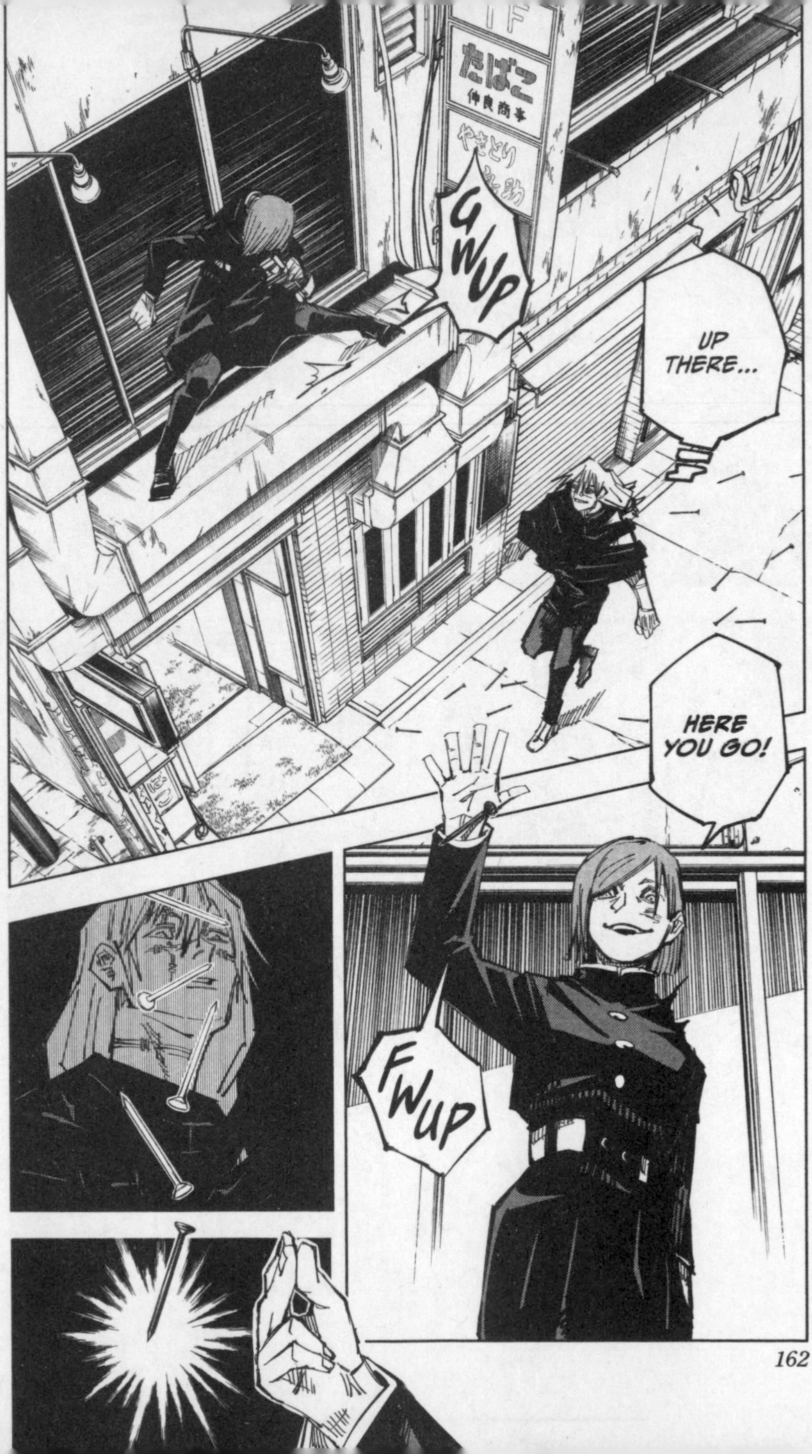
たばこ
仲良商事
やきとり
GWUP
UP THERE...
HERE YOU GO!
FWUP

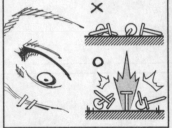

THE FIRST ONE RATTLED THE NAILS TO MAKE THEM POINT UPRIGHT!

THOK THOK THOK THOK THOK

!!

HAIR-PIN!!

THUNK

...

I'VE BEEN THINKING ABOUT IT.

BUT WHAT DOES THAT MATTER?

...THIS...

EVER SINCE I WAS TOLD ABOUT YOUR CURSED TECHNIQUE, I'VE THOUGHT...

!!

...WOULD BE EFFECTIVE AGAINST YOU.

SHE WAS BLUFFING TO MAKE IT SEEM LIKE SHE DIDN'T HAVE A PLAN!

BEFORE...

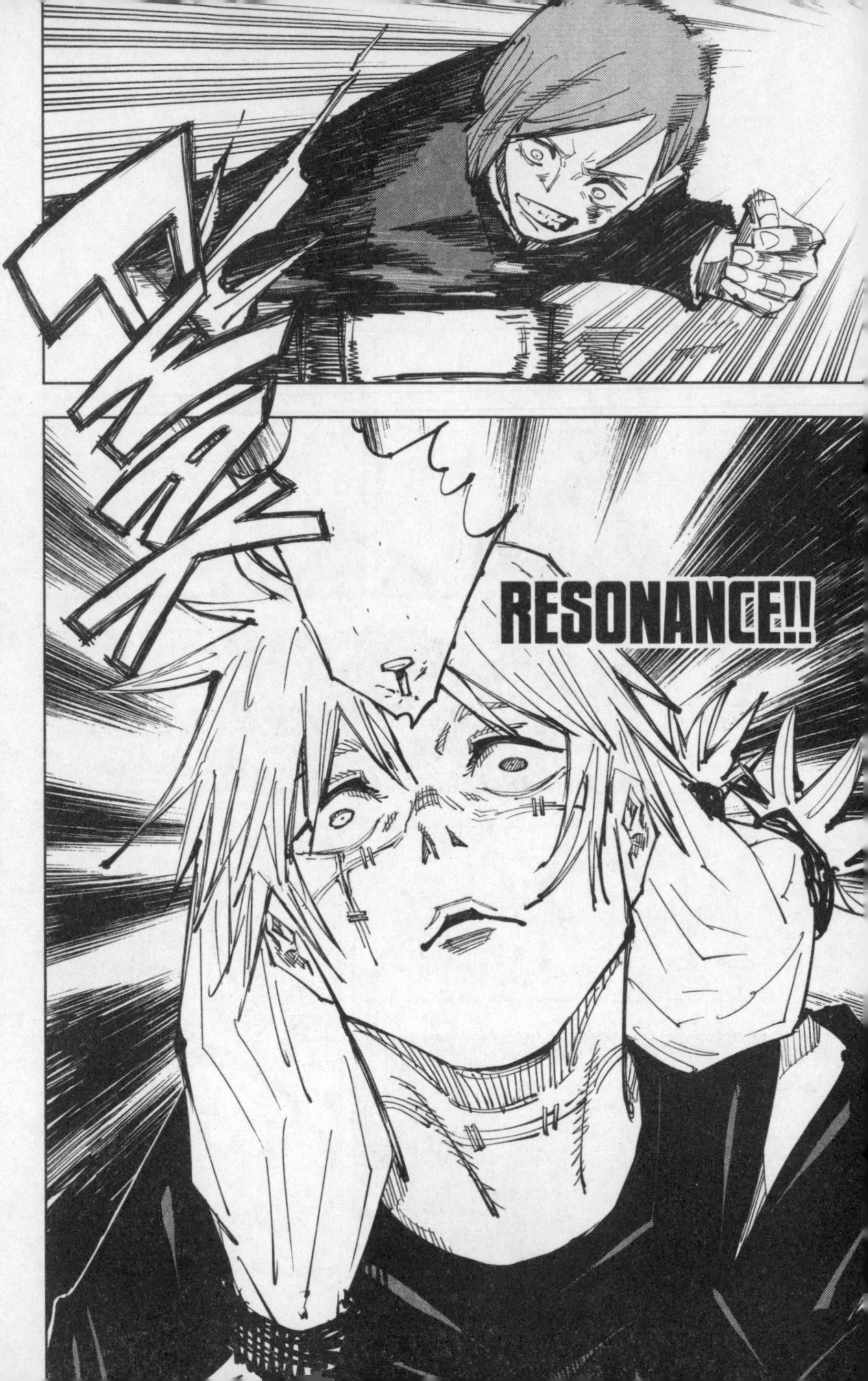
RESONANCE!!

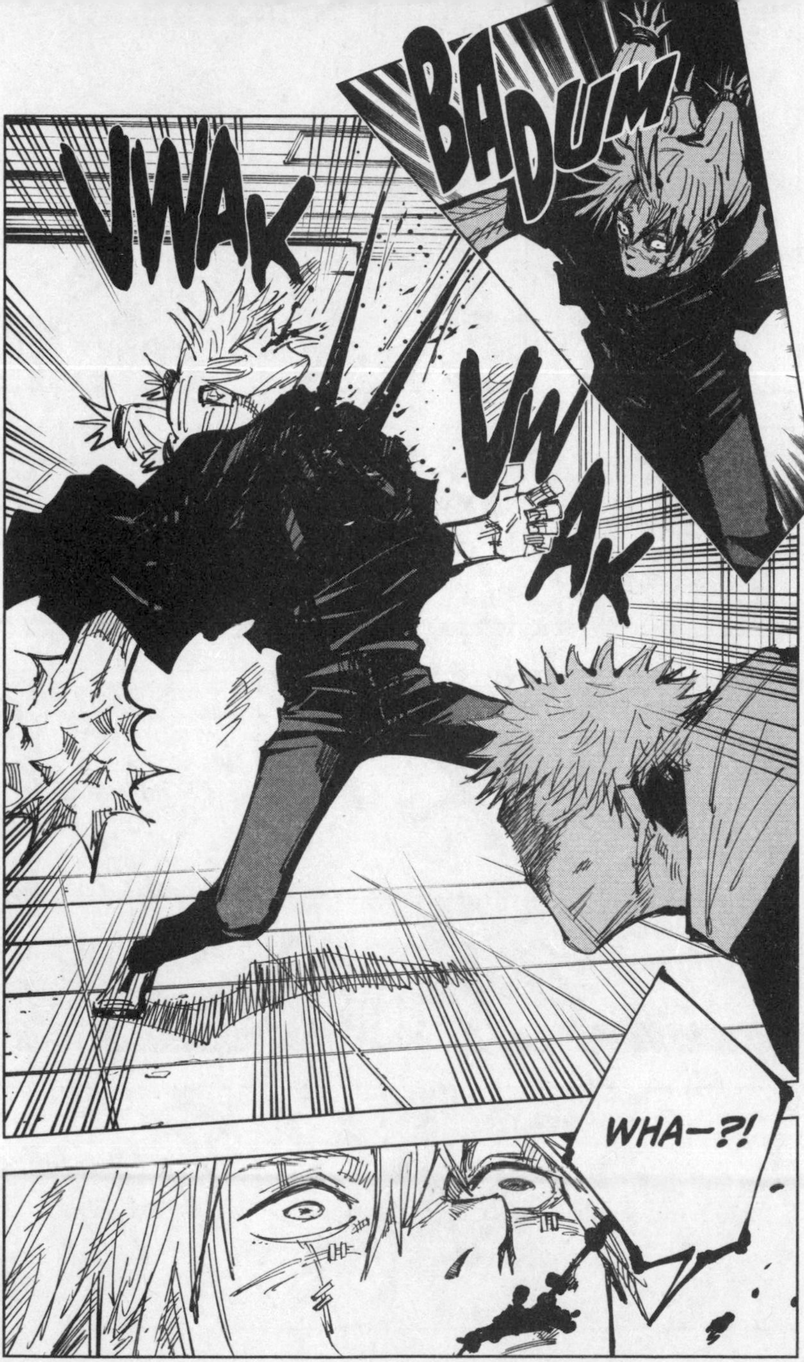
BADUM
VWAK
VWAK
WHA—?!

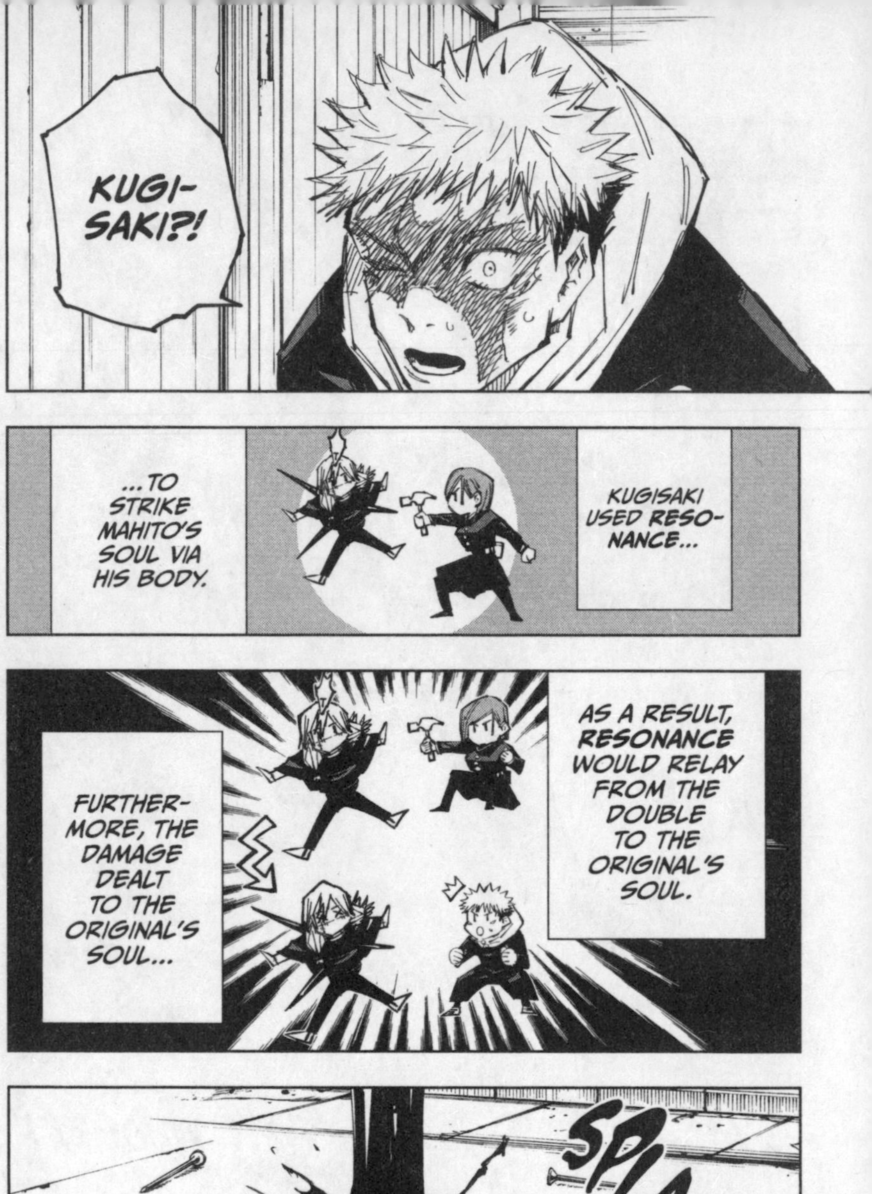
KUGI-SAKI?!
KUGISAKI USED RESO-NANCE...
...TO STRIKE MAHITO'S SOUL VIA HIS BODY.
AS A RESULT, RESONANCE WOULD RELAY FROM THE DOUBLE TO THE ORIGINAL'S SOUL.
FURTHER-MORE, THE DAMAGE DEALT TO THE ORIGINAL'S SOUL...
SPLACH

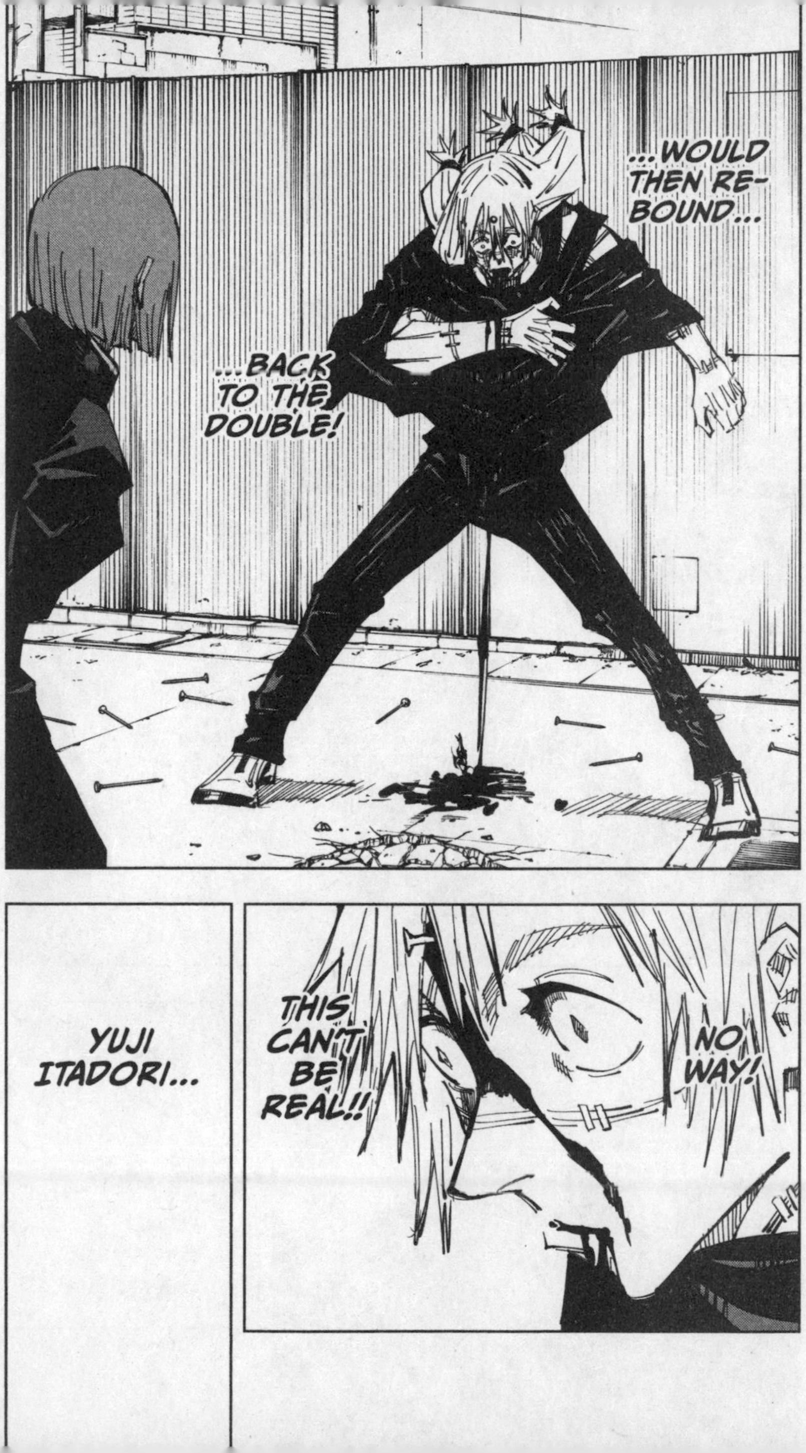
...WOULD THEN RE-BOUND...
...BACK TO THE DOUBLE!
NO WAY!
THIS CAN'T BE REAL!!
YUJI ITADORI...

...ISN'T MY ONLY...

...NATURAL ENEMY!

...DETONATE SOMEWHERE ELSE NEARBY.

I JUST FELT MY CURSED ENERGY...

HM... THAT'S WEIRD.

...YOU COULD'VE JUST GRABBED ME.

AND BACK THEN...

KREE

YOUR CURSED ENERGY ISN'T REALLY ALL THAT STRONG.

HOW DO I PUT THIS...

...SO YOU CAN'T USE YOUR CURSED TECHNIQUE, AM I RIGHT?!

YOU'RE LIKE A DOUBLE OR SOMETHING...

GRChK

CORRECT...

A Nice Story

• Hiramatsu-san drew this design
of a young Kugisaki for the anime,
and I used it in the manga too.
• When Hiramatsu-san draws
Kugisaki, she's actually cute.

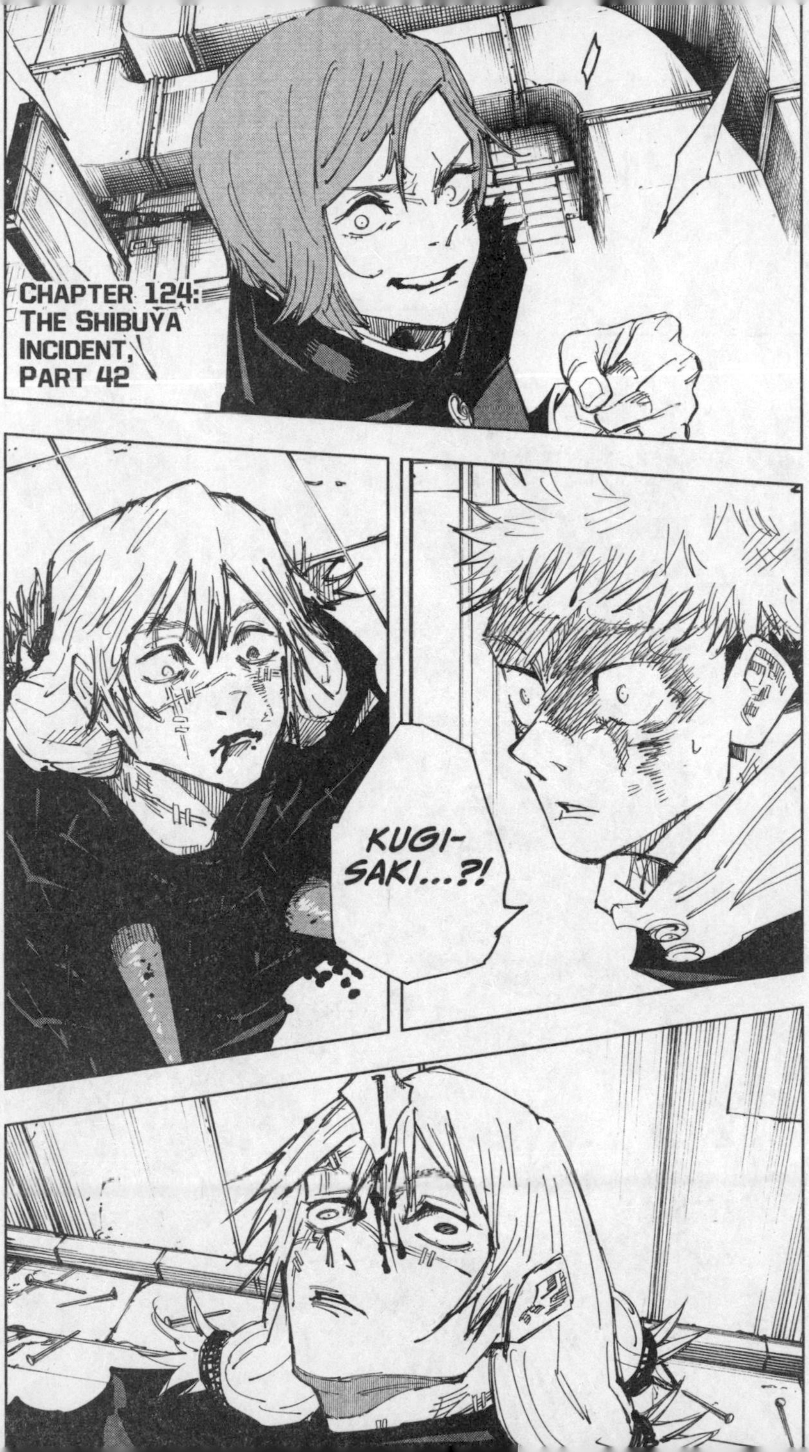
Chapter 124: The Shibuya Incident, Part 42
Kugi-saki...?!

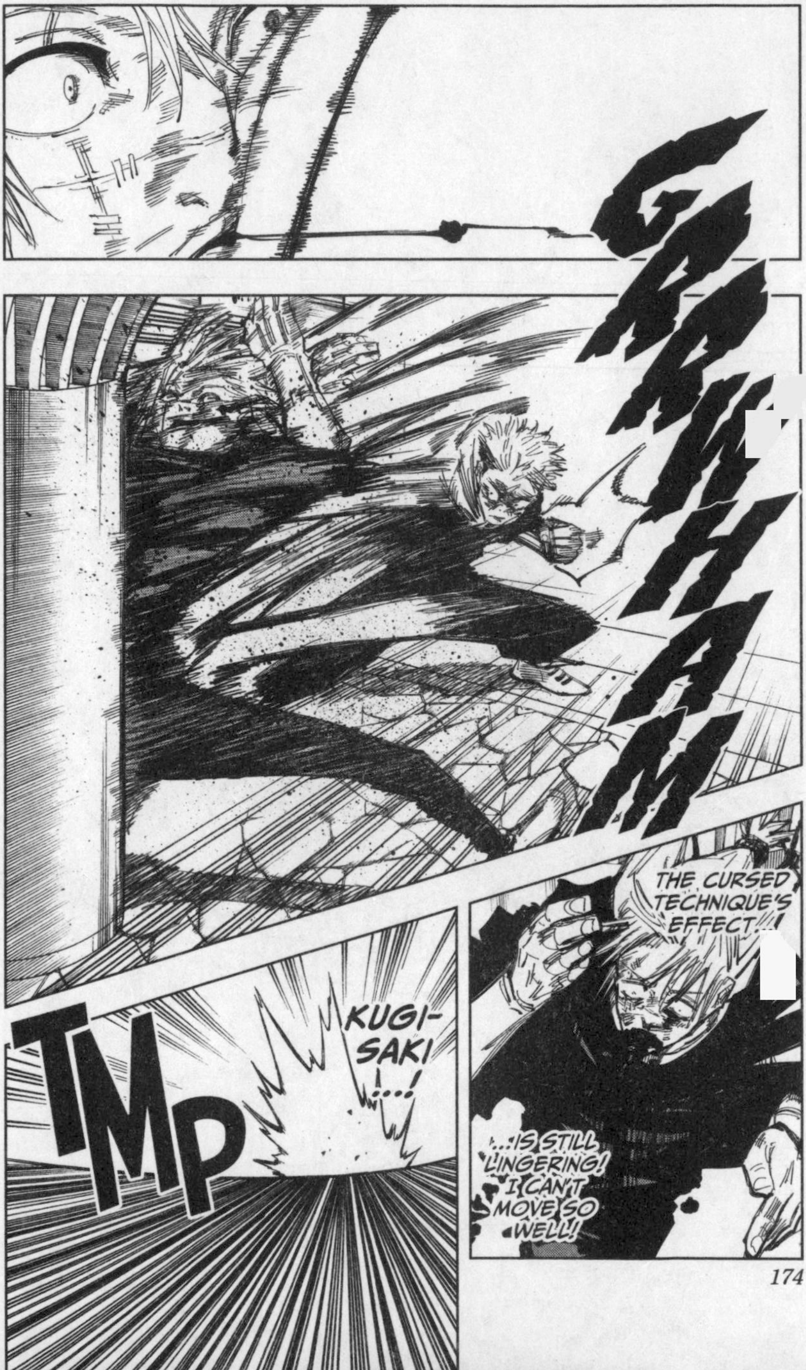
GRNHAM
THE CURSED TECHNIQUE'S EFFECT...
...IS STILL LINGERING! I CAN'T MOVE SO WELL!
KUGI-SAKI...!
TMP

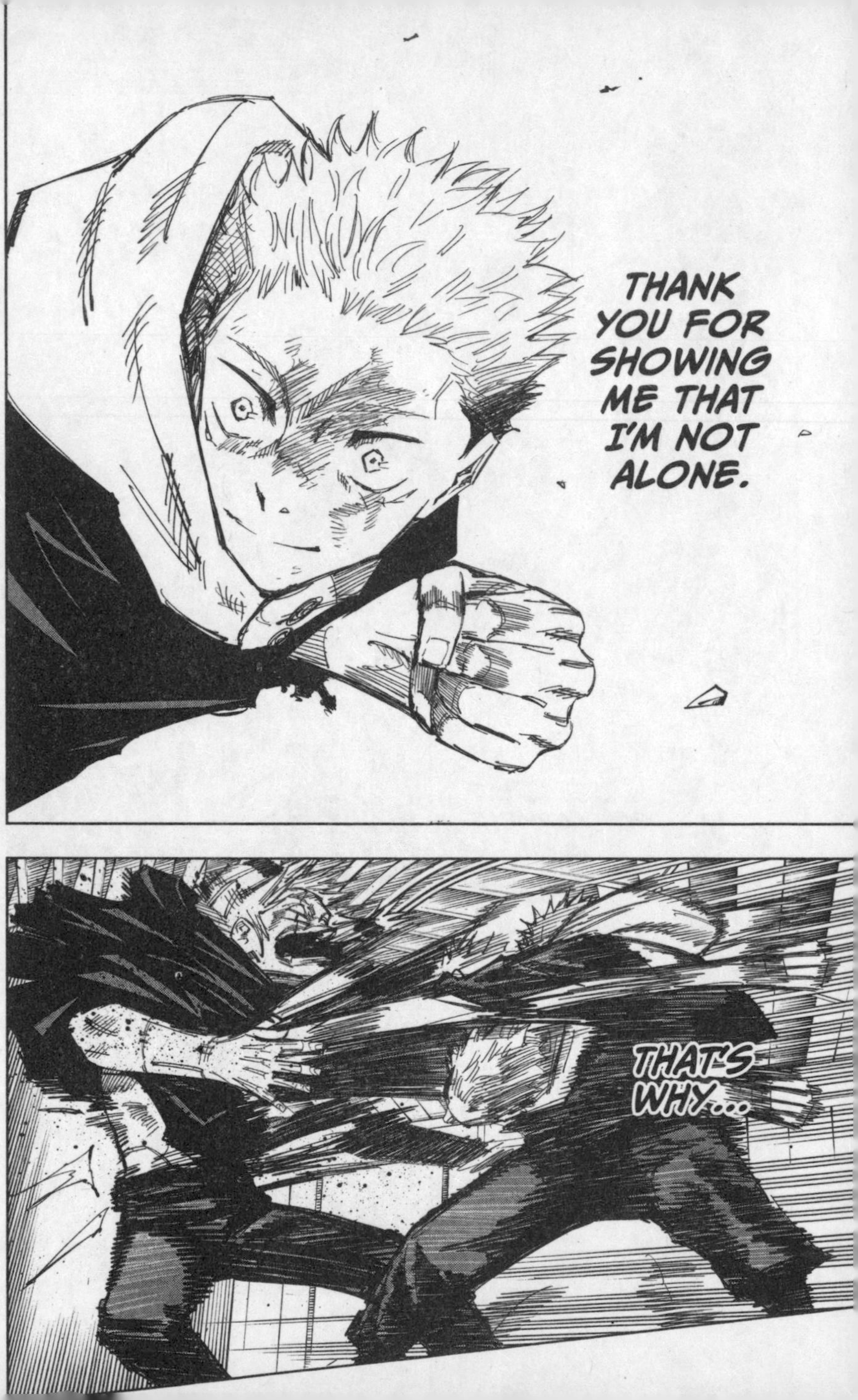
THANK YOU FOR SHOWING ME THAT I'M NOT ALONE.
THAT'S WHY...

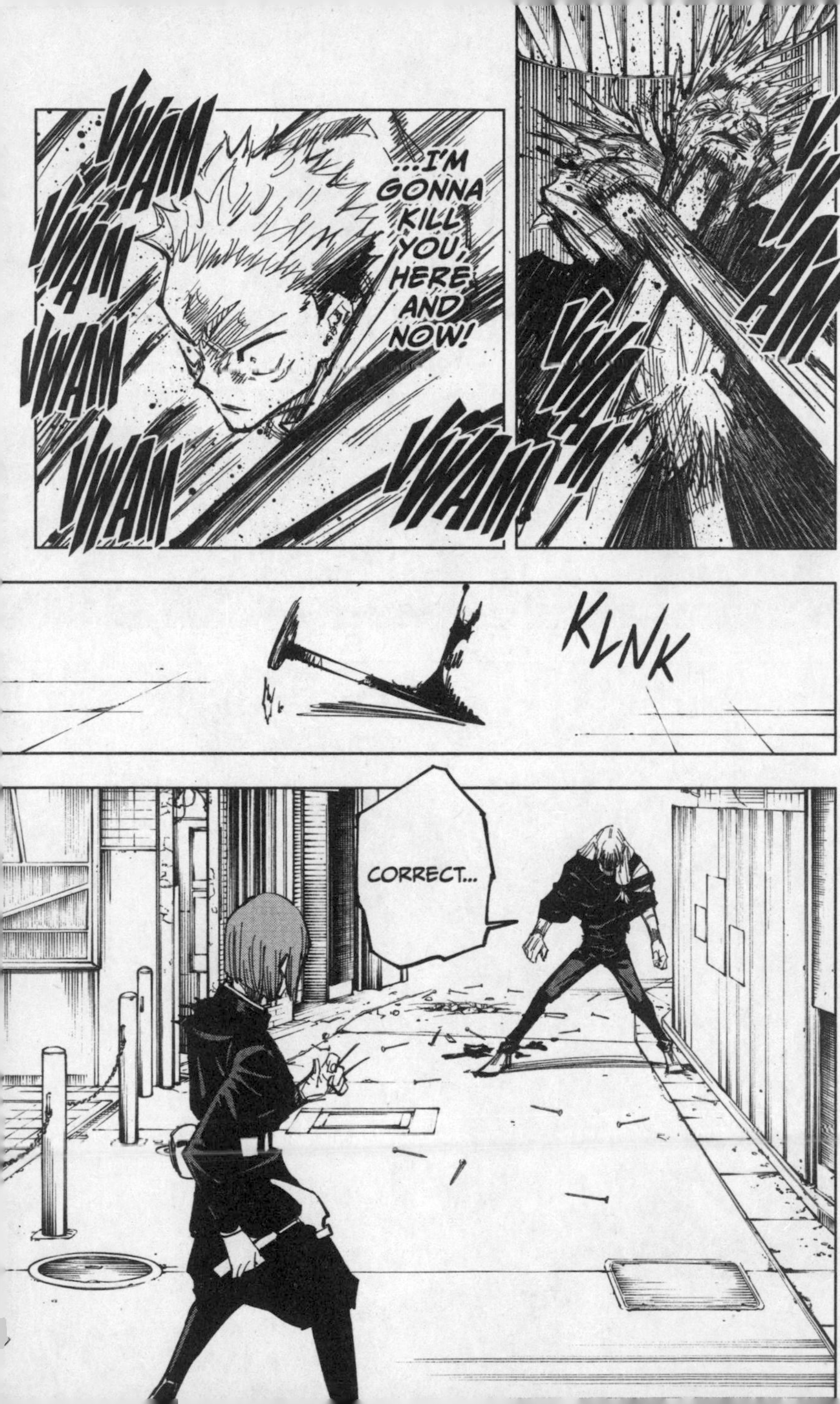
VWAM
VWAM
VWAM
...I'M GONNA KILL YOU, HERE AND NOW!
VWAM
VWAM
VWAM
VWAM
VWAM
KLNK
CORRECT...

NOW THAT RESONANCE IS WORKING, THE ATTACKS SHOULD SLOW DOWN A BIT.

THIS IS WHERE THE BATTLE REALLY BEGINS.

ACTU- ALLY...

TWITCH

I'M GONNA RUN AWAY!

WHAT ?!

!

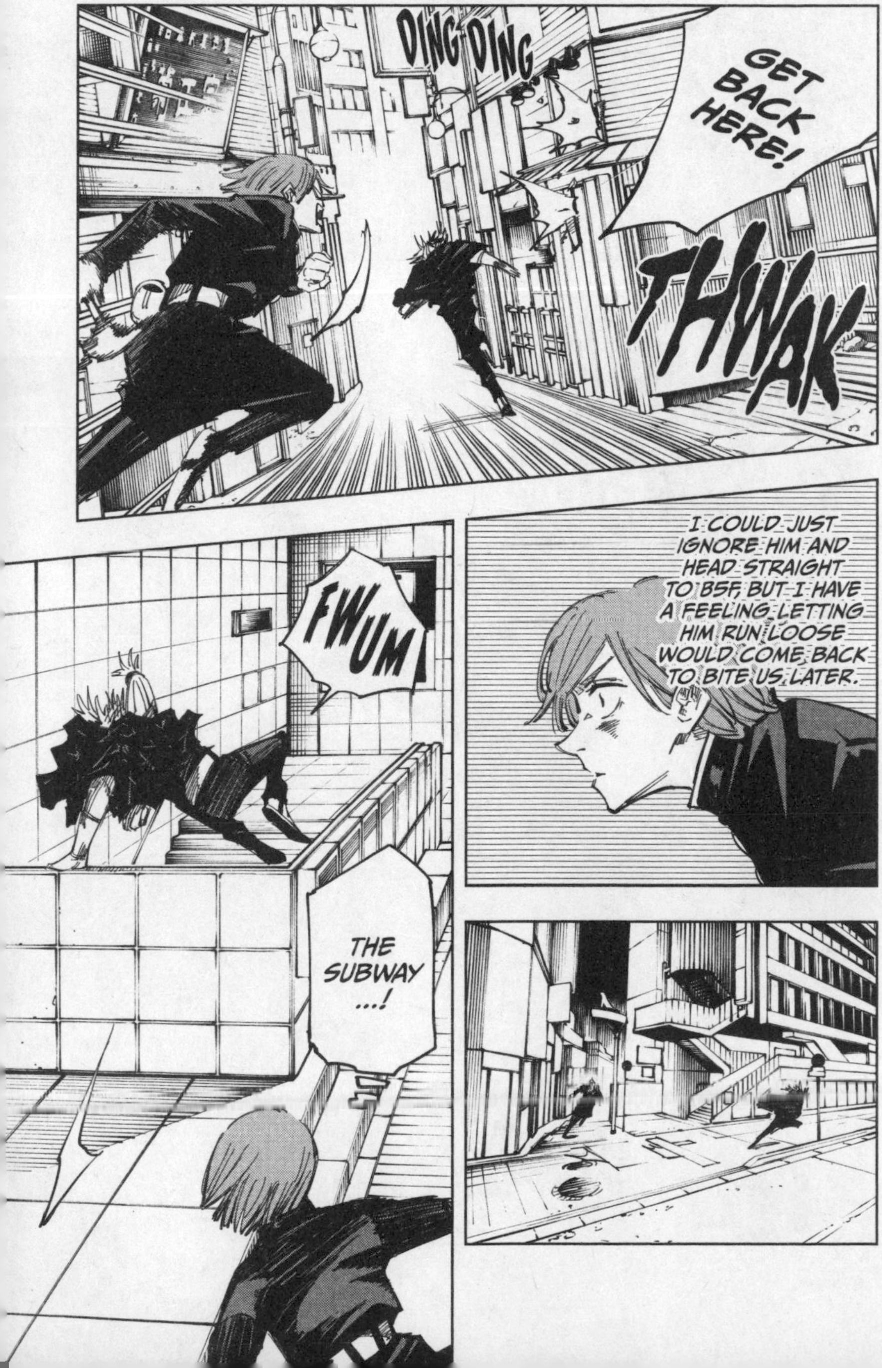
GET BACK HERE!
DING DING
THWAK
I COULD JUST IGNORE HIM AND HEAD STRAIGHT TO B5F, BUT I HAVE A FEELING LETTING HIM RUN LOOSE WOULD COME BACK TO BITE US LATER.
FWUM
THE SUBWAY ...!

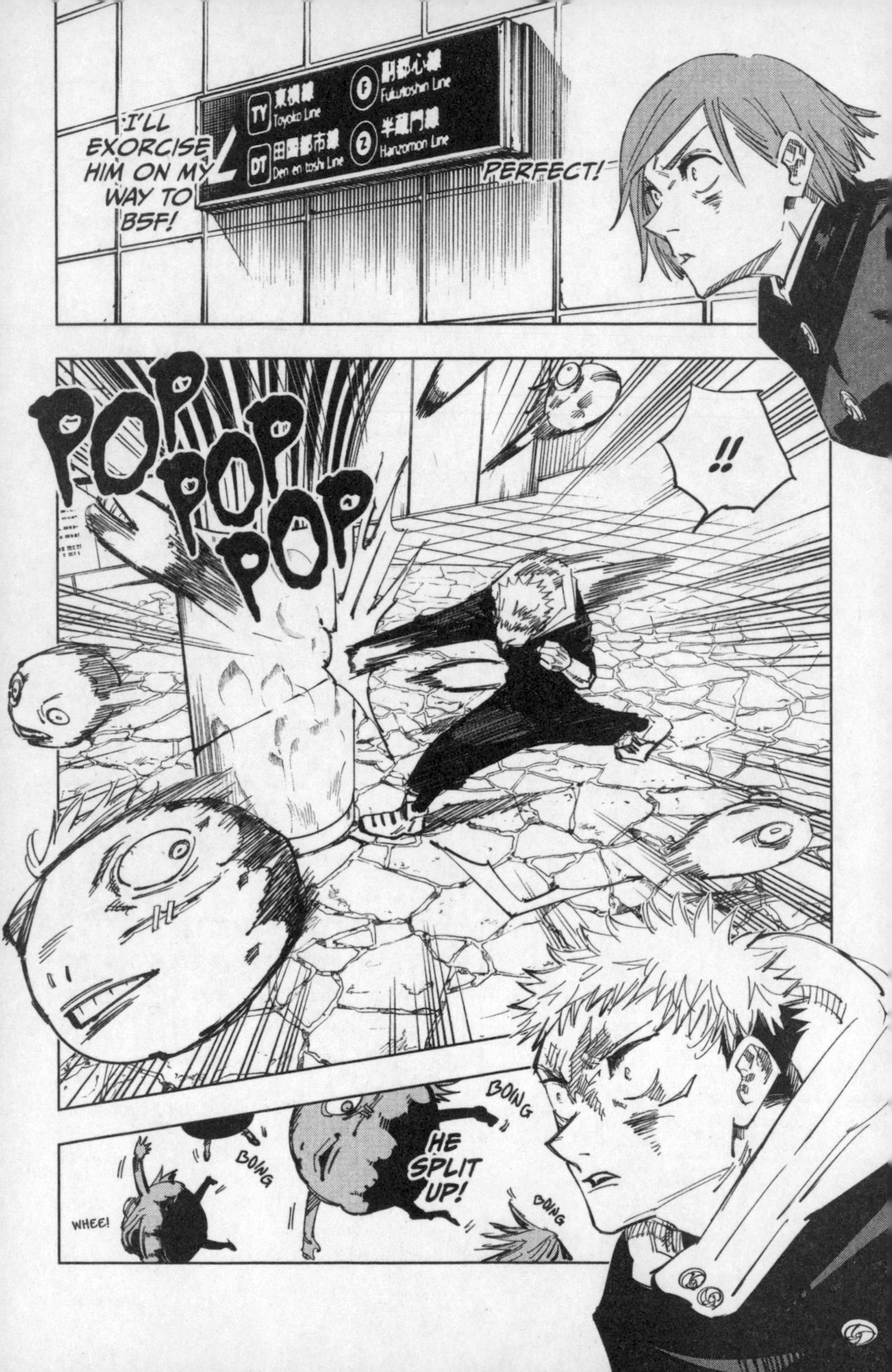
副都心線
Fukutoshin Line
東横線
Toyoko Line
半蔵門線
Hanzomon Line
田園都市線
Den en toshi Line
PERFECT!
I'LL EXORCISE HIM ON MY WAY TO B5F!
!!
POP POP POP POP
BOING
HE SPLIT UP!
BOING
BOING
WHEE!

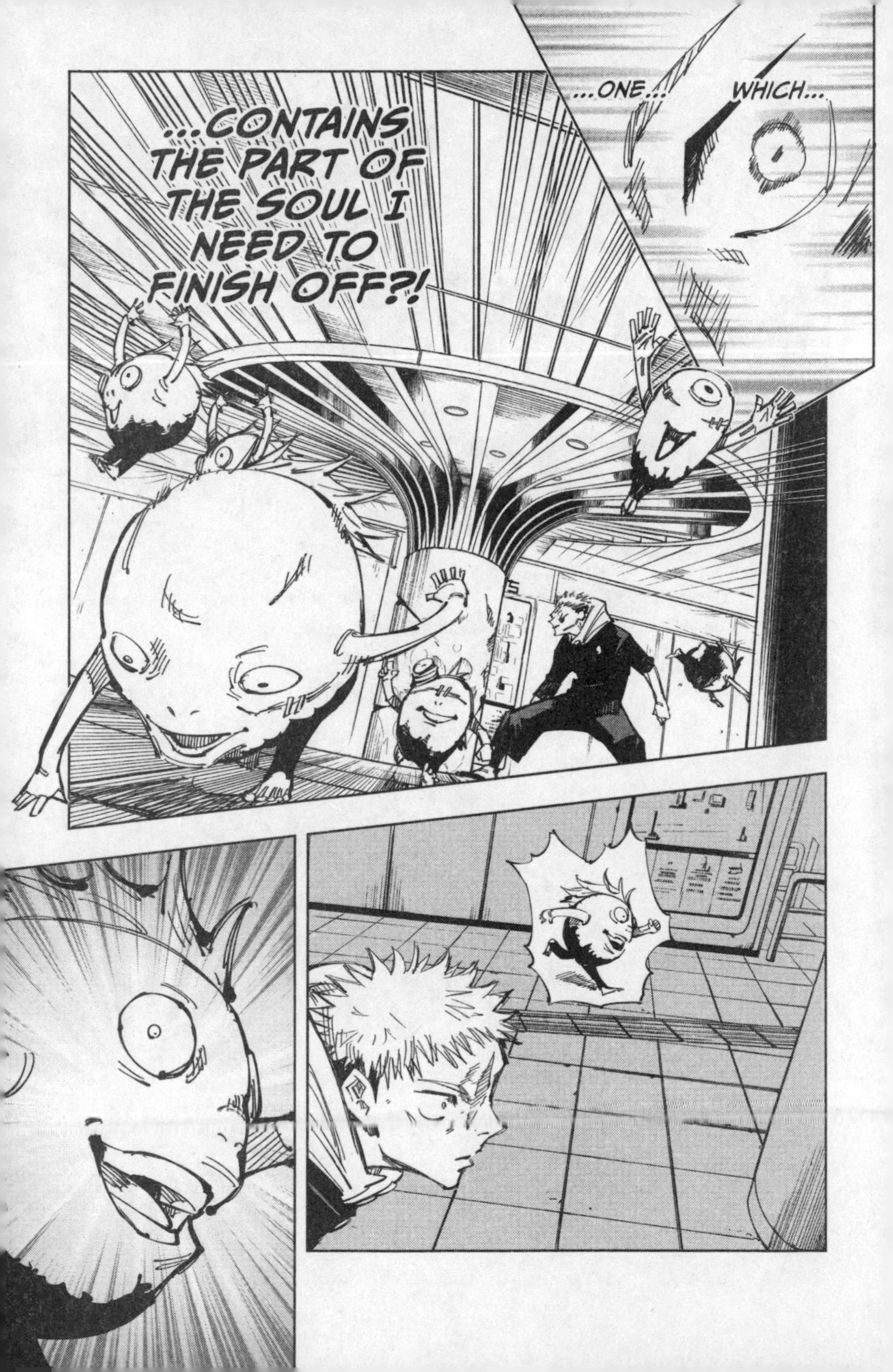
...ONE... WHICH...
...CONTAINS THE PART OF THE SOUL I NEED TO FINISH OFF?!

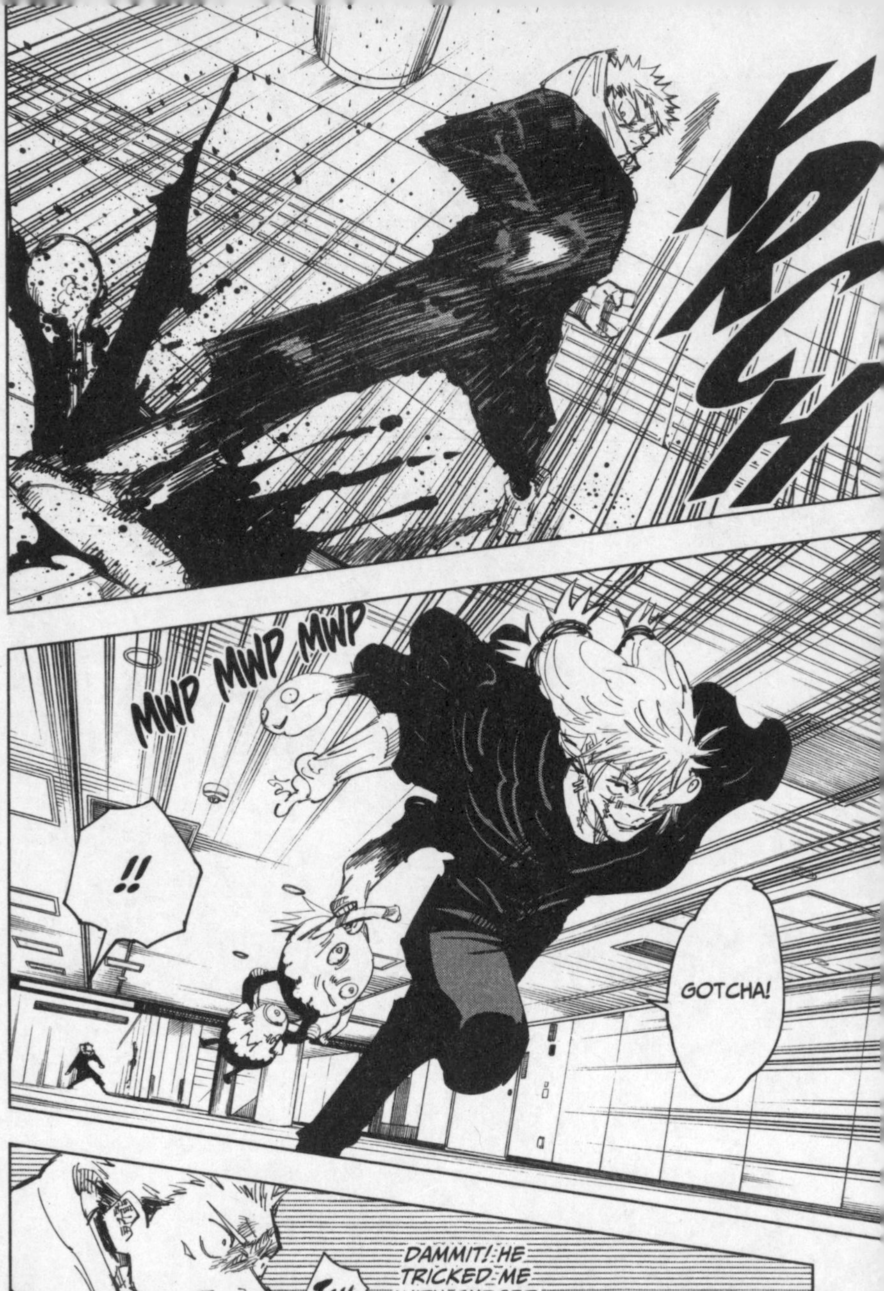
KRNCH
MWP MWP MWP
GOTCHA!
!!
DAMMIT! HE TRICKED ME WITH CURSED ENERGY!
TCH!

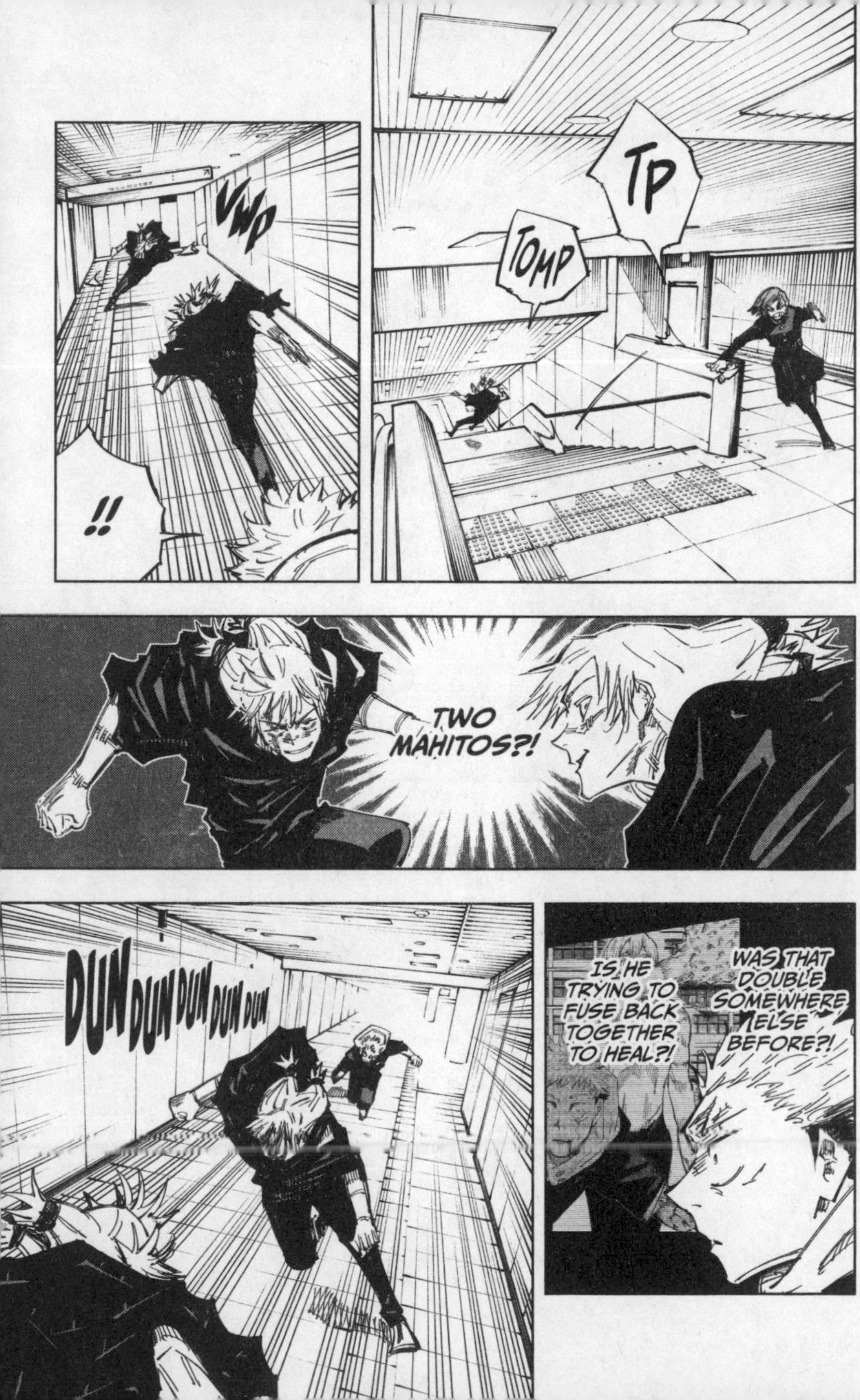
TP
TOMP
VMP
!!
TWO MAHITOS?!
WAS THAT DOUBLE SOMEWHERE ELSE BEFORE?!
IS HE TRYING TO FUSE BACK TOGETHER TO HEAL?!
DUN DUN DUN DUN DUN

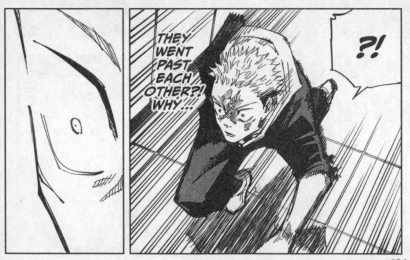

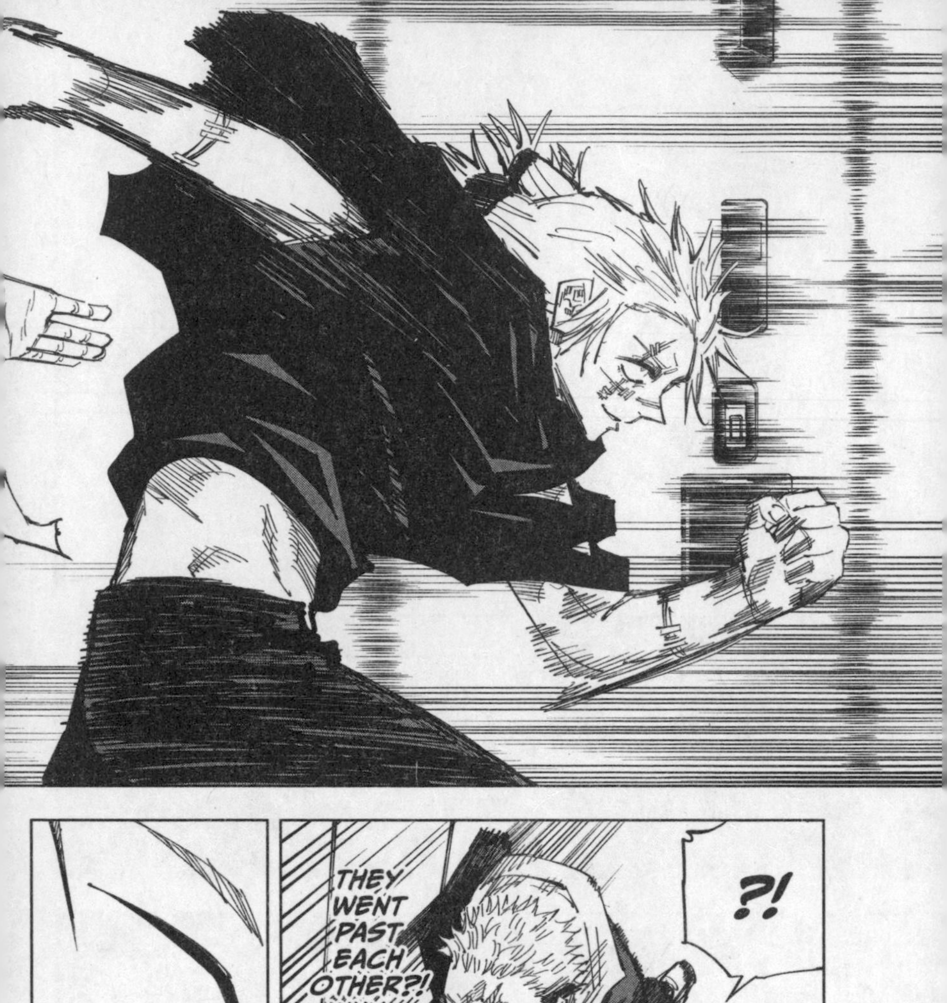
?!
THEY WENT PAST EACH OTHER?! WHY...

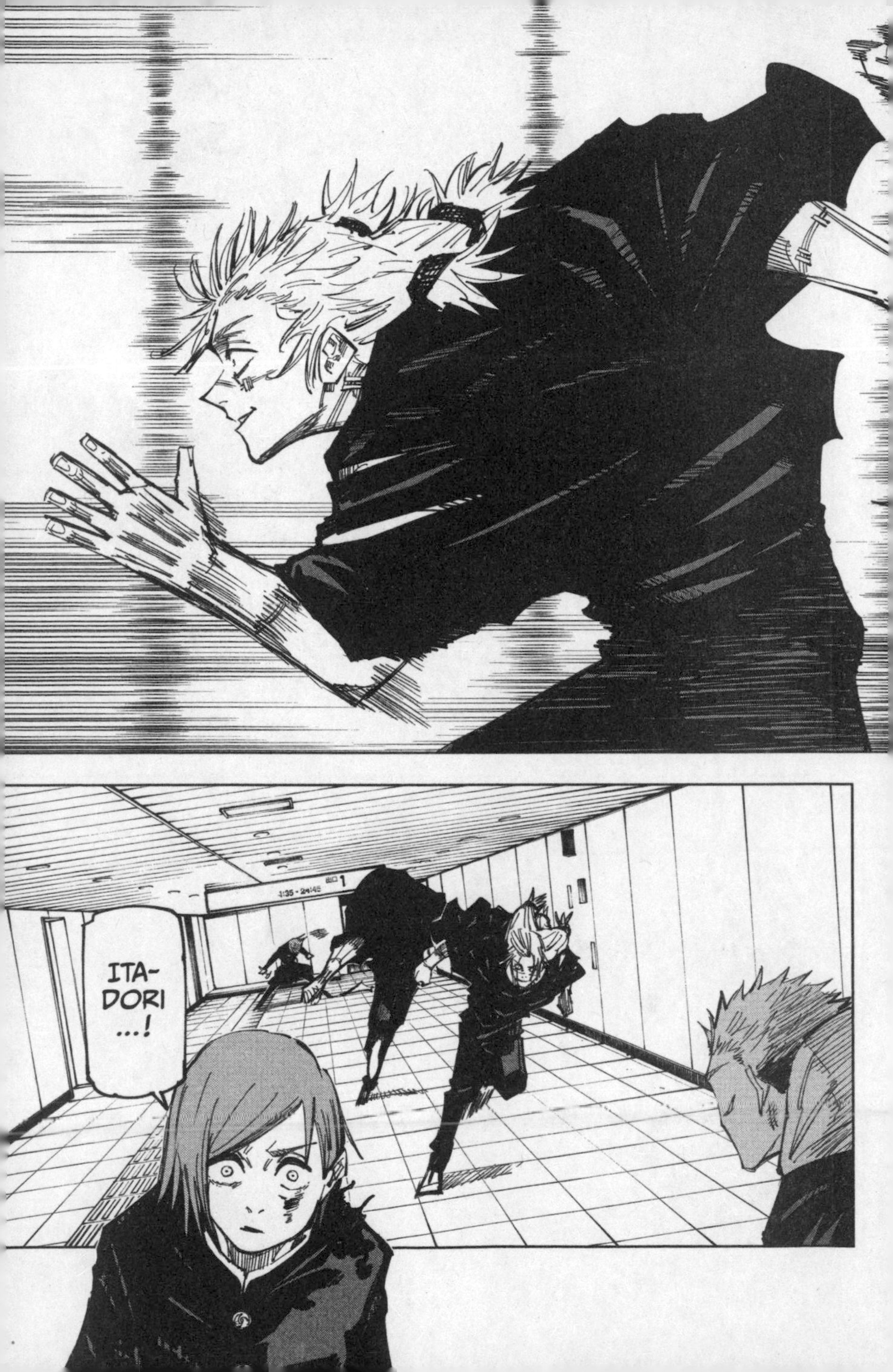
ITA-DORI ...!

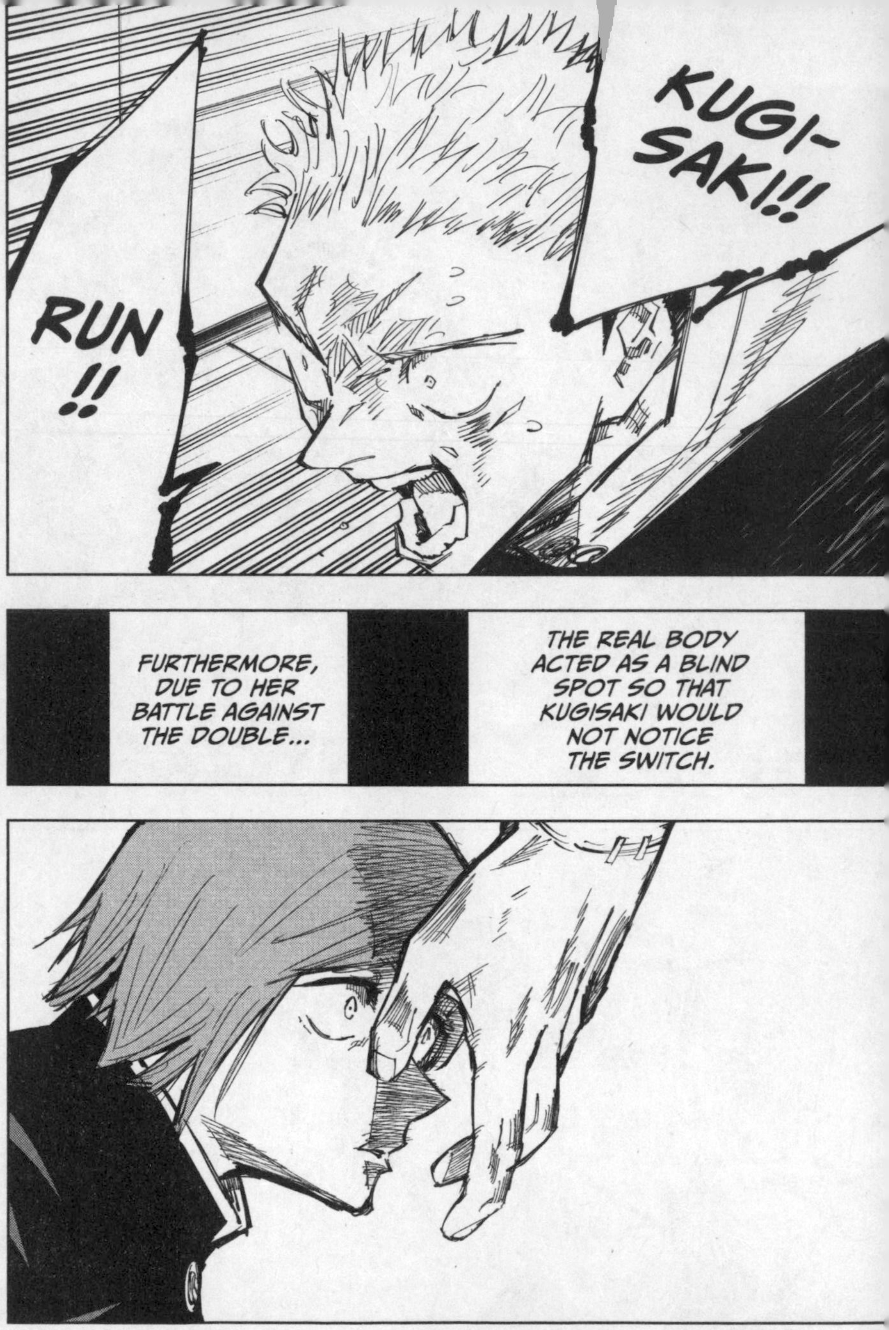
RUN!!
KUGI-SAKI!!!
FURTHERMORE, DUE TO HER BATTLE AGAINST THE DOUBLE...
THE REAL BODY ACTED AS A BLIND SPOT SO THAT KUGISAKI WOULD NOT NOTICE THE SWITCH.

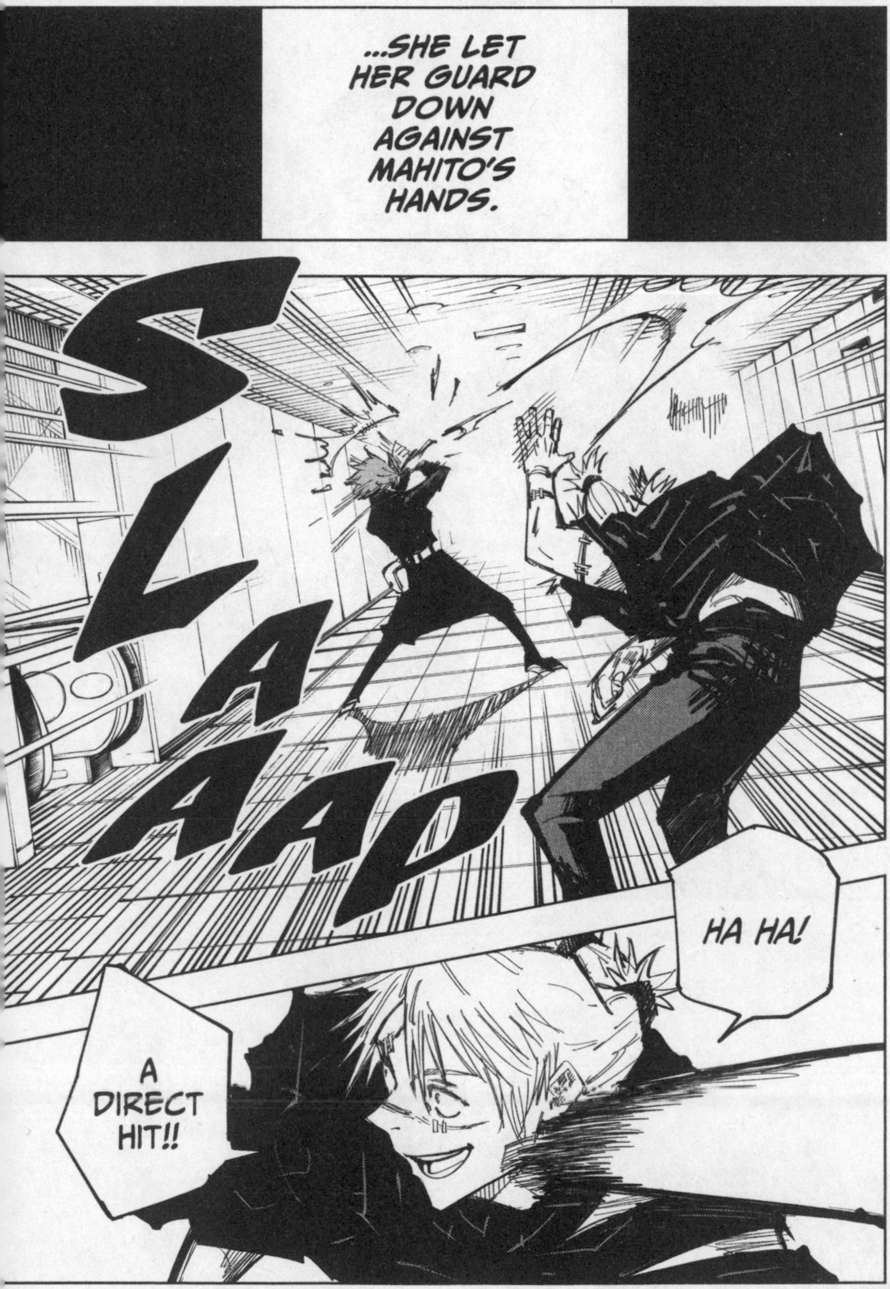
...SHE LET HER GUARD DOWN AGAINST MAHITO'S HANDS.
SLAAAP
HA HA!
A DIRECT HIT!!

188

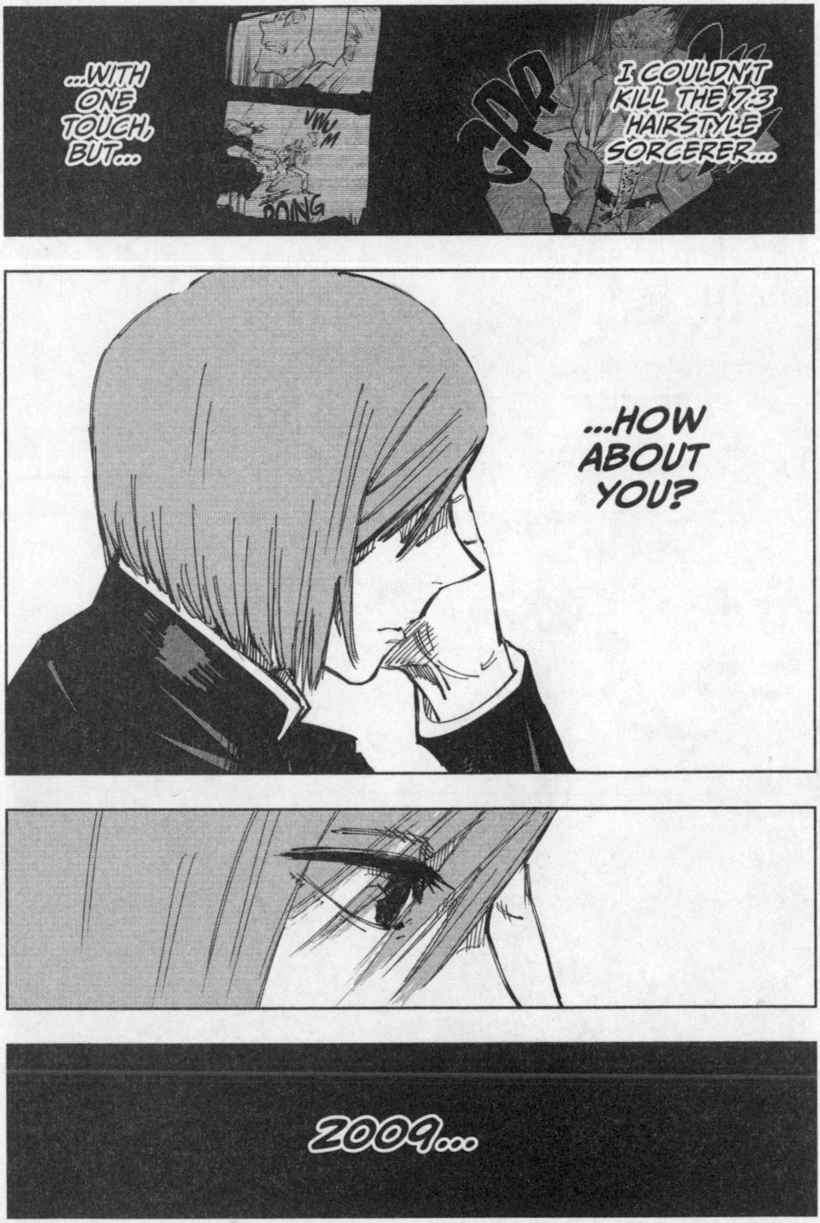
I COULDN'T KILL THE 7:3 HAIRSTYLE SORCERER...
...WITH ONE TOUCH, BUT...
VWUM
BOING
...HOW ABOUT YOU?
2009...

GRAA-AHHH!! DIE!!

NOBARA KUGISAKI
(SIX YEARS OLD)

YOU HAFTA MAKE SURE TO GO FOR THE KILL WHEN THE OPPONENT IS RECOVERING.

MAYBE NEXT TIME, NOBARA.

TO BE CONTINUED

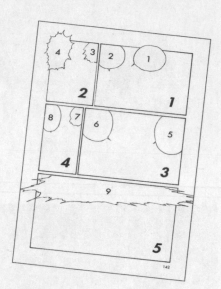

JUJUTSU KAISEN

reads from right to left, starting in the upper-right corner. Japanese is read from right to left, meaning that action, sound effects, and word-balloon order are completely reversed from English order.